GLORIOUS TIMES

GLORIOUS TIMES

Adventures of the Craighead Naturalists

TOM BENJEY

UNIVERSITY OF
MONTANA
PRESS

UNIVERSITY OF MONTANA PRESS
University of Montana
Corbin Hall 147
Missoula, MT 59812

First University of Montana Press soft cover edition November 2016

UNIVERSITY OF MONTANA PRESS and colophon are registered trademarks of University of Montana Press.

ISBN # 978-0-9909748-9-5

Library of Congress Cataloging-in-Publication Data

Names: Benjey, Tom, author.
Title: Glorious times : adventures of the Craighead naturalists / Tom Benjey.
Description: Missoula, Montana : University of Montana Press, 2016. | Includes bibliographical references and index.
Identifiers: LCCN 2016001322 | ISBN 9780990974895
Subjects: LCSH: Naturalists--United States--Biography. | Craighead family.
Classification: LCC QH26 .B36 2016 | DDC 508.092/273--dc23 LC record available at https://lccn.loc.gov/2016001322

TABLE OF CONTENTS

PART I

Who Are the Craigheads?

JUST WHO ARE THESE CRAIGHEADS people keep telling me about," I wondered shortly after moving to Cumberland County, Pennsylvania in the mid-1970s. Backyard neighbor Frank Hefelfinger told me they lived at Craighead Station, near where he grew up, and they had saved the grizzly bears in Yellowstone Park. Bill Coyle, operator of the planing mill that, generations earlier, had belonged to the Craigheads, reminisced about their exploits and feats of strength. Perhaps his story of the twins, Frank Jr. and John, walking on their hands as they raced each other across the top of the old one-lane, iron-truss bridge was exaggerated a bit. No one else saw them do it, but all who knew them said they could have. Over the years, I'd heard lots of fragments about the Craighead family but not enough to get a full picture. That changed when philanthropist Dr. David S. Masland came into my life in the very early two thousands.

"The trip with the twins out to the Tetons was the highlight of my life." In the late-1930s when he was just fifteen, Dave accompanied twins Frank Jr. and John Craighead on a ten-week trip to the Tetons during which they slept under the stars every night, ate no meals in restaurants, and didn't call home a single time. In spite of the indignity of riding in the back seat of the twins' '28 Chevy, with only a sheet of newspaper to shield him from the exhaust of the hawks and owls perched on the front seat backs, at ninety, Dave still considered this, his first trip out west, to be the most memorable, most exciting adventure of his life. By the time of that adventure, the twins already had an article published in *National Geographic* about training Cooper's hawks to become falcons. Seeing the impact the Craigheads had on him, I figured there must be something to them. He also mentioned their sister, Jean Craighead George, his unrequited first love. She was the older woman and four years difference was far too great for such an attractive girl to even consider this mere boy as more than a good friend. And so, at David's urging, I started doing a little research.

It didn't take long to get me hooked. While doing some genealogical work to get the names and ages right, I learned that, in spite of having no money, Frank Craighead (father to Jean and the twins, and son of Charles and Agnes Craighead, who lost their businesses around the turn of the 20th century) and his four siblings graduated from high school at a time when most people, especially those living out in the country, didn't. Not only did they all graduate from high school, they all graduated from college—even the girls! Few people—generally just the elites and mostly males—attended college in those days. One of them, Frank, earned a Ph.D. A little more research discovered that this couple's grandchildren, all eleven of them, also graduated from college. Two of them, Frank's twin sons, even earned Ph.D.s. The Craigheads were surely an extraordinary family that deserved further investigation.

Dave arranged a visit with Jean. Soon I was off conducting interviews with family members and friends. I soon learned it wasn't just Jean and the twins who were naturalists: starting with their father's generation, the family had produced a veritable army of naturalists that grew generation by generation. It didn't take long to convince me that, other than a little background on their Scots-Irish pioneer ancestors, I would have to limit myself to studying only the first two generations of Craighead Naturalists or the project would quickly become unmanageable. Because so many people I wanted to interview were already in their eighties or nineties, I prudently prioritized interviews with the older generation. That turned out to be a wise decision because several of them died or became incapacitated before this book was completed. If I'd waited, it would have been too late.

Jean mentioned her hypothesis of a naturalist gene that runs through her family. Empirical evidence in the numbers of people in her father's, hers, and following generations of Craigheads who work in or are interested in some aspect of nature supports her supposition. My challenge was to explore whether this Craighead naturalist bent is caused by nature or nurture.

Studying Craigheads is a challenge because they are not navel-gazers by nature: they are doers; they succeed. They don't write memoirs, with the exceptions of Jean's *Journey Inward* and her thinly veneered *The Summer of the Falcon*, so I had to glean information from interviews, newspaper and magazine articles, public records, and from school yearbooks (my personal favorite because they were so gossipy in those days). Occasionally, details about their lives crept into their notes, such as in later editions of *Hawks in the Hand* and *Life with an Indian Prince*. A year before her death, Jean said, "You know more about us than we know about ourselves." I responded, "Not really," and sidestepped to discussing education and accomplishment. She responded, "That was always assumed. We were expected to do well."

In June 2014, I was approached by two school teachers about giving talks about the Craigheads to junior and senior high school students. Fearing that adolescent children might not enjoy the talks I normally give adults and knowing that my school talk would have to fit into a single period, I concluded that it would be necessary to focus on a single aspect of the Craigheads and make it relevant to teenagers. While mentally outlining the talk about the twins first training falcons, it became apparent to me that, although the details of the talk would deal with the difficulties the twins overcame in studying and training hawks, the point of the talk would be that teenagers can and did make an impact.

Before the twins took up falconry at age fifteen, only four Americans were involved in the sport, all adult males. The twins soon influenced a dozen other boys, a sister, and a female cousin in Pennsylvania and Washington, DC to give it a try. Their first *National Geographic* article attracted the attention of an Indian rajah. Either their first book, *Hawks in the Hand*, or their sister Jean's novel, *My Side of the Mountain*, or both convinced virtually every American involved in falconry since 1932 to pursue this tedious and time-consuming activity. Such is the impact these youngsters had and continue to have.

The Craigheads were not one-act wonders; they had second and third acts of even more importance than the first. Saving the grizzlies in Yellowstone Park or writing the Wild and Scenic Rivers Act or receiving a Newbery Award would have been capstone achievements of most people's careers. These accomplishments were all in a day's work for Craigheads, for they are not people who rest on their laurels. They couldn't afford to because they had to keep on working to support themselves as significant financial rewards did not accompany their scientific and literary successes. The Craigheads are a shining example of how people of ordinary means can change the world.

Biographies have been written about naturalists such as John Muir. A young adult biography of Jean was written two decades ago, and numerous magazine articles have been written about Jean, her father, her brothers, and some first cousins, but no full-length biographies have been written about them individually or collectively. I contend that Craigheads are best understood when looked at collectively rather than individually because they are more tight-knit than most families and, according to their reflections on what it means to be a Craighead, they share some common traits, curiosity being first and foremost to them.

Craighead twins in wrestling fettle, 1939. (William Moore Craighead)

1

The Dangerous Boys Train Their First Hawks *Spring 1932*

THE BOYS SCOURED THE BANKS AND ISLANDS of the Potomac River looking for hawks. Already experts at sling shooting, blow gunning, marble shooting and street fighting at the age of fifteen, identical twins Frank Jr. and John Craighead were embarking on a grand new adventure: falconry, the ancient sport of kings. Two neighborhood friends, Julian Griggs and Morgan Berthrong, followed close at their heels.

First, the boys needed to catch some hawks. Not just any hawks: they needed Cooper's hawks, which were few in number. The easiest way to find a Cooper's hawk's nest was to spot the hawk flying and then follow it home. The boys readily found barred owls and red-shouldered hawks but, unfortunately, these birds had proved unsuitable for falconry. Cooper's hawks have short, rounded wings and rudder-like tails that are well adapted for hunting in the woods and open country then found near Washington, DC and in central Pennsylvania, places the Craigheads called home. After countless hours mastering the intricacies of the Library of Congress's book retrieval system, Frank and John found some old *National Geographic* magazines and a few books on their topic, including one written in 1615. Now they could study the observations of falconers from ancient times in far-off lands and learn of the attributes that made these particular accipters (hawks that inhabit deeply wooded areas) good candidates for falconry.

The twins decided the Cooper's hawk was the ideal bird for their experiment. It didn't bother them that Cooper's hawks had never been trained as falcons anywhere in the world. Frank Jr. and John would be the first. As they saw it, Cooper's hawks had all the attributes of other birds that had been successfully trained for falconry; however, the sport was almost exclusively practiced in the old world, and these predators lived only in North America. In the early 1930s, only four people practiced falconry in the U. S., and one of them, Army aviator Capt. Luff Meredith, had challenged them to become the first in history to train Cooper's hawks. The twins embraced their mission with unbridled enthusiasm, as did their friends Morgan and Julian. The four combed the rural Maryland countryside near Chevy Chase until they found their birds. This task required much patience, especially for teenage boys. On unsuccessful days, the twins had a favorite meal of their mother's beef roast and orange pudding as a consolation prize when they arrived home cold and empty-handed.

In early April, they spied a Cooper's hawk catching a blue jay. Over the next month, they glimpsed the same predator often. In early May, its mate appeared. The pair of accipters soared above a group of tall oaks where some hawks had built large nests of sticks. But which nest belonged to this pair? The boys noticed a new aerie in the crotch of a gigantic oak about 50 feet above the ground. They couldn't be sure it was a Cooper's hawk nest because the nest was at the upper elevation of where hawks build their homes. Needing to know, Frank climbed the tree to see the aerie up close. That woodland oaks had upward-pointing limbs and Cooper's hawks nested close to the main trunk, made the ascent easy for someone so practiced in tree-climbing. He shinnied up the trunk to the lowest branch and climbed up the oak from there. As hoped, he found a nest made of sticks and lined with thin flat pieces of pine bark. It also contained a surprise—five eggs with a slightly green tinge. Exactly what the boys had been searching for all this time!

Full-grown hawks are difficult to train; young ones are best and the nest held five future hawks. Knowing birds sometimes desert disturbed nests, the budding ornithologists exercised caution and stayed away until the eggs hatched.

The four boys took turns climbing high to watch the hawklings several times a week after school and on weekends. Between hawk viewings, they voraciously read the few falconry books they had found. Using the knowledge thus gained, they developed a plan to take the young birds from the nest at the state of development that would give them the best chance of success. So, on Friday, June 24, when the eyases (hawk nestlings) were almost ready to leave the nest, Frank and John climbed up to select their passages (immature wild hawks). One of the nestlings, apparently startled by the intruders, fluttered down to the ground by Julian. The twins lowered the two largest ones, both believed to be female because of their size, to the ground in a knapsack, leaving two behind for the mother to raise. Females were chosen because the Craigheads claimed, "Among the hawks, the female is 'deadlier than the male'—bigger, stronger, more spirited, and hence far better adapted for use in falconry." The nestlings still wore much down as they were just beginning to feather, yet they were old enough to be taken from their mother.

The twins recorded their observations in journals as their scientist father, Frank Cooper Craighead, Chief Forest Entomologist for the U. S. Department of Agriculture, no doubt had taught them to do. On the first day of captivity, the hungry birds ate English sparrows for breakfast, shared a starling for lunch, and ate another starling for dinner. The boys tore the meat from the sparrows and starlings into small enough pieces to stuff into the tiny hawks' mouths because the birds were too young to eat on their own.

The very next morning the Craighead family, birds, dog and all, left for summer vacation at Craighead Station, Pennsylvania. It was a good time to leave the nation's capital because 1932 marked the depths of the Great Depression. Bonus Marchers simmered in makeshift camps after the Senate voted down the Patman bill a week earlier, eliminating any hope of the veterans receiving their WWI pensions before 1945. Ultimately, Army troops under Gen. Douglas MacArthur swept them out of town in a violent, one-sided battle. The Craigheads did not let the Bonus Marches delay their departure, as vacationing in bucolic environs was far more desirable than staying in the hot, humid "Foggy Bottom" air, long before the advent of air conditioners. Each summer, the twins' parents Frank and Carolyn would stuff belongings, wildlife, the twins and their younger sister Jean into their Ford, strap suitcases onto the running boards and embark to Craighead Station.

Frank would drive his meticulously maintained car to his boyhood home in south central Pennsylvania, then leave the family behind the next day to inspect his experiments in forests of the southern and western states being devastated by spruce budworm infestations. But before the family could depart for their annual trek north, the birds had to be fed. Their parents insisted, if their children were to keep these hawks, they must be responsible stewards. After the two hungry little hawks choked down three sparrows for breakfast, the family left for what the boys called their "Ancestral Home." The twins considered the place ideal for the task at hand: "The country around Carlisle is open farmland, excellent for training and flying both hawks and falcons." It was also studded with groves of tall trees.

Today, the 100-mile trip from the Craigheads' home at 5301 41st Street, N.W. in Washington, DC to Craighead Station, Pennsylvania takes a little over two hours to drive, but in 1932 the drive took half a day—if the car was well maintained. Frank drove a few blocks from their home to Wisconsin Avenue and headed northwest on what had been re-designated U.S. Route 240 six years earlier, through the towns of Rockville and Gaithersburg, and continued westward to Frederick, Maryland. At Frederick, they turned north onto US Route 15 to wind their way over the Catoctin Mountains, across the Mason-Dixon Line and push on to Gettysburg. At the circle in downtown Gettysburg, they took Pennsylvania Route 34 north toward Carlisle, by way of Biglerville, past historic Thomas Brothers Country Store, and through the lush orchards of Adams County. They could see the apple and peach crops were more plentiful than in previous years. Their father may have told them prices would have been high had money been plentiful, which it never was during the Great Depression.

After crossing South Mountain, they descended into Cumberland Valley at Papertown and passed through Mt. Holly Springs, where they could pick up last-minute supplies. Continuing north on what was known locally as the Holly Pike, they completed the last leg of their trip. Two miles north of Mt. Holly, they turned east on Old York Road toward their long-awaited destination. The last, and shortest, stretch of the trip was over a dirt road that ran past their summer home and through the middle of the area that served as their playground. Depending on the weather, it was dusty, muddy, or rutted. Younger sister Jean recalled, "There weren't any places to stop then. Mother prepared sandwiches and a thermos of milk. No paper cups then either, or at least we didn't spend recklessly on them when we could wash cups when we got there…. It must have been a tough ride because I remember how glad we were to get there and run free down the lawn to the creek. Arrival is a very pleasant memory."

Craighead Station, was an unincorporated area adjacent to the tracks of the South Mountain Railroad (later the Gettysburg and Harrisburg Railroad Company) that extended for about half a mile in any direction, give or take. "Craigheads," as local people call it, indisputably included the store, feed mill, train station and other businesses along the train tracks, and that were originally operated by Craighead ancestors, west to the iron bridge—hence the name Craighead Station. Some considered the planing mill to be part of the hamlet; others didn't. The twins' paternal grandfather built the Victorian house in 1886 for his new bride and placed it diagonally across the tracks from the station and store. They raised their children in it and, after 1907, summered there until their deaths in the mid-1920s, after which their children used it as the clan's vacation home.

After arriving and stretching their legs, Frank and John fed their birds again, sating their appetites with two sparrows and a starling. The next morning was Sunday. The boys surveyed the spacious back yard extending from the back of the kitchen to the bank of the Yellow Breeches Creek and the side yard between the east side of the house and the railroad tracks to select a place to keep their hawks. They then set poles in the ground of the side yard and fenced off a large enclosure with screen wire for the birds' summer home in clear view of the young males' sleeping porch. The twins also hung a box on the maple tree within the enclosure and placed their young hawks inside it. Although the boys chomped at the bit to start the training, they knew they had to wait until the hawks feathered out. In the meantime, they had much work to do getting their birds—and themselves—ready to hunt.

The boys bent two bow perches low to the ground in the enclosure but the birds weren't quite ready to sit on them yet. Later on Sunday, for the first time, Frank and John did not have to tear the birds' food into pieces and stuff it into their little mouths. The little ladies devoured three sparrows, one starling, and almost a whole pigeon on their own. The hawks had gotten noticeably stronger; one sat on her perch for two hours.

The twins expended vast amounts of time and attention caring for their young birds. John later wrote, "Falconry requires patience, perseverance, and hard work. It also demands dedication and a full-time commitment needed for few other sports." He and his brother practiced these new traits while raising their Cooper's hawks that summer. Hawk food wasn't found in stores, and the twins didn't have money to buy it had it been. Instead, they found plenty of sparrows, starlings, pigeons, blackbirds and rodents nearby. All that was necessary to harvest them was a sure eye and steady trigger finger on the trusty .22 rifle. Jean, the twins' younger sister, their first cousins, Sam and Bill, and some neighbor boys assisted in filling the larder that occupied a corner of the icebox their mother shared with their aunts. The barn, located just across the tracks from the house, provided a virtual shooting gallery full of the much-despised sparrows, starlings, and pigeons.

On Monday, John's hawk sat on her perch from two o'clock until seven in the evening. Both birds acted more tamely than ever and ate more readily, ingesting two sparrows, a starling, a pigeon (breast and entrails) as well as a bit of beef. Their feathers continued coming in. The next day, the twins fitted their hawks with jesses and leashes in preparation for the start of their training. (Jesses are leather strips attached just above birds' ankles.) John wrote in his journal, "Frank's hawk twisted up his leash and hung himself upside down. It did nothing but frighten him. Must adjust the sliding ring." On Thursday, they bought heavy leather gloves for carrying their birds and changed the feeding location and schedule.

Birds of prey often ingest fur, bones and feathers along with the meat but cannot digest these things. They get rid of them by casting out indigestible material as pellets. The twins observed their birds casting each morning around nine or ten. They started feeding them twice a day, once shortly after casting, the other in the evening, both times on the perches, soon giving them whole birds to eat. The hawks tore up their food themselves and ate fresh-shot sparrows and starlings. Still-unnamed, the raptors balked at eating legs because of their low blood content. But when Frank and John dipped the legs in blood, the hawklings gobbled them. Hearts and livers were their favorites.

By the second week of July, the boys attempted to carry the birds on their fists. At first, it took plenty of effort to keep the birds in place, but soon the growing hawks learned to take off and land on fists and to take their food there as well. The arms of the twins were surely tired by being extended in one position for hours on end while they walked around, providing perches for the birds on their gloves.

Training was finally in full swing. Once the birds could be carried on fists, Frank and John granted them occasional freedom. The hawks loved to bathe in the stream, providing quite a show for the twins and their gang. As they matured, the differences in the personalities of the hawks emerged. Frank's bird was more active, responding excitedly to each and every stimulus. Her hyperactivity came with a price tag as she broke three tail feathers by mid-July. The twins learned to approach the hawks very slowly and deliberately, taking care not to startle them. They took a step-by-step approach to releasing the birds for flight. First, they prevented fly-aways by attaching strings or tethers to the birds' jesses. Prior to feedings, the boys allowed their raptors-in-training to fly ever-increasing distances before returning to the glove for food. Eventually, the birds returned promptly after hearing one of the boys whistle.

After considerable practice with tethered flight, the time for moving to the next step arrived: "Now at last we were ready to set them free. It was a thrilling moment when we turned our first hawks loose. The birds skimmed along the ground, then rose up, up to the topmost branches of a pin oak tree. They ignored us while taking account of their surroundings, and then tested their wings with a few short flights directly away from us. Were we really going to lose our hawks after months spent in patient training? No. They were just seeing how it felt to be free. As the novelty of their first real flight wore off and they became hungry, they recalled their two months' training and at last dropped down to our gloves."

The boys learned more than did the birds they were teaching. They observed the difficulty of providing young hawks proper nutrition as their birds developed hunger streaks and weak spots in their feathers. They fed the birds more to eliminate hunger streaks and supplemented the regular food, pest birds, with bone and liver to ward off rickets. Our apprentice falconers also learned to make the equipment they needed. With only four other people in the country practicing this sport, paraphernalia specific to falconry wasn't readily available. Using pictures from books as guides, they fabricated jesses and leashes with snaps and swivels out of long, supple strips of leather less than a half inch wide and fitted them to their birds. They fashioned perches of various styles out of wood they cut from nearby trees. If something they needed couldn't be found among ordinary, inexpensive household supplies, they made it themselves or adapted something else to their purpose.

Perhaps most of all, they learned the differences between birds—not just by species, but also by individuals within a species. Frank observed, "Some are spiritless, puny, slow. Some are much faster than others; they are just born faster or are more spirited and try harder." His bird provided a ready example of high spirits. She loved to hunt rabbits and could spot them well before human eyes could detect them and would be off. In her first overeager attempts, she swooped at a rabbit hiding in thick undergrowth, hitting the bushes hard and damaging her feathers. But soon she learned to follow her quarry to a clearing where she could make a clean strike. One day, she followed a wily rabbit for a half mile from tree to tree until he entered a little open space. She saw her opportunity and struck. However, her wily target dove through the crotch of a small locust tree, leaving her in his dust as she hit the "Y" hard enough to wedge herself between the branches.

Falconry was anything but a solitary activity for these boys; they worked with a constant audience. Their sister Jean, cousins Sam, Bill, and, on holidays, Nancy and Barbara, along with several neighbor boys watched their every step and participated to whatever extent possible. Frank and John were natural teachers with patience even for much-younger children. David Masland, Barbara Gawthrop, and Bill Craighead were seven, eight, and nine years younger than the twins but were still included in their activities. These kids weren't just tolerated; the twins patiently taught them what they were learning as they were learning it. Not surprisingly, David, Bill, and Barbara idolized these innovators, as did their older friends.

Time-consuming training left the boys little time to log their activities in their journals for the rest of the summer. On September 14th, after returning to Washington, one of the twins wrote:

"We continued to train our hawks throughout the summer, flying them frequently to strengthen their flight muscles. We entered them on any type of live quarry we could capture. The preferred prey, cottontail rabbits, were scarce at our summer home, so starlings and pigeons had to suffice. In early September we returned to Washington, D.C., and began flying our hawks at wild quarry. Frank's hawk was always keen and aggressive; John's hawk had a poor appetite and showed little interest in capturing prey. It frequently took hours to retrieve her after a flight. She was finally released and our efforts were concentrated on hunting with Frank's hawk. Cottontails were unusually abundant near our home in Washington, D.C., in the fall of 1932."

On September 15, Frank finally named his bird. He dubbed her Comet, probably because of her speed. This was a landmark date in her training: "Her first real flight was at a full-grown pigeon thrown from my hand. She started fifty feet from behind the pigeon and overtook it in a hundred yards. She bound to the pigeon fifteen feet in the air. She was flying against the wind, which enabled her to rise fast. I walked up to Comet slowly and took her on my glove."

This was a marked improvement over the first time Comet flew at free birds, who fooled her completely. Using her keen eyesight from far above, she spotted a flock of pigeons feeding in a field of wheat stubble and dove toward them at top speed. They scattered. She selected as her target the last pigeon to take flight. With a 100-yard head start, the foxy old pigeon flew through an open barn door and out another door on the far side, banked sharply to quickly circle the barn, then reentered the barn through the first door and hid among the rafters. Baffled, Comet perched on the barn roof, perhaps too ashamed to come down. She wasn't fooled so easily in later hunts, though. Learning quickly was one of her greatest assets.

Another attribute of Cooper's hawks is their quickness on the ground. Comet put her foot-speed to work when her quarry shook off her strike from the air. Once, when one cottontail ducked under a fence as she raced in hot pursuit, Comet almost knocked herself out when she hit the wire. Another time she chased a full-grown rabbit down a groundhog hole, which is not a wise idea considering the strength and sharpness of rabbit claws. All of these incidents took a toll. By late September, she had broken the last of her tail feathers and could no longer make sharp turns or stop quickly when flying at prey. So, Frank and John found it necessary to learn yet another skill.

From the falconry books, the twins discovered Comet was far from the first hawk to damage her feathers. Centuries earlier, falconers developed a procedure, called imping, to replace broken feathers. The twins couldn't find Cooper's hawk feathers, so they substituted marsh hawk (later called hen harrier) tail feathers. They inserted long needles they fashioned from hacksaw blades into the stubs of the broken feathers, slid the new quills onto the needles, and glued them fast. Books recommended salt water to attach the needles to feather stubs, but some of Comet's tail feather stubs were so short or split, glue was necessary. Comet's new tail worked well before going the way of her original one. A crow's tail was tried but didn't last long. The twins imped in a barred owl's tail next. This proved to be the most satisfactory due to the flexible nature of the feathers, although it turned Comet into a rather odd-looking bird.

Their interest in falconry immediately attracted their friends and relatives to the sport. The twins captured young birds for their sister and cousins, including the youngest ones, Bill and Barbara. Pennsylvania friends David Masland and Chestin "Chet" Eshelman also took up the hobby as did Washington buddies Julian Griggs, Morgan Berthrong, and Gates Slattery. Alva Nye and Otho Williams may have been out of school already but joined with the boys because of their common interest in the sport. Frank, John, and their Washington friends continued to fly their birds through the fall and winter, becoming minor celebrities along the way. On November 19, The *Washington Star* sent a reporter out to photograph them, their friends, and birds for a story about them in the Sunday edition. Hawks are often released into the wild after a season of hunting, but the twins decided to keep Comet through her molt. They planned to get John another Cooper's hawk and also to try their hands at training sparrow hawks (American kestrels) the following spring. All this and more for two boys who had just turned sixteen in August and only two years earlier had set the city-wide record for the 200-meter relay in the under-70-pound class.

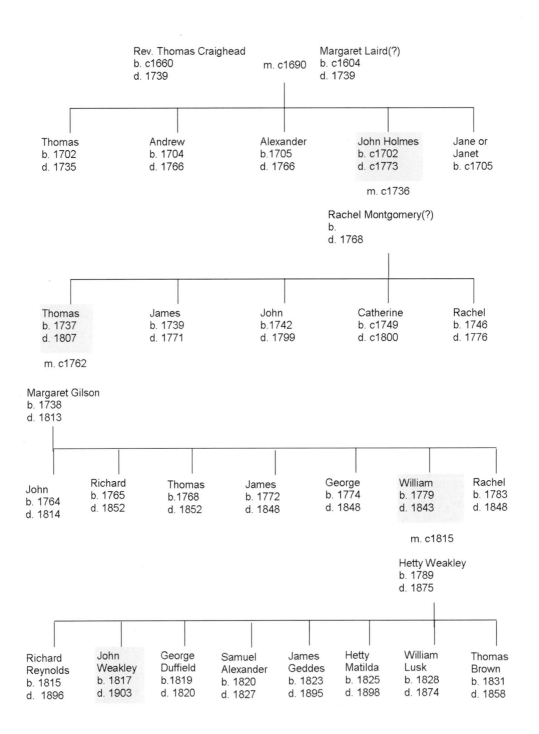

The Craighead Naturalists' ancestors.

2

Craigheads Come to Pennsylvania

F ROM MY SCOTCH CRAIGHEAD ANCESTORS I have inherited a sense of
'clan' and enjoy the comradeship it brings with it. People write me that they are
'Craigheads' and I bond with them," began Jean Craighead George when asked what
it meant to her to be a Craighead. She recalled Cotton Mather's description of Rev.
Thomas Craighead, the first of the family to come to the New World and the man from
whom all American Craigheads are descended: "He is a man of singular piety, meekness,
humility, and industry in the work of God." To understand the Craigheads, one needs to
know a little of their history.

In *Truman*, David McCullough portrayed the Scots-Irish as "tough, courageous, blunt,
touchy, narrow-minded, intolerant, and quarrelsome. And obstinate." Others described
them as adventurous and cautious, taciturn to a fault, but speaking their minds freely
when aroused. They were a serious people who rebelled against perceived injustice but
loved sports and had a sense of humor. They intensely disliked restraints of any kind,
loved the whiskey they distilled, and hated taxes.

Modern-day Craigheads descend from a long line of well-read, rugged individualists.
Some generations had money; others didn't. Most have had very clear principles but
don't necessarily follow accepted conventions. Leading is preferred over following. Not
suffering fools gladly is a common Craighead trait. Jean Craighead George wrote, "The
descendants from these ancestors would become minister-farmers, teachers, professional
people—and terrible businessmen."

Immigrants typically relocate for one of three reasons: economic opportunity, religious tolerance, or to escape war. Lowland Scots left for all three reasons. Ayrshire, the ancestral home of the Craighead clan, is rugged land located on the Firth of Clyde a bit north of Scotland's border with England. Lowland Scotland, due to its close proximity to its ancient enemy, was the all-too-often site of battles beginning with the English invasion in 1295. The Scots waged wars for independence over the next 400 years but ultimately failed. After combat ceased, religious friction and lack of economic opportunity continued to chafe Presbyterian Scots, who shuttled back and forth between Scotland and Ulster in Northern Ireland whenever political, religious or economic winds shifted.

Expecting no change for the better, Rev. Thomas Craighead (born c1658), one of the most eminent clergymen of the Presbyterian Church in Scotland and Ireland, boarded the ship *Thomas and Jane* in the fall of 1714 at Londonderry, Ulster bound for Boston in the Massachusetts colony. He brought with him his wife and children: four sons, only daughter, plus his sister Catherine, and her husband Rev. William Homes (or Holmes). Although endorsed by his friend Cotton Mather, Father Craighead was unable to establish himself in New England, probably because the Congregationalists were already serving like-minded colonists and the waves of Scots-Irish Presbyterians were yet to arrive. After several failed attempts to settle at a number of locations in New England and Delaware, he relocated to Pequea in Lancaster County, Pennsylvania in 1733. Although "...respected for his talents and learning, and loved for his genial spirit and piety..." and successful in "...planting and building up churches in the region," his family problems moved the Presbytery to "dissolve the pastoral relation." He was left to supply (a Presbyterian term meaning to serve as a temporary pastor) for the Meeting House Springs parish near present-day Carlisle and, later, at Big Spring near present-day Newville, both west of the Susquehanna River in what would later become Cumberland County, Pennsylvania.

That Rev. Craighead barred his wife from taking communion for treating their youngest son's wife in a less-than-Christian manner continued to block his installation as a permanent pastor until November 1737. The Presbytery then instructed him that, "his son John and family must no longer continue to live with him." The obstacle eliminated, Thomas was installed as pastor at Big Springs in October 1738, with his son Alexander (who had become the first minister of any denomination to preach west of the Susquehanna three years earlier) conducting the service.

The elderly Craighead's tenure at Big Spring was short. Although seventy-three, he was still near peak performance. Congregants hearing his sermons were often brought to tears and to emotional reactions so intense they were unwilling to disperse at the end

Big Spring Presbyterian Church (Cumberland County Historical Society)

of his services. In late April 1739, while giving one of his typical impassioned sermons, exhausted, he rushed through the benediction, waved his hand exclaiming, "Farewell! Farewell," collapsed, and died in the pulpit. He was buried in the cemetery adjacent to the log meeting house, but his remains were later re-interred and placed under the cornerstone of the new church when it was built in 1789. They repose there still.

John Holmes Craighead was born in Ireland c1710 and, being the youngest son, may have been a bit spoiled by one or both of his parents. He decided to preach the gospel, as had his great grandfather, grandfather, father, and brother, attended school (most likely in Scotland), but failed at the family profession. He returned to Pennsylvania, where he met and married an English heiress named Rachel (probably Montgomery) around 1736. He tried several other occupations, quickly depleting the bulk of his wife's fortune, leaving them to live with his parents out of financial necessity. Thomas's reaction to the friction between John's and his wives surfaced as an issue for the Presbytery to resolve. To restore domestic tranquility, church officers required John to move out of his parents' home.

Around 1738 (records are unclear), John invested the remains of Rachel's riches, a few webs of linen left from his failed tailoring business, as a down payment on a tract of land in the fertile limestone soil along the Yellow Breeches Creek in what would later become Cumberland County. The land was located four miles south of present day Carlisle and three miles west of present day Boiling Springs. Family members still have the parchment deed from 1773 when John Craighead's original tract was split among his sons after his demise.

Broke and with his parents deceased, John Craighead had little choice but to work and support his family (son Thomas had arrived in 1737). And work he did. He built his first house, a log cabin, just outside the right-angle bend in the Yellow Breeches Creek. John probably employed the same basic architecture as the Scots-Irish had used in the Old Country; only the building material changed from stones to readily available wood. They just filled in the gaps between the logs with dirt, mud and clay as they had previously filled in the gaps between stones. Their log cabins had the same floor plans as had their stone cottages in Scotland and Ireland, but the walls were made of a different material.

John positioned his cabin so he could see both up and downstream in case of an impending Indian attack. Restive Shawnees and Delawares were a constant threat during much of his lifetime. Because attacks were expected to come via the waterway, he placed the cabin to allow ample time to call people working in the fields to reach relative safety. Living under these conditions would have been terrifying for most people, but the Scots-Irish were accustomed to it due to the chaotic conditions they had experienced in the borderlands of Scotland and England.

The counties on either side of the border between Scotland and England where the Craigheads originated were disputed territory and lawless for centuries before Thomas Craighead's minister father left for Ireland. The English and Scottish armies took turns crossing a border that was accepted by no one and, when in enemy territory, raped, killed, pillaged, and burned everything in their way. This almost constant warfare created a state in which criminal activity thrived. Certain clans made a profession of preying upon their neighbors, reiving, as it was called in that area. Other families specialized in rustling livestock. Border reivers also served as the first line of defense for their respective kings—until their allegiances shifted, sometimes in mid-battle. Such effective cavalrymen were these reivers, Queen Elizabeth I claimed, "with ten thousand such men, James VI could shake any throne in Europe." Common people's only viable choices were to run or hide when they approached.

Life wasn't easy for John and Rachel, even though major Indian attacks did not materialize. Although the soil was fertile, they had to clear it or break the sod before crops could be cultivated. The Cumberland Valley in that area is believed to have been largely grassland at the time colonists first arrived. However, the valley is strewn with boulders and limestone outcroppings near the Yellow Breeches. The labor required to remove stones offset the ease of having relatively few trees to fell and stumps to dig out. They hewed and sawed the downed trees into beams and boards used to build structures to house people, grain, and animals.

The Scots-Irish didn't have a reputation for being as skillful at farming as their German neighbors in Lancaster County, who were highly adept at tilling the land. Before coming to the American colonies, Scots-Irish had generally farmed marginal soil, often on rocky terrain, for subsistence only. Over time, John and his children built several houses for servants and tenant farmers. They also cleared land to rent to tenant farmers. Starting as an almost penniless farmer, John Craighead rose to being a wealthy landowner and businessman due to his industriousness. He provided his descendants land and businesses, and his place in the community allowed his offspring to marry into the best families. The land his family owned or controlled increased to over 1,000 acres.

Thomas's grandson, also named Thomas, wrote in 1845 that his grandfather and great-uncle James had difficulty paying for their land and built a saw mill to raise the money. *Manufacturing and Mercantile Resources of the Cumberland Valley* (1882) published by the Commonwealth of Pennsylvania dated the construction of the mill to 1750, the year Cumberland County was separated from Lancaster County, and informed of its purpose, "In connection with the flouring mill is an excellent saw mill, which annually turns out many thousand feet of prime lumber, for all of which there is a steady and active demand." Tax rolls date the addition of the grinding operation to 1767.

Upon or prior to his death in 1773, John Craighead deeded his holdings over to his three sons. Thomas inherited the western half of John's original tract, referred to as the "Mansion Farm"; second oldest son John received the easternmost "third" but didn't live on it because, upon becoming a minister, he preached in the vicinity of Chambersburg; and the youngest, James, apparently was to receive the section between them, but he died before his father, resulting in land and his interest in the mills being acquired by his oldest brother. Except for the time Thomas briefly served as a Private in the 3rd Battalion of Cumberland County Militia in the Revolutionary War before George Washington furloughed him due to his having camp fever (typhus), Thomas lived on Craighead land continuously until his own death in 1807, by which time he had expanded it considerably through purchasing neighboring properties.

John and Rachel's middle son, John, followed his ancestors and family tradition by pursuing a course in classical studies at Princeton College and then studying for the ministry. Presbyterian ministers weren't pacifists: they wanted independence as fiercely as did the lay people. Rev. John Craighead was no exception. According to Rev. James Geddes Craighead in his 1876 genealogical memoir of the Craighead family:

"Mr. Craighead, like nearly every other Presbyterian minister in the Cumberland Valley, and indeed in this country, was an earnest patriot in the war for Independence. He could scarcely have been different, descended as he was from a Scotch-Irish ancestry, who in Scotland, Ireland, and in this country, were ever foremost in their resistance to all forms of oppression, and in their maintenance of civil and religious liberty. His uncle, Rev. Alexander Craighead, as early as 1742, while residing in Lancaster County[1], published such advanced sentiments on the subject of political freedom, he incurred the displeasure of the Governor of the Colony and also of his fellow ministers. He removed to North Carolina, where his opinions and teaching were said to have been more influential than those of any other individual in the final production of the celebrated Mecklenburg Declaration of Independence."

Presbyterians were biased toward a republican form of government rather than a monarchy, in great part, because of the organization of their church. They had a representative government within the colonies when other religious and governmental organizations looked across the Atlantic to England (or Rome) for directions. King James I declared, "Presbytery agreeth with monarchy like God with the devil." So, it was not without justification that King George III called the American Revolution "The Presbyterian Revolution."

Almost a third of the population of the thirteen colonies were Presbyterian. More, if similarly-minded Calvinists were included. This situation occurred because Scots-Irish colonists were more prolific than other denominations.

Unsurprisingly, Craighead ministers were firebrands for independence long before the Revolution; they, their congregants, and neighbors maintained this fervor throughout the war. On August 31, 1775, Rev. John Craighead "raised a company from the members of his own congregation, put himself at their head, and joined Washington's army in New Jersey." He and his men demonstrated their commitment to the cause as they "gave undoubted evidence that their courage was of no mean order." Historian E. H. Gillette wrote that the good reverend, "fought and preached alternately."

Rev. James Geddes Craighead summarized the performance of Cumberland County men under arms:

"These were not holiday soldiers, but men inured to toil and exposure; accustomed to the use of firearms, but unacquainted with the discipline of the regular army. What they lacked in experience, was largely supplied by the clearness and firmness of

1 Cumberland County was cut out of Lancaster County in 1750. References to Lancaster County previous to that date often refer to places that were later part of Cumberland County.

their convictions of the justice of the cause that had summoned them to arms. They were able, if circumstances required the sacrifice, to march without tents or baggage wagons; their knapsacks furnishing them their food, and their blankets their only covering at night. Many of their officers were either ministers or ruling elders of the Presbyterian congregations, from which the men in the ranks had been enrolled. The suspicion of being even lukewarm in the service, much more that of being a Tory, was a reproach and stigma upon a man's character; if it did not, as there is evidence that it sometimes did, bring upon him the discipline of the Church. It is not surprising, therefore, that when, three years after the war closed, in a notice for the sale of forfeited estates of persons attainted of treason, *there was not one in the County of Cumberland.*"

Such were the type of people local to the Craigheads who served in the revolution. Rev. John Craighead and his uncle, Rev. Alexander Craighead, were only two men, but both had major influences on the fight for independence. The elder minister spread Presbyterianism from Pennsylvania to Virginia and North Carolina as well as making the earliest case for separating from England, while the younger took up arms himself and led his congregants into battle. Cousins Capt. William Craighead and Col. George Craighead also fought in the Revolution. After independence was secured, Craigheads returned to their peacetime occupations and flourished.

On Thomas's death in 1807, *Kline's Gazette* reflected, "In his death his family have lost an affectionate head, and society a very useful member, whose activity and zeal, in matters both of a civil and religious nature, were conspicuous and exemplary." Because Thomas had already given son James £1,000 and son Thomas other lands and a mill, he left the Mansion Farm including "...my cash, bonds, notes, debts, stock, the services of my negroes, and all my other personal property..." to sons Richard and William. William, his youngest son, was just eighteen when his father died. Richard and William were to divide the 380-acre parcel equally by running an eight-foot-wide roadway (known now as Bonnybrook Road) up the middle of it. Thomas also left explicit instructions for how his widow, their mother, was to be cared for by her sons. Richard never married. He lived with William's family on the Mansion Farm his entire life.

Ancestry.com lists Thomas Craighead Sr. as having three slaves on the 1800 federal census, Richard as having two slaves on the 1810 census, and William as having three "free colored persons" living on the farm in 1820. The shift from slaves to freemen was likely a result of An Act for the Gradual Abolition of Slavery passed, by the Pennsylvania legislature in 1780, the first such law passed in the United States.

William married Hetty Weakley in 1815 and lived on the Mansion Farm until his

Craighead Mansion Farm House (Cumberland County Historical Society)

death in 1843 at which time his pastor, Rev. George Duffield described him thus, "he was a decided, energetic, and exemplary Christian, and his loss will be seriously felt by the church, as well as his family. He was zealously affected towards all the benevolent efforts of the day, and his name is recorded among the liberal contributors to those different objects. As a husband, father, brother, friend, and neighbor, he was justly beloved by all who stood connected with him in these various relations."

After William's death in 1843, the half of the Mansion farm west of Bonnybrook Road, the part on which the Mansion house sits, passed from William to his second son John Weakley Craighead, then aged twenty-six, perhaps because his oldest son,

Richard, was in the ministry. After Richard died in 1852, the eastern half of the Mansion Farm, including the grist mill, passed to William's second youngest son, William Lusk Craighead, who was then twenty-four years old. John Weakley married in the year following his father's death and William Lusk married the year following the death of his uncle. The marriages followed the inheritances so quickly because they enabled the two to support families and to have sons needed to work the farms.

Prosperity that began with John Craighead around 1740 continued through the generations that followed, and Craigheads continued to educate their young with their offspring going into a business or profession, farming ancestral lands, cutting timber, or, not surprisingly, preaching the Gospel in a Presbyterian church. When the Civil War erupted, Craigheads fought gallantly for their side depending upon which side of the Mason-Dixon Line they lived. John Weakley's son, Richard Reynolds, was wounded by a mini-ball while fighting for the Union but survived.

In the nineteenth century, Pennsylvania became a major industrial state while maintaining its primary industry, agriculture. Cumberland County's iron industry predated the Revolution. In fact, Boiling Springs, the village located closest to John Craighead's lands, grew up around two furnaces along the Yellow Breeches downstream from his farms. Across the Susquehanna River, Harrisburg became a rail center from which the Cumberland Valley Railroad ran tracks from the capital to Carlisle in 1837. Rebel forces were heading for the rail center at Harrisburg in 1863 when they were intercepted by Union forces at Gettysburg. After the war, railroad expansion happened in parallel with and was stimulated by the post-Civil War expansion of the iron industry, particularly in iron-producing areas such as Cumberland County. The iron and rail industries soon changed life on the Mansion Farm immensely.

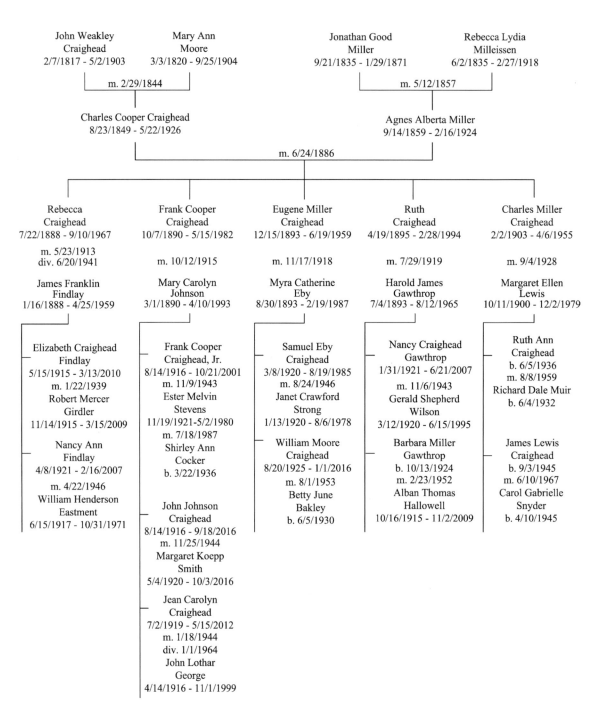

John Weakley
Craighead
2/7/1817 - 5/2/1903

Mary Ann
Moore
3/3/1820 - 9/25/1904

m. 2/29/1844

Jonathan Good
Miller
9/21/1835 - 1/29/1871

Rebecca Lydia
Milleissen
6/2/1835 - 2/27/1918

m. 5/12/1857

Charles Cooper Craighead
8/23/1849 - 5/22/1926

Agnes Alberta Miller
9/14/1859 - 2/16/1924

m. 6/24/1886

Rebecca
Craighead
7/22/1888 - 9/10/1967
m. 5/23/1913
div. 6/20/1941

James Franklin
Findlay
1/16/1888 - 4/25/1959

Elizabeth Craighead
Findlay
5/15/1915 - 3/13/2010
m. 1/22/1939
Robert Mercer
Girdler
11/14/1915 - 3/15/2009

Nancy Ann
Findlay
4/8/1921 - 2/16/2007
m. 4/22/1946
William Henderson
Eastment
6/15/1917 - 10/31/1971

Frank Cooper
Craighead
10/7/1890 - 5/15/1982

m. 10/12/1915

Mary Carolyn
Johnson
3/1/1890 - 4/10/1993

Frank Cooper
Craighead, Jr.
8/14/1916 - 10/21/2001
m. 11/9/1943
Ester Melvin
Stevens
11/19/1921-5/2/1980
m. 7/18/1987
Shirley Ann
Cocker
b. 3/22/1936

John Johnson
Craighead
8/14/1916 - 9/18/2016
m. 11/25/1944
Margaret Koepp
Smith
5/4/1920 - 10/3/2016

Jean Carolyn
Craighead
7/2/1919 - 5/15/2012
m. 1/18/1944
div. 1/1/1964
John Lothar
George
4/14/1916 - 11/1/1999

Eugene Miller
Craighead
12/15/1893 - 6/19/1959

m. 11/17/1918

Myra Catherine
Eby
8/30/1893 - 2/19/1987

Samuel Eby
Craighead
3/8/1920 - 8/19/1985
m. 8/24/1946
Janet Crawford
Strong
1/13/1920 - 8/6/1978

William Moore
Craighead
8/20/1925 - 1/1/2016
m. 8/1/1953
Betty June
Bakley
b. 6/5/1930

Ruth
Craighead
4/19/1895 - 2/28/1994

m. 7/29/1919

Harold James
Gawthrop
7/4/1893 - 8/12/1965

Nancy Craighead
Gawthrop
1/31/1921 - 6/21/2007
m. 11/6/1943
Gerald Shepherd
Wilson
3/12/1920 - 6/15/1995

Barbara Miller
Gawthrop
b. 10/13/1924
m. 2/23/1952
Alban Thomas
Hallowell
10/16/1915 - 11/2/2009

Charles Miller
Craighead
2/2/1903 - 4/6/1955

m. 9/4/1928

Margaret Ellen
Lewis
10/11/1900 - 12/2/1979

Ruth Ann
Craighead
b. 6/5/1936
m. 8/8/1959
Richard Dale Muir
b. 6/4/1932

James Lewis
Craighead
b. 9/3/1945
m. 6/10/1967
Carol Gabrielle
Snyder
b. 4/10/1945

Craighead Naturalists and Their Immediate Ancestors

3

Charles and Agnes Craighead

JOHN WEAKLEY CRAIGHEAD, GREAT GRANDSON of John Craighead, signed an agreement on December 4, 1868 that changed the fortunes of his branch of the clan forever. The Cumberland Valley at that time was very different than it was in the 1730s when Craigheads first crossed the Susquehanna River to minister to the Scots-Irish settlers who had ventured out to the frontier. "[A] rich luxuriance of grass is said to have covered the whole valley; wild fruit abounded, and in some parts the trees were of singularity variety." A century and a quarter later, the grasslands had long been plowed for cultivation and many descendants of the Scots-Irish who first settled the county had migrated west or followed the mountains southward to avoid hearing the bark of a too-close neighbor's dog. German family names, such as Gutshall, Zug and Erb, replaced some Scottish ones on local maps, but many Craigheads still remained and prospered. Like their ancestors, these Craigheads preached, operated mills, or tilled the fertile limestone soil along or near the Yellow Breeches Creek in the southern part of the valley. Overall, the Cumberland Valley was an intensively farmed, prosperous area. About the only forest that remained after settlement was on the mountains that delineated the valley or on land unsuitable for cultivation. But fertile land and forests weren't the only things of value in the Cumberland Valley.

Iron ore in the form of hematite, limestone, springs, and streams, coupled with the presence of lumber in close proximity to water power, made this an ideal site for ironworks. Thus, it should be no surprise that iron furnaces began popping up in the first half of the eighteenth century, creating the foundation for the industrial revolution in Pennsylvania. By the nineteenth century, iron furnaces operated up and down the valley, nine of which were in Cumberland County alone. In the early 1830s, railroads began transferring goods and people within the valley as well as to and from other parts of the country, due in significant part to the need to bring in materials used by the ironworks and to ship out their finished goods.

This iron industry that brought much commerce and the railroad to the valley also denuded the mountains to produce the incredible amounts of charcoal—an acre of forest cut per day for each furnace—needed to stoke the furnaces. A twenty-first century analysis of an aerial photograph of South Mountain in the general vicinity of Pine Grove Furnace revealed 5,000 circles thirty feet in diameter, the size of the wood piles colliers burned to make charcoal. Because of the proximity of some of these piles to one another, it is believed that timber was harvested more than once in some places, with decades between harvests. About the only trees that remained were on the mountain wood lots belonging to nearby farms, and those were endangered by tree poachers.

Pennsylvania was the earliest and, in 1870, the largest iron-producing state. It produced more than twice the iron of second-place New York. Iron furnaces and forges were usually located at the center of iron "plantations" that employed hundreds (or, in some cases, over 1,000 workers), generally in rural areas near forests, streams, and iron ore deposits. The iron master almost always lived in a mansion from which he managed the company's numerous operations. The workers lived in houses clustered nearby, shopped in stores operated by the company, and worshiped in churches built by the iron master. Some small towns that still remain, such as Boiling Springs, developed around an iron furnace. The iron industry and railroads were large businesses and served as the foundations for Pennsylvania's leading place in the Industrial Revolution, however agriculture remained the commonwealth's largest industry for at least another century.

Four generations of Craigheads had thrived farming the rich limestone soil found in the southern part of the county along the Yellow Breeches. They also dug mill races to divert water from the creek to power mills to grind grain or shape wood. Of course, a son or two from each generation usually went into the ministry. The daughters played their parts by marrying into the best families. An 1858 map of Cumberland County identifies several properties near the original Craighead tract still owned by family members as were a number of others a bit farther away. The 1872 atlas reflected no decline for the clan. If anything, more properties and businesses were owned by Craigheads than there were adult males in the family.

John Weakley Craighead, the second son of William and Hetty Weakley Craighead, lived in the white, painted-over brick colonial Mansion House and farmed the land instead of his older brother, Richard, who went into the ministry. John W.'s grandson Frank considered him to be a "very deep thinker and reader, excellent scholar; very reserved and quiet in manner" and a "great reader, bible student."

In 1844, John Weakley married Mary Ann Moore, a "very hospitable, very attractive and beautiful" daughter of a successful area farmer whose favorite study was music. The couple had public and common school educations, respectively, which probably meant they were better schooled than their less well-off neighbors. Beginning with William Weakley, in 1845, the first three of their six sons were born in consecutive odd-numbered years. The births of the last three sons were spread out more over time. Both John W. and Mary Ann aged well, as their grandson Frank considered both of them to be "remarkably well preserved" late in life and her "mind [as] very active." They were, of course, members of the First Presbyterian Church in Carlisle and had their sons baptized in that church.

Their first son, William Weakley Craighead, died in 1867 at age 22. Fourth son James Geddes had died at 10 years and 2 months of age in 1862. The four other sons all lived to adulthood. Second son Richard Reynolds was only 18 when he survived a mini-ball wound from a Confederate musket shot in the heavy fighting at the battle at Fort Steadman [Stedman], Virginia just two weeks before Lee surrendered to Grant at Appomattox. Afterwards, he returned home where he, his red-haired next oldest brother, Charles Cooper, who was too young for the war, and their two youngest brothers lived on the Craighead Mansion Farm with their parents, paternal grandmother Hetty, widowed aunt Sarah, Elizabeth Hiester, and Alice Kennedy. The last two were probably employed as domestics. One assumes that the boys worked the farm alongside their father before embarking on businesses on their own.

Shortly after the Civil War's end, increased activity at the iron works at Pine Grove Furnace convinced the operators to risk some of their money in developing the South Mountain Railroad (SMRR) to connect with the Cumberland Valley Railroad (CVRR) east of Carlisle near Ashland Cemetery to serve the iron works at Pine Grove. SMRR issued bonds and land acquisition soon commenced. They purchased a right-of-way 5,400 feet long and variable in width (but not wider than 50 feet at any point) through John Weakly Craighead's farm and to bridge the Yellow Breeches Creek. SMRR staked out the path the tracks would take as stated on the purchase contract. However, the legal description for this particular right-of-way was not included, a factor that makes determining its precise location problematic long after the tracks were removed. They paid John Weakley $6,000 or $1.095 per linear foot or $576,000 in 2010 dollars, a princely sum for 1868. He also negotiated direct access to the tracks within the right-of-way on both sides of Old York Road adjacent to where the tracks crossed and installed a siding parallel to the main tracks to provide temporary storage for a few boxcars.

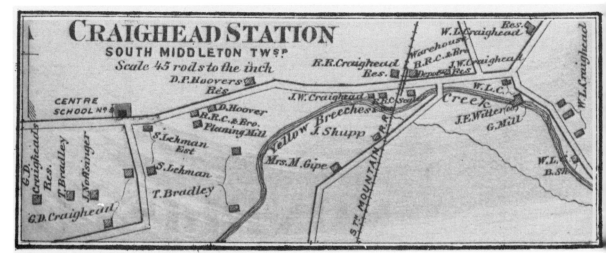

Craighead Station from the Beers 1872 Atlas (F. W. Beers & Co.)

By 1870, he or his sons built a railroad station (Craighead Station), general store, warehouse, feed mill, and coal shed and installed a scale to weigh wagonloads of grain and coal. John Weakley's two adult sons, Richard R. and Charles C. Craighead, operated the businesses and were listed on that year's census as "Clerk in warehouse." The next year, R. R. Craighead and Bro. built a planing mill a short distance west along the Yellow Breeches from the Mansion House on the site where Burkholder's mill had been located. Beers's 1872 *Atlas of Cumberland County* lists R. R. Craighead and Bro. as "Forwarding and Produce Merchants. Also Dealers in Flour, Feed, Grain, Lumber, Coal, Hay and Straw, and Manufrs of Doors, Sash and Blinds. Proprs of Planing Mill." The brothers surely had their hands full running all these businesses, but they also reaped the profits from them as their reward. As their businesses flourished, the brothers expanded their operation by starting or acquiring additional enterprises. An excerpt from the 1882 *Manufacturing and Mercantile Resources of the Cumberland Valley* published by the Commonwealth of Pennsylvania stated:

"...Mssrs. Craighead are conducting a very large and growing business in the purchase and shipment of grain, seeds, and other agricultural products, and in supplying contractors and builders with choice building material, embracing all kinds and grades of lumber etc. They are also proprietors of the Summit Quarry, which produces a superior quality of limestone, in practically inexhaustible quantities, and the shipment of which reaches the average of twenty tons daily. Their premises are extensive and improved by fifteen to twenty different buildings…their productions being shipped as far as Europe and South America."

In addition, their uncle William Lusk whose properties adjoined the Mansion Farm, operated a large flour and feed operation "…which he ships in large quantities to Philadelphia, New York, Baltimore, and also to Europe, his shipments in flour alone reaching an average of four hundred to five hundred barrels per month, exclusive of the large quantity distributed throughout Cumberland Valley." Arranging shipment of these products surely netted R. R. Craighead and Brother something.

The previously quoted publication also commented on the Craighead brothers' characters:

"Suffice it to say that in every relation, social and commercial, as merchants, agriculturalists, and as citizens, they have ever enjoyed the highest esteem of all the classes of the community of which they have been for so many generations formed a valued part, and the present members of the family are known to all as chief among the promoters of the welfare of this section, and as gentlemen who have done much to enhance the distinction of the honored name they bear, and to maintain the sterling character which is their chief heritage."

Because their businesses were so successful, R. R. Craighead and Bro. had enough excess cash to buy other businesses. In 1887, they further expanded their business holdings by purchasing the nearby four-story flour mill on Lerew Road near its intersection with Old York Road for $3,300 at a public sale to settle the debts of their uncle William Lusk Craighead. In addition to the mill, the property also included a two-story brick house and a frame tenant house. This purchase ended the Craighead brothers' expansion. Their challenge for the future was to maintain what they had.

Richard Reynolds Craighead, senior partner in the business, was a "stout 5'7" tall and was of good business qualities & physique." Apparently, he suffered no serious, long-term effects from his Civil War wound and lived an active life, including participating in reunions of his army outfit, Gen. Hartranft's Division of the Ninth Army Corps, and serving as Treasurer of the 209th Regiment. He married Mary Alice Leidich in 1871 and built a large Victorian home across the tracks and directly behind the station. They attempted to start a family almost immediately but met with much sadness. Their first four children died in infancy and two others died in childhood. Only three of their nine children survived to adulthood.

Junior partner, Charles Cooper Craighead, married Agnes Alberta "Aggie" Miller, who was ten years his junior, on June 24, 1886, when he was 36. Rev. West of Westminster Presbyterian Church conducted the ceremony in Aggie's mother's home in Harrisburg. Agnes was thin, very pretty, and well-educated for a woman of her day. Her hair was believed to have been light brown with a bit of red mixed in. Charles was shorter than average as were most Craighead males, and she was shorter than him. The whole family had blue eyes. Having graduated from high school, she had more schooling than her husband, who had only completed "common school," the public elementary school available to him locally. Boiling Springs High School would not graduate its first class until two decades after their wedding, and boys generally entered the work force at much younger ages at that time. Charles's favorite subject was mathematics, where Agnes enjoyed history and music.

Although she was a city girl, having grown up in relative affluence in Harrisburg, Agnes re-adapted to life in the country as she had spent her earliest years on the family farm across the Susquehanna River in Dauphin County. Agnes's father, a farmer and part-time lawyer, died when she was just eleven. Her grandfather Miller bought her mother a house in Harrisburg in which she raised her six surviving children on the income generated by the farm.

After their wedding, Charles and Agnes caught the 3:40 p.m. train from Harrisburg to the beautiful Victorian home Charles built for her directly across Old York Road from Richard. Charles's house and lot were a bit smaller than his older brother's but, with five sizeable bedrooms, a sewing room, and a servant's bedroom, all upstairs, was large, even by contemporary standards. Its decorative walnut millwork, flooring, sashes, doors, windows, shutters and rusticated siding were shaped specially at the family's planing mill. The unusual wood siding was milled with beveled edges to resemble quarried limestone blocks. These boards were painted and sprinkled with sand before being hung in the same manner as those at Mount Vernon. Charles's elegant late-Victorian

Charles Cooper Craighead

Agnes Miller Craighead

(Barbara Gawthrop Hallowell)

house with Italianate features was situated alongside the railroad tracks, and the back yard sloped gently toward the Yellow Breeches Creek, which meandered behind it on its way from its source on the northwest side of South Mountain to its mouth at the Susquehanna River.

Charles's modern home had no well for potable water, perhaps because the property was so close to the creek or to save the (sometimes considerable) expense of drilling a well. Drinking water was hand pumped into pitchers and other containers from the shared well just across the road in his brother's front yard and carried back to the house for use. Another absent feature, central heating, was never installed.

Charles and Agnes started their family in 1888 with the birth of their first daughter, Rebecca. They had their first son, Frank Cooper, two years later, followed by Eugene Miller in another two. Ruth came two and a half years after Eugene in 1895. Perhaps unexpectedly, their fifth child, Charles Miller, arrived in 1903, almost eight years after their fourth.

The children reveled in life at Craighead Station; it was an idyllic setting for nurturing children. The railroad bridge that spanned the creek was situated perfectly to attract Charles and Agnes's children and grandchildren to engage in sometimes dangerous activities such as waiting for a train to get close then jumping off the bridge. The

Charles & Agnes Craighead home in 1899 (Barbara Gawthrop Hallowell)

creek, that bridge, the fields, woods and meadows around Craighead Station provided a playground and natural laboratory for the next two generations of Craigheads, as well as their friends. They could hunt, fish, swim, and play games in their back yard. Frank even had a favorite sinkhole nearby that he used for hiding things he didn't want people stumbling onto accidentally. And Craighead children were far too inquisitive to ever get bored.

Charles and Agnes, both of whom enjoyed good health, had much better luck than most because all five of their children lived to adulthood. Their children had common childhood diseases but survived them all. One assumes their active life styles and getting plenty of fresh air playing outdoors helped them fare better than many children of this era.

Charles and Agnes shared the same religion, regularly attended First Presbyterian Church in Carlisle, and expected their children to do the same. Charles hitched Old Maud to the horse-drawn wagon for the hour-long trek to church each Sunday morning, even in the dead of a Pennsylvania winter. Daughter Ruth remembered huddling under buffalo robes to keep warm in the back of the wagon.

Ruth recalled watching horses and mules turn the huge grindstones that ground the grain into flour in the grist mill by walking on a treadmill. Several decades later, she took her daughter, Barbara, to see the ruins of the mill. Part of the flour they ground was placed into bags adorned with a distinctive red rose to identify their own brand, Rosedale; the remainder was sold under their Yellow Breeches brand. Other nearby businesses included a blacksmith shop and a cider press that operated seasonally, attracting hordes of flies to the juice. Based on later accounts, it appears that Charles did the accounting for the businesses, while Richard managed them and handled customer relations.

Agnes loved to garden and filled almost the entire yard with flowers of various types. Hers was no English garden that appeared to be wild; it was highly manicured and required a considerable amount of attention. "The dirt was as fine as pepper and the flowers were gorgeous" in the opinion of her daughter-in-law, Carolyn. Her granddaughter Jean, then 91, sketched the layout of her grandmother's flower gardens as they were in 1926, to the best of her memory. The phlox, irises, roses, hollyhocks, herbs, zinnias, marigolds, violets, day lilies, tulips, and lilies of the valley Agnes cultivated created a sea of color in her yard. Her daughter, Ruth, recalled, "Mother was a great gardener, very involved in keeping it blossoming through the seasons. And she had a flock of chickens which she loved. They'd talk to her and she to them. They were great friends." Another of Agnes's granddaughters, Barbara, recalled a canyon of white phlox towering over her on either side of the walk from the kitchen to the outhouse when she was very young.

Grandson Bill, like Barbara, was born after Agnes died but remembered her gardens as they were kept in his early childhood. "Grandmother Craighead's perennial flower beds were always a sight worth seeing with holly hocks and phlox. The phlox usually attracted many insects like butterflies, bumble bees, moths and hummingbirds. Well, speaking of insects, just before it got very dark, the fireflies would put on a magnificent display as they hovered just above the wheat fields."

Agnes Craighead was also musical and played the piano. That piano, or a successor, was a center of entertainment at Craighead, as it was called by friends and family, for generations to come. Barbara remembered her mother Ruth relating something unusual about her own mother: "Grandmother Craighead let the kids go swimming in the creek even during thunderstorms, seeming unconcerned about any danger. 'She loved a thunderstorm and got me to loving them, too,' said Mother. And she passed that along to me, an incorrigible storm watcher, though with great respect for the electricity involved."

Agnes Craighead holding oldest son Frank Cooper Craighead 1891
(Barbara Gawthrop Hallowell)

A source of willing workers to help tend her flower gardens—one assumes that her mother, sisters, and children could not be classified as such, with the possible exception of her eldest daughter, Rebecca—was the Carlisle Indian School[2]. Even before Agnes married Charles, Richard and Mary Craighead supported Carlisle Indian School, attended events at the school, and provided a home for students in the outing program. Agnes followed suit after she married into the family. She participated even more than most other "Outing Mothers" as evidenced by the number of mentions of her in the school's newspaper. The November 14, 1902 edition of *The Red Man & Helper* included a small piece about a teacher's visit with a student's outing family:

"Miss [Fannie G.] Paull spent Sunday with Mrs. Charles Craighead, at Craigheads, where Emma Strong lives. She had a delightful time and was pleased with Emma's progress. Emma is happy. Mrs. Craighead has discovered she has a voice, and Emma sings to her accompaniments. She goes to school and is to sing two solos in their Thanksgiving entertainment. [Emma was probably attending the nearby one-room elementary school.]"

Decades later, granddaughter Jean met a former Carlisle Indian School student who had helped tend Agnes's gardens. He wanted to show his wife what he had done, and, perhaps, see some of the people at Craighead he had known. He was disappointed to find Agnes's carefully tended flowers turned into a playground by her grandchildren.

---

2 Carlisle Indian Industrial (1879-1918), located on Carlisle Barracks, was the first government off-reservation Indian boarding school. Integral to the program was an outing system that sent students to live and work with families in eastern Pennsylvania and New Jersey to better integrate them into the majority society.

Later articles report of Rebecca and Miss Paull becoming friends and of Rebecca staying with Miss Paull when she visited Carlisle Indian School. That education was important was imparted to Agnes by her mother Rebecca Miller. Charles and Agnes sent Rebecca and Frank to Carlisle High School rather than to the much closer, but smaller, school in Boiling Springs. Whether they commuted via the train or stayed in Carlisle during the week is not known. Another possibility is that they walked, or rode a horse, a couple of miles to catch the trolley to school. Rebecca and Frank likely used one or more of these options to make getting their high school diplomas from Carlisle High possible. Their younger siblings, however, went elsewhere. Their idyllic world at Craighead Station was shattered by events not of their making.

★ ★ ★

Insular Cumberland Valley could not always avoid being affected by things happening elsewhere, even back then. Major national and international events affected life at Craighead Station almost as much as anywhere else at that time. The Craighead brothers could hardly have picked a worse time to be in business. The Panic of 1873, sometimes called the Crisis of the Gilded Age, initially a real estate bubble in Europe caused by cheap mortgages, ultimately triggered a financial crisis in the U. S., where railroad companies had overbuilt by relying heavily on credit. Eighty-nine railroads went bankrupt, 18,000 businesses failed, and, in 1876, unemployment reached 14%, long after the panic had ended. Some see this panic not as an isolated event but as part of something larger.

The Panic of 1893 was, in many ways, similar to the Panic of 1873, so similar that some call the period from 1873 to 1900 The Long Depression. Railroad overbuilding, based on shaky financing, caused bank failures and set off the Panic of 1893. To make matters worse, a rush on the gold supply coincided with the bank failures. Some consider the Panic of 1893 to be the worst economic depression the country has experienced. The country had barely caught its breath in the early 20th century when F. Augustus Heinze attempted to corner the market on American Copper Company shares in 1907. His attempt failed but exposed the existence of close associations between bankers and stock brokers, raising anxiety levels of depositors in New York banks and trust companies. All that was necessary to start runs on these institutions was for depositors to learn that a few men controlled multiple banks or served on the board of directors of several of them. The Panic of 1907 led to the creation of the Federal Reserve Bank System, but that was much too late to help R. R. Craighead and Brother.

★ ★ ★

The trade from the local iron furnaces flagged in the latter decades of the 19th century as the demand for steel increased and the giant U. S. Steel in Pittsburgh was able to produce steel more efficiently and less expensively than the old iron furnaces. The operators modified the furnaces to take advantage of more advanced processes, but that wasn't enough. They just couldn't compete with larger plants that had less expensive access to higher grade iron ore from Minnesota. The fluctuations in the iron business wreaked havoc with the Craighead brothers' finances. Their iron trade came to an end in 1895 when the Pine Grove Furnace was shut down permanently. The Carlisle Furnace in nearby Boiling Springs had ceased operation the previous year.

To inject additional capital into their businesses, the Craighead Brothers took on a partner, William G. Coyle, for the planing mill, which took the name Craighead & Coyle. Coyle, born in 1849 and listed in the census as a carpenter, would have been in his late 30s at that time. The reason for taking on a partner was surely something they did out of necessity rather than desire. Regardless, this move proved unsuccessful.

In August of 1895, probably in reaction to the loss of income from their rail-related businesses, they ran an advertisement in the Williamsport *Gazette and Bulletin* in an attempt to sell the planing mill, complete with "sash and door factory with latest improved machinery." They didn't advertise the sale of their mill locally because the mill at Mooredale had been advertised in *The Evening Sentinel* for months, with no taker. Their attempts to divest Craighead & Coyle proved fruitless. The brothers also borrowed from a C. Stayman, optimistically expecting business to improve and to be able to repay him in the future.

Richard Craighead suffered a massive stroke on the evening of December 5, 1895 and died at 6:30 the next morning. His fellow elders from First Presbyterian Church served as pallbearers at his funeral. It is quite possible the stress from two decades of running businesses in extended periods of recession brought about the stroke. Speculation that a war injury brought about his premature death at only 48 years of age seems unfounded, particularly when one considers how his nephew, Frank, described him as being "of good business qualities and physique."

Charles not only lost his older brother and neighbor; he also was left without his senior partner. But he soldiered on. It probably wasn't easy because he had surely relied on Richard's good business sense, and major changes over which they had no control were disrupting their business at the time. He also lost a worker who would have been very hard to replace, especially one who had experience maneuvering through turbulent times.

Daughter Ruth, born in 1895, only had one toy, a doll, and never considered asking for a bicycle as she knew her parents could not have afforded to buy her one. Charles's parents had means and helped keep the business afloat until they, John W. and Mary Ann, died in 1903 and 1904, respectively, after accruing debt that exceeded the value of their estates. John W. had even mortgaged his farm for $2,500 to Valeria Penrose. He apparently had no expectation of ever being able to repay the loan because he stipulated that his wife Mary Ann have the use of the Mansion House for the rest of her life. The farm was sold to George B. Otto for $8,667.20 to cover their debts. Richard's wife, also named Mary, must have had some money of her own because she loaned the business money after her husband's death; his debts were also considered uncollectable when she died in 1904. Rebecca Miller, Agnes's mother, was a woman of some means and may well have helped her daughter's family financially.

Richard and Charles Craighead valiantly attempted to protect their families from the consequences of the decades-long economic depression with every tool at their disposal. That the 1900 census listed a white servant girl, Agnes Bogner, as a member of Charles's household and that Agnes Craighead continued to host Carlisle Indian School students on their outings imply that the family still had some disposable income. Richard's widow Mary and three of their children continued to live in the house across the road from Charles, something that certainly required some income. Charles's parents (83 & 80), brother John and his wife (40 & 39), a white servant girl (19), and a black servant boy (9) still lived in the Mansion house. The implication is that enough resources remained in the family at least five years after Richard's death to maintain some of the lifestyle to which they were accustomed. That Mary and her children were living in Carlisle when she died in 1904 might not indicate that she no longer had sufficient income to maintain her large country house by that time but that she preferred the comforts living in town provided or perhaps needed to be closer to medical facilities.

In addition to family members, Charles likely borrowed money from some or all of his planing mill partner, neighbors, or banks. He also had difficulty collecting what was due to the business. The Pine Grove Furnace's files in the Pennsylvania State Archives include correspondence from R. R. Craighead & Bro. to the iron works, over half of which are dunning letters. These letters crescendoed from asking to be paid to pleading for money to pay their creditors to getting the furnace owners to sign promissory notes to make installment payments. Charles's grandchildren understood that he was generous with credit to the local farmers at a time they had difficulty paying him. Some think that he may have been too nice to his creditors, ultimately causing his family to suffer the consequences.

Lenders demanded payment in 1905, but Charles didn't have the money to pay them. The businesses were lost, and the Craighead brothers' homes were put up for sale but did not change hands. In spite of all this, Agnes was still able to sponsor Joseph Tarbell on his outing from Carlisle Indian School in the fall of 1907. However, her attempts to save the businesses ultimately failed because, by 1908, Charles found it necessary to take a job in Harrisburg as treasurer of the Harrisburg Leather Products, a position he held for several years. The next year, the Craigheads' remaining business property was sold to George Otto, but Agnes was still able to retain possession of their home along the Yellow Breeches.

The bitter details of the Craigheads' economic demise were not saved for posterity, but some tidbits were passed along. Their daughter, Ruth, shared with her daughter, Barbara Gawthrop Hallowell, "He couldn't be hard on people to pay their bills. He was too nice!" Charles's granddaughter, Jean Craighead George, recalled that many of his customers were farmers who had been hit hard by poor economic times and were unable to pay her grandfather what they owed him. Losing the businesses due to being unable to collect what was due him shattered him and put great stress on his marriage. All that remained was their home by the creek.

No longer having a business or employment at Craighead Station, around 1908, Charles, Agnes, Eugene, Ruth and young Charles M. Craighead were forced to leave for the City of Harrisburg in order for Charles to find employment. Rebecca and Frank were finishing high school or attending college by this time. In 1909, the *Harrisburg City Directory* listed the family's address as 1821 N. Second Street, Harrisburg, in a house believed to be owned by Agnes's mother, Rebecca Miller, who lived at 1207 Third Street. Family members recalled her being a strong advocate for education. Charles and Agnes no longer had any servants; niece Bessie, a public high school teacher, and nephew Richard L., children of Charles's older brother Richard R., lived with them after their mother Mary died. Young Richard appears to have only lived with them a short time before leaving for Worcester, Massachusetts, while Bessie stayed with them for several years before moving to New York City. Their daughter Rebecca, then a public high school teacher, rejoined them around 1912 and lived with them in the Second Street house until she married. Charles and Agnes most likely needed extra income from boarders to make ends meet.

Harrisburg City Directory did not list Charles and Agnes after 1920, likely indicating that they, then 70 and 60, respectively, had retired to Craighead Station. Agnes's mother died in 1918 and may have left her enough money for them to get by on their last few years. Agnes died on February 16, 1924 while staying with her daughter, Rebecca Findlay,

Rebecca Milleissen Miller (Barbara Gawthrop Hallowell)

in Bethlehem, Pennsylvania. Charles died on May 22, 1926 while living with daughter Ruth in Kennett Square, Pennsylvania.

Back at Craighead during summers and after retirement, Agnes maintained her flower gardens the best she could with her children grown and gone, and, as Carlisle Indian School had closed in 1918, its students were no longer available to assist her. Her estate at the time of her death implies that she had retained enough for them to live on, although not as well as she had previously been accustomed to. Charles is remembered by his grandchildren as spending most of his declining years just sitting quietly in a chair. Frank's son, John, told a Carlisle *Sentinel* reporter, "For the short time our grandfather was alive, we'd catch eels and turtles and bring them to him.

Grandad said it reminded him of when he was a boy." John and his twin brother, Frank Jr., would rise early, race the short distance to the creek, and pull out the trout line to see if they had caught any eels overnight. After removing any eels caught from the line's large hooks, they would skin them, and nail the skins as trophies on a board that was mounted on a sycamore tree along the creek as a challenge to other boys in the vicinity.

Despite his business failures, Charles's oldest son Frank had a positive view of his father's business acumen, describing him in 1914 as a "methodical, good business director; very active and energetic; generous to a marked degree. Very fond of hunting and fishing and good observer of nature." He then described his mother, Agnes, as being "very neat; orderly; exact; strict." Younger daughter Ruth, known for not saying anything bad about people, said little about her mother. Barbara opined, "I gathered that it all wasn't peaches and cream," but things were different with her grandfather. "Mother had glowing things to say about her father: He was very kind and helped a lot of people who couldn't pay their bills. They had hit on hard times." Her cousin Jean recalled the final straw that broke Charles, "[M]y grandfather had loaned most of his money to the farmers and had little in the bank. It was a Friday night. It broke my grandfather and ruined his marriage."

The adjustment to living in reduced conditions wouldn't have affected just Charles and Agnes. It couldn't have been easy for their children, at least the older ones, who had been used to a life of relative affluence. The land, farms, mills, and businesses that had been the lifeblood of previous generations were all gone. The younger generation of Craigheads would have to make their own ways in the world by very different means than had their forebears. Education would be the key to unlock their futures. In that regard, Charles and Agnes, with the likely assistance of Agnes's mother, prepared all five of their children to survive and flourish in this new world to a far better degree than most.

PART II

Focus on Education

THAT THEIR FATHERS FAILED IN BUSINESS turned out to be a well-disguised blessing for the children of brothers and business partners Richard Reynolds and Charles Cooper Craighead, but it was a long time in coming to fruition. While Craigheads had a long history of being intelligent and better educated than most others, few had pursued academic careers. Many had been educated for the ministry, but almost no others had chosen vocations that required higher education. Losing the farms and businesses forced the current generation to look elsewhere for their sustenance. Rather than seeking out employment as unskilled wage earners or apprenticing themselves to tradesmen, they determined their brains would be the key to flourishing in what was an entirely changed world for them.

What they did is documented. Why they did it is obvious. But how they did it is not clear, as they probably considered their actions too mundane to record at the time or to reflect upon later. We can only piece together fragments from which to form a picture. R. R. Craighead's oldest daughter, Elizabeth (called Bessie in her youth, Bess in later years), was attending Carlisle High School, Pennsylvania's first public high school, when he died in 1895. Although family finances were strained, tuition would have been manageable; however, commuting or lodging costs also had to be covered. But how did they pay for tuition, transport and, if needed, lodging? We will never know; we can only speculate. We do know that for centuries Craigheads had been sending sons to university in preparation for the ministry, their family tradition of educating the young. Also, the first family member to come to America, Rev. Thomas Craighead, was highly educated and sent his youngest son John (the original settler on the land lost in the twentieth century) back to Scotland to be educated. Thus, it could be said education is in Craighead genes, by making schooling a top option when tides turned. Educating their children was relatively easy for these Scots-Irish compared to other challenges they had overcome in the old countries and on the frontier of the New World.

★ ★ ★

The Craigheads' physical attributes may have had an influence on their choices of vocations. Charles C. Craighead was about 5' 7" tall with light brown hair with a reddish cast. He, like other family members, had blue eyes and was small-framed and trim, neither skinny nor heavy. Agnes's specifics aren't known, but from photographs it is clear she was petite and quite attractive. Charles and Agnes passed their physical characteristics directly to their children and indirectly to their grandchildren. Eugene, at 5' 9 1/2" tall, was the tallest of their children. Frank and Charles were an inch or two shorter. Gene, weighing 130 pounds at age 49, was quite active throughout his life as an avid hunter and fisherman. His build was typical for a Craighead. Frank was thin and physically fit well into his 70s. Little is known about Rebecca's build, but it is likely to be similar to other Craigheads. Ruth, who is said to have inherited her auburn hair from her father, was about 5' 5" tall, trim, and attractive. Both Rebecca and Ruth met future husbands while in college. The following chapters tell of Frank, Eugene, Ruth and Charles until the U. S. entered WWII. Rebecca's life story will be told up to the time she broke with the family.

4

Rebecca Craighead

CHARLES AND AGNES'S FIRST CHILD, Rebecca, was born at home in 1888. Nothing was written about her childhood, but a few things can be surmised from what was written about her later. Agnes surely recruited her to help tend the flower gardens and assist with chores around the house. She must have swum in the creek behind the house, explored the nearby fields and meadows, and, occasionally, accompanied her father when he fished the local streams.

Rebecca's education was important to her parents, even though or, more likely, because they had fallen on hard economic times as she entered adolescence, and she would not be able to support herself in the family businesses. Their lowered economic status could also affect their daughter's chances of marrying someone from their former social strata. Charles's older brother Richard and his wife Mary, who lived across the road from Charles and Agnes, educated their daughters as well as their son. They undoubtedly influenced Charles and Agnes regarding the importance of education as did Agnes's mother, Rebecca Miller.

Richard and Mary sent their daughters, Bessie and Hettie, to Carlisle High School. After graduating, Bessie enrolled at Dickinson College, also in Carlisle, completing her degree in the Latin Scientific track in 1901. She was elected into Phi Beta Kappa and learned the secret handshake. In 1912, Bessie was awarded a Pi Beta Phi scholarship to cover a year of advanced study in Paris. Her sister Hettie graduated high school in 1904 but waited two years, probably because of finances or her mother's health, before enrolling at Dickinson College as a special student in the Latin Scientific track. She left Dickinson in 1908 to enroll at Wellesley College, where she earned a B. A. degree in

1910. The following year, Hettie completed her B. S. degree at the Columbia University Graduate School of Education, her second undergraduate degree, after which she embarked on a career as an educator. Bessie and Hettie surely influenced their younger cousin across the road.

When a mere Carlisle High freshman in 1902, Rebecca argued successfully in a school debate. For graduation in June 1906, the faculty chose her to give the address immediately following the salutatory oration. "Nature is God's Mirror" encompassed two themes close to her heart: nature and religion. She then matriculated into the Classical track at Dickinson College as a member of the Class of 1910.

How Rebecca paid for her education isn't known, as her father had lost his businesses and her paternal grandparents were dead. Perhaps her mother, who had resources of her own, or her maternal grandmother, who had money and was a staunch supporter of education, helped cover her college costs. An education was more attainable then because tuition was proportionally much lower than it is now.

Rebecca's classmates considered her rustic, if her yearbook entry can be a guide:

"When she first came to college, she was a simple country maiden always bedecked with *'flaers,'* but since then she has become accustomed to the frivolities and strenuosities of college life, and has lost all of her Freshman greenness except her fondness for *'flaers.'*"

To reinforce that point further, her Senior yearbook entry began with the first stanza of William Cullen Bryant's "O fairest of the rural maids:"

"O fairest of the rural maids,

Thy birth was in the forest shades,

Green boughs and glimpses of the sky

Were all that met thy infant eye."

Her favorite studies were "Greek, Latin, nature." Her brother Frank considered her to have a "special taste for language and classical literature, also very fond of nature study." But Rebecca didn't spend all her evenings studying. "She is always willing to help a fellow-sufferer less studious than she and spends much of her time in working out a certain young man's lessons. It is in this little class of two that Dan Cupid finds a chance to shoot his arrows." More information concerning her beau was found in James F. Findlay's entry: "He often calls at a dominie's house on Louther St. We hope that these calls portend nothing serious." That Rebecca lived with a teacher or minister's family seems likely. It's clear the classmate who wrote the piece on Findlay disapproved of him.

"Foggy," as Rebecca was called by her classmates, "since she fails to comprehend the slightest joke," may have been too naïve to accurately assess her suitor. James Franklin Findlay's yearbook entry began with a Shakespeare quote: "Oh [God,] that men should

B. LOUISE COLLINS . . . . Crisfield, Md.
Harman Literary Society; Y. W. C. A.

"Be good and you'll be happy, but you'll miss a lot of fun."

This is "Weezer," our friend from the "Eastern Sho'," and a very loyal friend she is. She came to us from the Wilmington Conference Academy and started with 1911, but wisely deserted its ranks for those of illustrious 1910. "Weezer" conscientiously lives up to her motto, and always has a smile for everyone. If a happy smile denotes a clear conscience, hers is certainly exceptionally clear. She is still heart-whole and fancy free, we believe, but the naughty little twinkle in her eye sometimes seems to say, "I know something, but I won't tell," "Weezer" is a true friend and comrade and is always ready to do a kindness for anyone.

REBECCA CRAIGHEAD . . . . . Craighead

"O fairest of the rural maids,
Thy birth was in the forest shades,
Green boughs and glimpses of the sky
Were all that met thy infant eye."

Rebecca, better known as "Foggy," since she fails to comprehend the slightest joke, is one of 1910's most loyal supporters. When she first came to college, she was a simple country maiden always bedecked with "*flaers*," but since then she has become accustomed to the frivolities and strenuosities of college life, and has lost all of her Freshman greenness except her fondness for "*flaers*." She is always willing to help a fellow-sufferer less studious than she and spends most of her time in working out a certain young man's lessons. It is in this little class of two that Dan Cupid finds a chance to shoot his arrows.

62

Rebecca Craighead's senior yearbook entry (Dickinson College Archives)

put an enemy in their mouths to steal away their brains." This followed immediately:

"Just why Hanover ever gave up this good judge of bad whiskey is more than we are able to say, but he is here and we are rather glad for his presence, for there are some good points about him. His most admirable quality is that he generally minds his own business. But there are stated times when he wants to fight, for he often wants to try to lick about a dozen fellows, but of course his friends won't let him…. Dam is his favorite expression, when he doesn't use something stronger. There is a place down town called 'Hock Shop' that often comes to his aid. Findlay goes to classes just as often as he is compelled in order to pass off some of his work."

After three years of vexing the faculty for failing his coursework and committing infractions of their rules, Dickinson College had seen enough of James F. Findlay, Class of 1910. On April 24, 1909, he was suspended, returned home to live with his parents who had moved to Allentown, and took a job as a clerk at a steel company.

Rebecca graduated with her class and began a teaching career. Her first job was in Netcong, New Jersey, about which she wrote:

"What have I been doing this year? Trying to be a dignified school marm, and oftentimes in the midst of a recitation the situation strikes me so funny I can't help smiling. My children are so amusing. A foreign element predominates, and funny answers never end. 'A river is a pond what runs down the lane.' 'A prairie is a large flock cattle.' 'The earth running on its axles cusses day and night.' A week or so after I came to Netcong I found a stranger in the town was a rarity. Everyone knew it, and it was even versed, much to my embarrassment."

She must have enjoyed her first job because she wrote, "Hoping all my classmates have enjoyed this first year half as much as I have." Why she didn't stay isn't known. Perhaps a poem a mischievous student, 'Hugh,' wrote about her had something to do with her leaving:

"Red, white and yeller,

Teacher's got a feller.

What's the matter with teacher—

She's alright."

In the first half of the 20th century, it wasn't uncommon for unmarried female teachers to be disallowed from dating. The school board in a community in which "a stranger is a rarity" could easily have become aware of her boyfriend and might not have rehired her for the 1911-12 school year for having a "feller." Rebecca moved to Harrisburg to teach Latin at Central High School and live with her parents.

In May 1913, James Findlay was offered the Manager Accountant position for the Bethlehem Steel iron mines in Chile. Either he had curtailed his drinking—as young men frequently do—or kept it under control enough to not affect his job performance. He accepted the promotion on the condition he be allowed to return to the U. S. for Rebecca in June 1914. But, the day before he was to sail, he learned the magnitude of the work waiting for him in Chile was so great he wouldn't be able to be away for the three months necessary to make a round trip to marry and return with his bride. However, the company would bring his wife down once a house had been built for them. But he had no wife and wouldn't be able to return to Pennsylvania to marry Rebecca. So, on May 23, 1913, likely without her parents' blessing, they married in a quiet service in New York City. Afterwards, he sailed off for Chile while she waited for the company to build them a house.

Rebecca resumed her life as an unmarried school teacher living with her parents and remained active socially under her maiden name. One such event was a pair of basketball games and dance for Central High School for which she was a patroness. Portraying herself as being engaged, friends feted her at a miscellaneous shower in January 1914. The guests did not include her mother or sister. Perhaps her mother was ill or was not enthusiastic about her supposed upcoming marriage or her sister Ruth could not arrange transportation from Swarthmore where she was then attending college. On April 2, Rebecca resigned from her teaching position and revealed the fact of her marriage the previous year. This revelation created such a scandal the *Philadelphia Inquirer* covered it in its State News Notes:

> "Harrisburg.—When Rebecca Craighead, teacher of Latin in the Harrisburg High School, resigned her position yesterday, announcement was made that she and James F. Findlay, Jr., had been married for nearly a year."

Rebecca left Harrisburg on April 6 for Bethlehem, where she visited her husband's parents, who then accompanied her to New York. Her own parents attending neither her wedding, shower, nor sailing may indicate their disapproval of her marriage. She sailed for Chile on April 11, 1914. The Findlays' first daughter, Elizabeth (Betty) Craighead Findlay, was born on May 5, 1915 at Minas del Tofo, Coquimbo Region, Chile. The three of them returned to the U. S. on the S. S. *Cabrillo*, docking in New York on February 3, 1916.

The Alumni column in the April 22, 1914 edition of Dickinson College's newspaper, *The Dickinsonian*, stated, "Both Mr. and Mrs. Findlay are Dickinson graduates." But Mr. Findlay was most definitely not a Dickinson graduate. However, it is quite possible this was a student reporter's assumption rather than a misrepresentation on Rebecca's part.

After sailing back from Chile, the three Findlays returned to Allentown where Rebecca managed the household and cared for Betty. James continued to work for Bethlehem Steel and rose to the rank of accountant. After their second (and last) child Nancy was born in 1921, they moved to Bethlehem to a likely larger home closer to his work. He must have continued to do well at Bethlehem Steel because he moved up to an auditor's position. Rebecca's mother, Agnes, lived with them during her declining months leading up to her death on February 16, 1924.

Rebecca split from her family after their father's death in 1926, but neither Rebecca nor her siblings shared with their children the cause for the alienation. One grandchild conjectured a disagreement arose between Rebecca and her siblings over their mother's care prior to her death. Who complained about what isn't clear. Some surmised she wanted to sell the house but the others didn't. She sold her share to her siblings for $600 on July 30, 1927. After completing the transaction, Rebecca burst out of the house, taking the original parchment deed with her. As far as anyone knows, she returned only once when she visited a friend in the area and drove up to the house. She parked at a place in the road from where she could watch her siblings' children play without getting out of her car.

Rebecca surely carried the naturalist gene as evidenced by her love of "flaers," but too little is known about her later life to know how it manifested itself in her.

5

Frank Cooper Craighead

FRANK COOPER CRAIGHEAD WAS BORN on October 7, 1890 to Charles and Agnes Craighead at Craighead Station, joining older sister Rebecca in the family. Aggie attempted to raise Frank much like town boys of his day were, but he thwarted her at every turn. She dressed him for Sunday church in a ruffled shirt and long curls like Little Lord Fauntleroy, but he refused to go. One Sabbath, he walked onto the railroad bridge and, without hesitating, proceeded to its center over the creek. When a train approached, he just *had* to jump to avoid it. He couldn't go to church with his Sunday best soaking wet. Another time, he retrieved his pet skunk from its home in the sinkhole about 100 yards upstream from the iron bridge and intentionally irritated it, getting the expected result. He could hardly go to church smelling like that! Agnes planned on Frank becoming a minister but had to accept he was never going to be a man of the cloth.

Frank described his boyhood in the country: "I was interested in insects and birds' eggs. I was alone on my grandfather's farm. I hadn't any playmates, and I just ran around the countryside since there wasn't enough farm work to do." The work part might have been true after his grandfather's farm was sold, but is more likely a matter of perception. Beside his older sister, he had cousins Hettie and Bessie (five and ten years older, respectively) and their brother Richard (his age) across the road. Frank viewed his male cousin as "dull, but with a peculiar gift for mechanics." Apparently, Dicky, as his Harrisburg Technical High School classmates called him, agreed with Frank's assessment, as he was allowed to spend his afternoons in the machine shop but was unable to follow simple directions from his football coach. Frank may have considered himself alone because his younger brother, Eugene, had different interests. Gene's favorite activities were hunting and fishing rather than poking around the woods looking for bugs. The age difference between Frank and Gene could also explain why he didn't accompany Frank on his South Mountain bug-hunting expeditions, at least at first. Ruth and Charles were far too young for Frank to take with him.

Since there is seldom a shortage of work to be done on a farm or in the family businesses, it seems more likely there wasn't enough work of the type he found appealing. Frank's daughter Jean observed, "Craighead men don't like to work." A more accurate way to put this would be they find or create jobs that interest them. They turn their hobbies into jobs, and those hobbies generally have something to do with nature. No nine-to-fivers, Craighead men work long and hard on things they find interesting.

Frank was inventive and resourceful, if not always successful. The Yellow Breeches Creek in his backyard beckoned to the young boy, but Frank had no canoe at his disposal. So, he made one from materials readily available at his father's business. He built the skeleton out of wood hoops from flour barrels, then stretched burlap across it, gluing it in place with flour paste. "It didn't hold together very well," he recalled with a smile late in life.

His first school was a typical Pennsylvania little red brick schoolhouse about a half mile west of his home along Old York Road. Years later he recollected, "There were about 25 pupils in one room and a teacher, Mr. Stuart, I believe, encouraged me."

Frank started his study of nature in earnest early in life. Just after his 12th birthday in 1902, he agreed to help Miss Paull, a teacher at Carlisle Indian School, by providing stock for the terrarium in her classroom. In gathering those specimens, he became the first of the numerous Craighead naturalists of his generation and those who followed. His next "job" was assisting entomologists from the Pennsylvania Department of Agriculture:

"My first contact with the Harrisburg group (that very definitely shaped my life) was at Gettysburg Junction about two miles south of my home 'Craighead Station,' a post office on the Phila. & Reading R. R. I was in high school then, about 1904-5, and met several of these men collecting [plants] along the foot of the South Mountain. I was becoming much interested in natural history and frequently tramped these mountains and, as our friendship developed, took these men to many interesting collecting spots....They wanted to find and collect a certain plant when it was in bloom. I knew where the plant was growing and took them there. That started a lasting friendship that really shaped my life, because I was in contact with them on many weekends for years, until I went to college. ...[T]he men that frequently met me there were [William R.] Walton, [Henry L.] Vierick, [Alfred B.] Champlain, [Harry B.] Kirk, [Wilber R.] McConnell, [Warren S.] Fisher and others. I began collecting insects and taking them to their office at Harrisburg…. During high school, I often spent Saturdays in their Harrisburg, Pa. office and picked up much knowledge on insects and natural history."

In ninth grade, Frank attended Carlisle High School to obtain a better education than his parents thought he would receive at the local public school in Boiling Springs. How Frank got to and from high school is unknown. By 1907, his family lived in Harrisburg. His daughter Jean thought he might have lived with a relative in Carlisle through the school week:

"[H]e awakened to new worlds with the discovery of the literary classics in the library of a great-aunt. During his high school years, he read his way from the door, around the room and back again. Years later he told me that the library had indeed inspired him to go to college and get his Ph.D."

Unfortunately, Jean didn't share where this great aunt who owned this library lived. Regardless, he received his Carlisle High School diploma on June 11, 1908 from Moses Friedman, Superintendent of Carlisle Indian School, who conferred at the ceremony.

Curiously, although never officially an employee of the Pennsylvania Department of Agriculture, Frank Craighead received more mention in the official history of the entomology program than did some long-standing employees of the Department because of his contributions, particularly to their insect collections, while in high school.

But he was just getting started. The fall after graduation Frank enrolled in the Forestry Department at Penn State College. His choice of schools was likely a combination of interests, economics, and geography. He wanted to become a doctor, but his parents couldn't afford to send him to medical school, so he selected something he liked and could afford. In spite of having to pursue his second choice, he very much enjoyed his years at Penn State:

"Dr. Baker was the head of the school then, but most of my contact was with the head of the Zoology Department. He gave me and a pal of mine, Doug Spencer (who was later a famous M. D.), the run of the laboratory. We could even work there at nights. So, I took all the courses in zoology, as well as forestry courses and botany. Dr. Buckhout, head of botany, was a great inspiration. At that time you registered in the Forestry School where you had to have certain courses in forestry, wood technology, silviculture, and management, but the rest of the time, I was permitted to take anything I wanted. I took mostly zoology and botany."

After his Freshman year, Frank roomed with George Drake, aka Duck, Gladys or

Drakie, who transferred from New Hampshire College. Frank and George roomed and spent summers together their last three years at Penn State. Drake recalled his introduction to forestry work:

"I went there as a sophomore. The school got us jobs with the Forest Service. Frank Craighead and I were supposed to go to Eugene, Oregon to work on a cruising party....Neither of us had ever been on a Pullman car before. We got on a Pullman at Pittsburgh to go to Chicago. A young lady had a lower berth, and she didn't know how to retire and we didn't know how to retire, so we sat up until about three o'clock in the morning wondering who in hell went to bed first. Finally, a porter came around and said, 'Don't you want me to make your beds?' We didn't know that the porter made them up. We didn't have much money, so we thought we'd take a lunch from Chicago, and we bought some ham sandwiches. It was terribly dry. There was no air conditioning on the train, and going across the prairies the second day, you couldn't bite through the damn things, they were that hard. Well, we survived to Portland, and then went down to Eugene.

Frank Cooper Craighead (Fairchild Tropical Botanical Garden)

"When we got there, we reported to the supervisor, Clyde Seitz. He was a very brusque individual. He told us he'd never heard of us. I said, 'Can't you check with the regional office?' He said, 'I'll call Portland. You come back tomorrow.' So we went back to the hotel. We didn't have much money. The next day we went back and he said, 'No, there's some mistake. You're not supposed to be here.' 'Well,' I said, 'We've got to do something. Aren't there any other jobs?' And he said, 'There's a job at McKenzie Bridge building trail. It's $1.50 a day and board.' I said, 'We'll take it.' So we went back to the hotel and found out McKenzie

Bridge was fifty or sixty miles away [between seventy-five and a hundred, according to Frank]. We made arrangements the next morning to send our baggage up on the stage, went down and put $10 in the bank out of our $20 we had left, and started hiking. The last mile we were barefooted, our feet were blistered so badly. When we got to this place, Vida, we stayed at a farmhouse…The next morning, the first mile we broke our blisters and finally went through a town called Blue River….Then we hiked into the South Fork of the McKenzie and started work. That's when our pay began."

Frank added, "Then later in the summer they called us for jobs on the timber surveys. We were running lines, taking the height and diameter of trees. We'd go out on a week's packing trip. George and I were always paired together in all that work. He was like I was—inquisitive, always seeking more information. He liked the outdoors and hiking trips. Bear Meadows was a famous cold water swamp where northern plants grew, and we'd often go over there. I had a great friend in George."

Back at Penn State in the fall, Frank was the lone entomologist in the Forestry School. "They all called me 'Bugs.' George Drake started it….We tramped the surrounding countryside many weekends, often with Doug Spencer." They found other ways to fund their education closer to home but not far from danger. Forester Joe Ibberson recalled how Frank earned another nickname:

"Back in the days when they used anti-venom for snake bites, Frank was up in a cabin in Clinton County where there was wire through the middle of the cabin. Frank and this other guy [George Drake] lived on the one side and the rattlesnakes lived on the other side of the wire fence….They'd milk those rattlers every day to get the venom out of them and sell it to the drug companies. That's how he got his money to go to college….We called him Rattlesnake Frank."

Frank explained how he, although a student in the Forestry School, became an entomologist:

"Through the Pennsylvania Department of Agriculture entomologists that I knew, I had been building up a collection of immature stages of insects, as a hobby. I had reared hundreds of insects and associated the adults with the larvae even before I went to college. Occasionally I would write Dr. Hopkins and send in specimens. They were also studying the immature stages, and could recognize them before they would have emerged. I had a lot of correspondence with them. The next two summers, while I was going to college, he put me on his staff as a temporary collaborator and I went out to Oregon and California. Then, before I graduated, I had an appointment with him as a specialist in Cerambycidae. The Cerambycidae are a group of insects that are wood borers. They do a lot of damage to saw logs and fallen timber. After college he sent me out west on several details. We had a very small organization—Burke and Miller and Edmonston and Snyder—in fact, I don't think there were more than a dozen of us."

Frank's senior yearbook page included more insect references:

"'Gee, ain't this a peach of a bug? This specimen must be a Psychomorpha epimenis which belongs to the order Sepidoptera, of the class Hexapoda.' This is quite a 'shark' and in his element when working with ordinary bugs, but when he chances to come in contact with that order known as 'lady-bug,' he does not seem to make much progress in classifying them, in other words, he 'gets fussed.' 'Bugs' is a loyal Forester and will be with us in June 1912."

The comment regarding Frank's dealing with the fairer sex was accurate, as his daughter described him as being really shy and sensitive.

Forest entomology was an emerging field in the early twentieth century. It flourished under the Pennsylvania Department of Agriculture when Prof. Harvey A. Surface was hired as Economic Zoologist in 1903. Between 1903 and 1910, he built up the staff Frank met at South Mountain and worked with in Harrisburg. The field's history with the federal government wasn't much different. The Department of Agriculture (USDA) was founded in 1862 as a result of the Agricultural Organic Act. USDA's original staff consisted of the nine members of the former Agricultural Division of the United States Patent Office, Department of the Interior. The USDA's Commissioner, Isaac Newton (not that Isaac Newton) immediately hired Townsend Glover as Federal Entomologist, a position he held until retiring in 1878 due to failing health. The USDA wasn't elevated to cabinet level until 1889. A primary function of early federal entomologists was maintaining the insect collection now housed in the National Museum of Natural History. Glover's successor, Charles V. Riley, devoted more attention to invasive pests. During Riley's tenure to 1894, the Division of Entomology was created to reflect the field's expanding responsibilities. Leland Ossian Howard succeeded Riley and held this post until 1927. In 1902, Howard made Andrew D. Hopkins Chief of Forest and Forest Product Insect Investigations within the Division of Entomology after he distinguished himself with his work on the southern pine beetle.

Frank took a job under Hopkins in the USDA's entomology division upon graduation from Penn State in 1912. When asked about the nature of early work done by the federal government regarding insects, Frank stated:

"In entomology, but not in forests, Dr. Hopkins was a professor at the University of West Virginia. He specialized in bark beetles and wrote a number of valuable

Frank Craighead visits a forestry service camp (Western Forest Insect Work Conference)

publications prior to his taking charge of the unit. I think when I went in they had only these men we've been mentioning, and an appropriation of $50,000 plus $75 each per month. We all started at that [$75], supposedly a good salary in those days." Frank also recalled what it was like to work with Hopkins:

"He was a very independent person and had very strong convictions about his work. He wanted his men to support him in every detail. But he was very good to his men and a tremendous worker, of course. He'd work at nights, and a lot of us worked in the National Museum, where our offices were, sometimes until twelve o'clock or two o'clock at night. We'd eat our dinner along about suppertime at a place called Sam's, where we'd get a great big beef sandwich and a beer, then go back and work all evening on our collections. I took charge of the collections of immature stages shortly after I came there. That was after Burke and Edmondston went

West. During the eight years our office was in the U.S. National Museum, I became acquainted with many of the specialists who built up various collections. I would bring material in to them from my various travels over the U.S. and they always welcomed the specimens and explained their habits and characteristics. Offhand I recall Drs. Swartz, Coleoptera; Cushman, Foraminifera; Bassler, Bryozoa; Clark, seashore animals; Mary Rathburn, crayfish; Schmitt, marine animals; Dr. Barutch, mollusks; Dr. Pilsbry, mollusks. These contacts greatly stimulated me and tended to broaden my education and approach to entomological problems."

Frank's exposure to naturalists from other specialties broadened him; however, his work for the federal government was confined to forest insects. Off the job, he stretched himself in other ways. Weeknights, he attended classes at George Washington University (GWU) in pursuit of a master's degree. Weekends also found him paddling his canoe the ten miles down the Potomac River from his home in Washington, D.C. to court co-worker Carolyn Johnson in Alexandria, Virginia. On the way, he collected wildflowers and gigged frogs to present as gifts to his intended. "I wasn't all that crazy about frog legs but yes, they did help him win my heart," admitted Carolyn decades later. Often, their "dates" were excursions up and along the then-wild Potomac. Seven months older than Frank, Carolyn was born on March 1, 1890. Christened Mary Caroline, in her school days she decided she didn't like her name and began using Carolyn, the name she used the rest of her life, even after she couldn't remember why she changed it. Like Frank, she had ancestors from lowland Scotland. Her mother's parents both came from Renfrewshire, a neighboring county to the ancient home of the Craigheads. Her father was an accountant who died of apoplexy at age 50. According to Frank, her mother had an artistic temperament and was broad-minded, reasonable and self sacrificing.

Carolyn dropped out of high school during her senior year out to help support her widowed mother and four younger siblings. She took a job as a scientific assistant at the National History Museum, where she made slides of insects for the princely sum of $25 per month. Working in the same building brought Frank and Carolyn in touch with one another. Frank coached Carolyn as she prepared for the Civil Service Exam, which was newly opened for women. Her supervisor promised her a promotion if she got the highest grade. Carolyn got a 97, the highest score of those taking the exam, greatly bettering the men, the best of whom scored only 89, but he reneged. Mustering her courage, she confronted him about passing her over for the men she outscored. After responding, "But I didn't think you'd beat the men," he promoted her to entomological assistant in the Bureau of Forest Entomology at the USDA. Thus Carolyn became the first woman to be hired by taking the Civil Service Examination. Carolyn's sister,

Pauline Johnson Zirpel, also worked in that office but may not have taken the exam.

Being a man of science and a very logical thinker, Frank didn't enter into marriage without examining all available data. With eugenics being all the rage, Frank submitted a Record of Family Traits for both Carolyn and himself to the Carnegie Institution of Washington in December 1914. In addition to basic data about themselves, their parents, grandparents, siblings, aunts, uncles, and first cousins, Frank also included his assessment of their intelligence, disposition, and general character. Relatives found curious that a so-called scientific foundation would base evaluations on the subjective assessments of a person only 24 years old. He described himself as being "especially fond of natural sciences; very active physically; very fond of outdoor life and hunting; absolutely without fear," all of which were accurate. He described Carolyn as "[having a] Nervous temperament, very artistic, very fluent talker and magnetic or attractive character."

The analysis done by prominent eugenicist and biologist Dr. Charles B. Davenport of the Station for Experimental Evolution in January 1915 included some interesting observations derived from the data Frank supplied, including, "I notice on your side that three of your four grandparents lived to a ripe old age, which indicates innate resistance on both sides of the house. The union of the highly emotional brother of your father [R. R. Craighead] with an emotional, hysterical woman was a bad combination that shows in the offspring; which is in striking contrast with the good mating that your more stable father made." Apparently, Dr. Davenport didn't consider the effects on Mary of losing her first four children within a year of their births and the next two by age six when he evaluated her "hysterical" personality. Nor did he consider her daughters' academic achievements. What follows is Davenport's analysis of Frank's proposed pairing in its entirety:

"The young lady clearly belongs to a somewhat more nervous strain but, as it does not seem to show itself in her in hysteria or lack of emotional control, it does not follow that there would be any tendency to over emotionalism in her offspring. In fact, it is to be expected that she might bring in a little more of brilliancy to the combination. The early paralysis does have an hereditary significance but we have not yet worked out exactly in what way. No doubt the absence of such paralysis on your side of the house would bring, in so far, strength to the children in this respect. Concerning the hay fever, we do not yet know how the tendency to it is inherited. It is quite likely that the children would have something of a catarrhal tendency which would have to be counteracted by the best of training, outdoor life and so on.

"On the whole, then, the examination of your family histories as given offers no reason for expecting that any children derived from the proposed mating would be other than normal, healthy children, having probably a better hereditary background than the great majority of children."

When learning about this assessment, Frank's daughter Jean responded, "Well, I guess we didn't turn out too bad." Younger readers may want to familiarize themselves with the meaning of hysteria in common usage in 1914.

Frank married Carolyn on October 12, 1915 in Alexandria, Virginia after completing the work for his master's degree. His thesis was an entomological study of the Prioninae larva he made for the Department of Agriculture, as part of his employment, one assumes. In 1915, he was sent to Florida for the first time to study pine bark beetles as part of research that would last for decades. Upon getting married, the young couple set up housekeeping in East Falls Church, Virginia in a house Frank built himself. On August 14, 1916, they were more than surprised when Carolyn delivered their first child—and his identical twin brother—both by breech birth. Frank Jr. and John were named later as two sons were not expected, so names for two boys hadn't been selected in advance. The older one was named after his father and the younger one after his mother's father. They did not cease being a handful after being born. Two and a half years later, they were joined by a sister, Jean, whose name was selected by Carolyn's mother, Agnes Aitcheson Johnson, because it was a good Scottish name. On Carolyn's 100th birthday, Jean praised her mother:

"Mother was extraordinary. She made our dresses, baked bread and pies every week, ran the house and walked a mile to shop for groceries. At night she would read the classics to us."

While starting a family, Frank focused on plant physiology and geology, completed his dissertation, and earned his Ph.D. from GWU in 1919. His dissertation topic likely dealt with protecting forests from the locust borer as the U. S. Department of Agriculture published his study of the insect in 1919 as *Bulletin Number 787*. His post-doctoral studies included two years of coursework in sedimentary geology under Raymond Smith Bassler at Johns Hopkins University.

In 1920, the year after Jean was born, Frank accepted an assignment in Ottawa, Canada under Dr. J. W. Swaine, head of Canada's forest insect unit, to study the spruce budworm, which was devastating pulpwood stands. Frank enjoyed the assignment: "I was headquartered at Ottawa, but I covered all the eastern provinces in both summer and winter. We traveled with dogs and sleds all winter, with temperatures twenty below. We'd set up our tent right on top of the snow." While technically not a leave of absence from the USDA, it was essentially one because, when Dr. Swaine asked him to come

Agnes Craighead with daughter-in-law Carolyn on railroad bridge over Yellow Breeches Creek
(Barbara Gawthrop Hallowell)

north, Frank asked his boss for permission. A. D. Hopkins responded, "Well, you can go if you [promise to] come back." Three years later, when he was ready to return, Dr. Hopkins had retired. L. E. Howard, who was then in charge of entomology, asked Frank if he would take the job as head of the Bureau. No other candidates were considered, and he accepted. He moved his family to a new house at 5301 41st Street NW in the Chevy Chase section of Washington, D.C. at the frontier with the Maryland countryside.

On weekends, the Craigheads took advantage of the opportunity to experience the nature so close to them. Jean recalled, "Almost as soon as we could walk, Mother and Dad took us along the Potomac and taught us the plants and animals. Our friends who came along all remember Mother's generosity and incredibly good food." Jean's father amplified this: "Our whole family, since the time the children could walk almost, lived out of doors and canoed and camped. At that time, the Potomac River was just as wild as any place in the United States. Moonshine setups all along. I knew every foot for a stretch of ten miles, and all the good fishing holes."

Frank emphasized his favorite thesis so often Jean memorized it: "Study an insect and you are soon studying the whole forest. Study the forest and you are soon studying the insect." This view served Frank well when interfacing with other governmental

Frank Craighead shooting a Muzzleloader
(Western Forest Insect Work Conference)

agencies and with the work he did in later life.

As much as she liked nature and "roughing it," Carolyn had limits. Frank bought an old house for weekend use, about 20 miles from their home, near Seneca, Maryland which the previous owner had built from lumber collected from the Johnstown flood. When they arrived at the house for a stay, Frank would jump out of his car, rush into the house before anyone else had a chance, grab the black snake that liked to sleep on their bed, and get rid of it before anyone else could see it, especially his wife. He knew Carolyn would not have liked to know a snake had been in her bedroom!

As head of the Bureau, Frank had responsibility for experiments underway in forests across the country, mostly in the south and west. As soon as school ended for the year, he and Carolyn loaded everything needed for the summer into his meticulously maintained car (Fords at first, Chevys later) and drove to the family home at Craighead Station owned by Frank and his siblings, where Carolyn and the children spent their summers. Carolyn enjoyed the relaxed life there which allowed her much opportunity to read and write. She especially enjoyed going to the market house in Carlisle where she could buy fresh produce and prepared meats, especially sausages. Frank's brother Eugene's wife, Myra, and their sons also spent their summers in the house. On long weekends and holidays, Ruth's family joined them. Charles, the youngest sibling, brought his bride, Peg, after they were married in 1928. But Charles and Peg's children didn't come along until later. Their oldest was still a toddler when WWII interrupted everything. Everyone—Craigheads, friends and neighbors—enjoyed their times in that house. Jean summed up those summers:

"Each summer, aunts, uncles and cousins—as many as seventeen altogether—filled the house and sleeping porch and spilled over into the yard. Ours was a naive existence. We fished, swam, rode the hay wagons and raised owls, falcons and guinea pigs. We really believed that if you were good, good would come back to you, and that work was salvation. Other virtues were sharing, being honest, minding your elders, and not having sex before marriage.

"In the evenings we sang by the creek or played softball, with the parents joining in. When we were bored and likely to get into mischief, Mother would send us into the meadows to collect wild flowers, which we pressed and identified; she gave me lessons in sewing and canning fruit, both of which also bored me numb. I much preferred to be out with my brothers, catching frogs and jumping off the limbs of a tree into a deep pool of the creek."

Local resident Donald Goodyear recalled how Carolyn and his grandmother, Grace Goodyear, became close friends who spent much time together. Grace lived in a cottage perched above the Yellow Breeches just downstream of the iron bridge, behind which was anchored a raft. Carolyn would snap the chinstrap on her cap, jump into the not always warm water, and swim up the creek to the iron bridge to visit her. Although Grace was a generation older, she and Carolyn cemented a strong friendship. They sunned themselves in wool one-piece swimsuits and relaxed away lazy summer afternoons on the raft removed from the noise and activity of the children.

Carolyn cried when summer ended, marking the time to return to Washington and the school-year grind. Being raised Southern, Carolyn tried as best she could to keep a proper home considering whom she had married. Once, she defended her housekeeping

Frank & Carolyn Craighead Family in 1933 (William Moore Craighead)

to her daughter, saying, "I always stood for gracious living. It was the Craighead men who let the owls fly through the house and who would come to the table in their bare feet. Not I."

Although it might appear Frank was lax regarding his children's upbringing, that was far from the case as he constantly taught them about the plants and animals around them. He was also exacting and wanted them to think before they acted. Jean recalled a weekend camping trip with him and Paula, a daughter of her mother's younger sister, Pauline Johnson Zirpel. While the girls set up the tent, he caught a fish for supper. "When he returned and I proudly showed him how smooth the tent was, he snapped, 'This won't do. You've pitched the tent right on the path. The fishermen come down this trail all night and day. Take it down.'" After moving the tent, he told them to collect some hellgrammites (stone-fly larvae) from Seneca Dam. After collecting a couple dozen of them, the girls accidentally slid down the slippery rocks, losing the bait bucket. "My father's nostrils flared when he saw us approach empty-handed. 'You lost the bucket because you were playing. I saw you out there laughing and having a big time.'" Frank's words were sharp at times, but they were the harshest tools he and Carolyn used against their children—instilling self-discipline was a common goal.

Frank was a serious man. He did not want his children to be frivolous. When asked if her father was a Phillies fan after she volunteered the results of the previous night's Yankee's game, Jean responded, "Lord no. He disdained comics, trashy books, radio (except news), liquor, cigarettes, lipstick, no stockings, and the like." Although he rejected religion, he internalized many of his parents' Calvinist practices. Frank was not flirtatious, far from it, but women found him attractive. Carolyn dealt with potential interlopers by befriending them. This strategy sidetracked rivals before Frank had any idea the women had any interest in him.

Frank and Carolyn were serious about educating their children and welcomed opportunities to improve learning conditions whenever they arose. Shortly after Robert F. Griggs, early explorer of the Katmai River Valley in Alaska, and his wife, Laura, moved to Chevy Chase, he and his family became close friends with the Craigheads. Finding Chevy Chase-Bethesda schools inferior to those they left in Columbus, Ohio, Laura took it upon herself to do something. She, Carolyn and Carolyn's sister Pauline founded the Chevy Chase Child Study Club to address the "everyday problems of the parents of every child, such as how to secure obedience, how to change unsatisfactory habits, [and] the relative merits of the child-centered school over the old type curriculum." The group grew to have considerable influence on the Chevy Chase and Washington, D.C. school districts.

The Craighead, Griggs, and Zirpel children also socialized with each other. Actually, the boys socialized with the boys and the girls with the girls—all three families had at least one daughter in the age bracket of the Craighead children—but getting the boys and girls to mix was exceedingly difficult. In the minds of their mothers, the boys—Julian Griggs and the Craighead twins—lacked social graces, particularly in dealing with girls. Robert Griggs recalled the reaction when the women tried to arrange a get together with a mutual friend who had two daughters of appropriate ages:

"A party with these girls and guests was suggested. Julian's reaction was immediate and violent. When we asked him what harm could come of it, Julian loudly proclaimed, 'Why, they might say hello.' We tried some specification. But the thought was too horrible a threat even to contemplate. Over and over Julian repeated, 'They might say hello.' It was clear enough that he was sure that any such party would queer him with the twins and therefore would be altogether out of the question.

"With the Craigheads, the Zirpels and the Griggses, however, there was a good nucleus without inviting strangers. So Mrs. Kincannon, a charming young woman, was engaged as a dancing teacher and the group began meeting in each other's homes on Friday nights. The first Friday night the boys had to be practically dragged from their corner and almost forced to touch hands with the girls for a Paul Jones."

Jean's friends Florence Kelton and Emma Shelton also joined in the dance lessons. Emma recalled "the lack of prowess shown by the brothers in dancing class." Frank didn't make this mixing easy for the women. He considered dancing feminine and proclaimed it "sissy" to his sons.

Throughout the many years Frank Craighead lived in Washington, D.C., he considered himself a Pennsylvanian. He claimed Craighead Station as his home and voted straight Republican, with few exceptions. Maintaining a Pennsylvania residency proved handy when time came to send his children to college. In-state tuition for three children in college at the same time posed a much smaller financial hardship than out-of-state tuition would have presented. By June 1941, all three had earned their bachelor's degrees and the twins their master's. Frank worked steadily during the Great Depression, never losing a day's pay and managing his money carefully. He and Carolyn had their children raised when WWII ended the Depression, but world events kept them from relaxing and taking it easy.

Eugene Miller Craighead as a baby (Laurie Craighead Rudolph)

6

Eugene Miller Craighead

EUGENE MILLER CRAIGHEAD WAS BORN at Craighead Station on December 15, 1892 or 1893, depending on which of his draft registrations is accurate. (Church records are fuzzy.) His son Bill and sister Ruth believed he was born in 1893. That Gene didn't accompany older brother Frank on his bug-hunting expeditions on South Mountain argues for the larger age difference. That the brothers chose different religions when it came to angling was significant. Where Frank was a cane pole man who fished streams and lakes for ordinary fish, Gene was a dry fly fisherman extraordinaire.

When Frank and Eugene were boys and when their children were young, the Yellow Breeches Creek had no trout, only bass, bluegills, eels, and mussels. Letort Spring Run, one of America's premier trout streams, flowed through Bonnybrook (the next stop on the railroad heading toward Carlisle) and provided Gene the perfect learning opportunity. Fishermen must crawl up to the bank to sneak up on the highly suspicious trout living in and near the watercress beds at Bonnybrook. Those in the Letort are reputed to be so smart only the most expert fishermen have a chance at hooking them. Eugene learned well, most likely by coming home empty-handed on his first few tries, and succeeded in becoming renowned for his skill at netting these most difficult of all trout to catch. Young Gene likely preferred spending his free time pursuing elusive fish while his older brother collected insects.

Gene probably attended the elementary school down the road from his home but, with the family's move to Harrisburg, attended Harrisburg High School rather than Carlisle as had his two older siblings. Like Rebecca and Frank, he was a strong student and was quite active in school affairs. In addition to serving as Exchange Editor of

Argus, the school's monthly literary magazine, his Junior and Senior years, Gene was a member of Omicron Pi Sigma social fraternity, Demosthenian Literary Society, and Philonian. His reputation as the family jokester was reinforced by a couple of quips in the June, 1912 *Commencement Argus*:

"—Eugene C., writing for information
Dear Sir,
   Venus is my love. However, I fear that I insulted
Her the other day when I said, 'Venus is statue?' I
Want to marry her, but I'm afraid. Can I?
E. M. C.
(Don't mind her, 'Gene, she's 'armless.)
AND
"—Dick Garner, attempting to humorize—'If 30 degrees Fahrenheit is the freezing point, when is the squeezing point?'
Craighead '12—'Two in the shade.'
That settled it."

Eugene M. Craighead graduated in the Latin Scientific track from Harrisburg High in June 1912, as his older brother Frank graduated from Penn State. During high school, Gene must have gained enough interest in the study of nature to choose to make it his life's work. That fall, in a manner of speaking, Gene replaced his brother there but as a biology major. His college nickname was "Egghead," but it had a different meaning in those days and conveniently rhymes with Craighead. His Senior yearbook entry listed his objective as "To become a bird interpreter" and described him as:

"'Egghead' is some 'Bugologist' and some day we expect him to find a new kind of bug. As a true lover, he delights in roaming through field and wood in quest of bugs. 'Gene' never becomes lonesome in the woods, for he has learned the language of the birds; in fact, he can talk intelligently with the crows. Often on a sunny day, should one be near the woods, he may hear the lusty call of a crow; but on further investigation, he will find that it is not a crow, but only 'Egghead' perfecting his vocabulary."

Gene shoveled coal and worked in the dining hall to pay his way through Penn State. A biology professor required all students taking his course to not only memorize all the orders of insects but to also collect an example specimen for each of them. Gene earned spending money by catching and selling bugs to students needing to satisfy this assignment. As a member of the Class of 1916, he also received two years of military training as a Private in, one assumes, ROTC. After graduating from Penn State in 1916, Gene obtained a position doing research with the renowned pathologist J. Homer Wright on Infantile Paralysis (polio) at Harvard Medical School. He tested Mark W. Richardson's theory that fleas might be carriers of the dreaded disease and authored two papers on the study. He was contributing to the support of his parents, aged 58 and 68, when he registered for the first WWI draft in May 1917.

In August 1917, Myra Eby's parents announced her engagement to Gene but set no specific date for the wedding. A young doctor was also courting Myra but she chose Gene when her mother was told he "comes from a good family" (or so the legend goes). Not long after the engagement, Gene enlisted as a

Eugene Miller Craighead graduation photo
(William Moore Craighead)

Pharmacist's Mate First Class in the Naval Reserves. His prior experience and ROTC training gained him a higher rank than most recruits. He was training for the Medical Corps in Chelsea, Massachusetts when the increased probability of going to war may have advanced some of his plans for the future.

Although classmates, Gene and Myra didn't date during high school. Myra and Gene's sister, Ruth, were friends. They both sang alto in the school choir and had other musical interests in common, especially playing piano duets. The summer after graduation, Myra visited Ruth at Craighead Station. There is a good chance Gene was present at least some times when she visited his sister.

The fall after high school, Myra enrolled in Briscol School, a finishing school in Washington, D.C. for several months, then transferred to Lasell Seminary for Young Women in Massachusetts, "the first successful and persistent junior college in the country." The yearbook didn't mention what Myra studied in her two years at Lasell but notes she was quite active in the Athletic Association, particularly with tennis, and acted in the Latin play her first, her junior, year. She was known for saying "Go dig a bean," something akin to "get out of my face." Someone at Lasell wrote a short poem about "Little Ebey [sic]":

"I would not grow too fast

For sweet flowers are slow, and weeds make haste.

In tennis she is awfully fast,

In chapel she's awfully slow.

Those in back she keeps till last.

For in marching she must slowly go."

After finishing her formal schooling, Myra took, and passed, the entrance examination for the public library training program in Harrisburg. The training led to Myra working in one of the city's libraries. She remained active in social affairs, the Covenant Presbyterian Church, and with music performances, both singing and playing the piano. When the United States entered WWI, Myra did her part by volunteering for the Red Cross Motor Messenger Service. Hold ups became of such great concern that Myra and the other motor messengers trained in the handling and shooting of revolvers with which they could ward off robbers.

The August 12, 1918 edition of *Tyrone Daily Herald*, the newspaper from Myra Eby's original hometown, announced, "The auspicious occasion was without any

Myra Eby Craighead in 1925
(William Moore Craighead)

special arrangements and was simple in its appointments" when informing its readers of the marriage of former resident Myra Eby to Eugene M. Craighead on August 6 at "the little church among the woods" near Saranac Lake, New York. Their ceremony was performed by Rev. Harry F. Klaer, pastor of Myra's home church in Harrisburg. Myra's family could well afford a wedding for her, but the war didn't allow time for planning large events in advance. The newlyweds stayed in Boston while Gene awaited his impending assignment to France. In the fall, he was assigned to accompany soldiers on a commercial ocean liner commandeered to serve as a troop transport. As a medic, he was very busy treating the sick, including those stricken in the influenza pandemic that was a major factor in ending the war.

The combatants signed the Armistice shortly after he boarded the ship, so his ship returned to port and he was discharged within days of the ship docking in America. Afterwards, he did not enroll in medical school as planned because he had a wife to support. He took a job as an entomologist with the Pennsylvania Department of Agriculture. Myra and he lived with her parents and younger sister in Harrisburg. She traveled with her parents to St. Petersburg, Florida in early February 1920, as had been their custom before she married, but probably for another very special reason. On March 8, Myra gave birth to their first child, Samuel Eby Craighead in Florida. It seems improbable Gene could have been present for his first child's birth due to the amount of time he would have had to take off work to be there. They continued living with the Ebys until at least 1923, when they moved to the small town of Guernsey north of Gettysburg. The move brought Gene closer to the Department of Agriculture's Chambersburg laboratory and situated him amongst the fruit orchards he was studying. He published several papers in *Entomological News* on topics such as emergence records of the peach tree borer and biological notes on Chrysomelidae and Siphonaptera. He also conducted life history studies of the peach tree borer and other fruit pests at the Chambersburg lab.

Their second (and last) child, William Moore Craighead, was born in Gettysburg on August 20, 1925. Gettysburg newspapers often published news of Gene and Myra's frequent social activities with the country club and bridge set. Gene's mother died the year before Bill was born and his father the year after, leaving their Victorian home at Craighead Station to Gene and his siblings. Myra loved that beautiful old house and used it as a site for social activities, hosting afternoon bridge parties there for her ladies group.

Having considerable money of her own made it possible for Myra to take the lead in maintaining the old house. In many ways, it was by default because the others had to use their money, scarce during the Depression, to support their families. Also, the Craighead brothers were neither big on home maintenance nor sentimental about preserving architecture. A case in point occurred when the house needed a coat of paint. Using hammers, Frank, Gene, and Charles knocked off some decorative elements to eliminate the tedious task of painting them. Rather than painting the house trim a different color than the walls according to Victorian fashion, they painted the whole thing battleship gray. (One wonders if the paint came from navy surplus.) Myra electrified the house and had indoor plumbing installed, neither of which were uniformly welcomed by family members. Gene's niece, Jean, preferred the romance of kerosene lighting and was opposed to electrification. She wanted to keep the place as it was in her earliest memories.

The men's dislike of indoor plumbing may have surfaced when they chose not to repair a gap in the siding, which allowed honeybees to nest in the wall adjacent to the toilet. The bees especially tormented the women. Sitting on the toilet was so risky at times it warranted a verse in the Craighead song (to the tune of *It Ain't Gonna Rain No More*):

Gene Craighead fishing off the railroad bridge over the Yellow Breeches Creek
(William Moore Craighead)

> "Oh, the bees are making honey
> Right near the bathroom seat
> It wouldn't be so bad except
> They seem to like fresh meat.
> "There's Carolyn and Myra
> Also Peg and Ruth
> Four finer girls you never found
> Underneath one roof.
> "They're always bright and cheerful
> They always tell the truth
> They'd like to please those doggone bees
> But they're not puncture proof."

Gene and Myra sent their sons to the local schools where they lived at the time but, after tenth grade, they made a switch. Craigheads hadn't previously gone to prep schools, but Myra started the tradition within the family by sending her sons, possibly because of her experiences at Lasell, an institution she supported financially as an adult. Myra was Presbyterian as was Gene, but a friend so highly recommended George School in Newtown, Pennsylvania that Myra sent her sons to the Quaker school for their last two years of high school.

Bill recalled fond memories of his father:

"On weekends my father, Eugene, was great. He often would take us and any of the neighborhood kids who wanted to go fishing, hiking, hunting, and ice skating. Often, we would go to the local zoo. Perhaps, one of the most outstanding activities was when a carload of us kids would go arrowhead hunting on an island 20 miles north of Harrisburg in the middle of the Susquehanna River. Years later, I can remember ending up with a half-bushel basket full of Indian artifacts. We did this over a period of years."

Regardless of where they lived, worked or went to school, Myra, the boys, and dog

Brownie spent their summer in the house at Craighead Station with Carolyn, Frank Jr., John, Jean, and dog Spike. Because his work was always somewhere in the state of Pennsylvania, Gene spent more time there than did Frank, whose work took him across the country. When at his boyhood home, Gene kept everyone entertained with his antics. His favorite trick was to take a bucket or pitcher of water to the upstairs bedroom directly above the living room and wait quietly for unsuspecting quarry to wander into his trap. There was no heat in the second story of the house, so a vent— basically a hole cut through the floor with a decorative metal grate covering it to keep people from stepping through it—was installed to allow warm air to migrate upstairs. When a visitor unwittingly stopped under the vent in the living room, Gene poured water on him or her, completely surprising his victim.

One particularly hot summer, Gene concocted a batch of home brew, bottled it, and stored it in the cellar. When the beer had fermented, loud pops reverberated throughout the house. Carolyn dispatched the twins to the cellar. Higher than expected temperatures had caused Gene's beer to go wild and escape confinement. Bottles exploded, spewing sticky liquid and broken glass all over the dirt floor, creating a rather unsafe situation.

Eugene & Myra Craighead family in 1933 (William Moore Craighead)

From the safety of the cellar stairs, the twins pacified the beer with their trusty .22. Over time, the beer soaked into the floor, the glass was crushed into it, and the mess cleaned itself up. Decades later, the dirt floor was covered with concrete, hiding the evidence permanently.

The families got along marvelously at Craighead, probably because the women wisely acquired three stoves and three tables for the kitchen to eliminate conflicts. Each mother shopped and prepared meals for her own family. Gene, however, was known to sample all of the available offerings before he sat down to eat. Always the jokester, he would amuse diners by quickly stamping his feet near Spike and Brownie as they lay under the table. The dogs immediately started fighting, raising quite a commotion to the enjoyment of the youngsters. The only known serious incident occurred when Frank suddenly dumped a large bowl of applesauce on Myra. No one recalls precisely why he did that. Perhaps the adults knew, but they aren't around today to tell the story.

In 1929, after cleaning the upper part of the south wall of the kitchen, on a whim, Gene painted rats that appeared to be running into the round opening in the chimney where the stove pipe had been. Soon, he added a cat to chase the rats. When the kids asked if they could put artwork on the walls, he told them to clean a six square foot area first. John enthusiastically tackled the cleaning and painted his first piece of kitchen art: the large owl on the west wall. Frank Jr. and John painted a kestrel, probably Bad Boy, on a perch and in flight. The Zirpel children painted on the left side of the north wall, creating what is called "The Zirpel Corner." Most notable in that section is the owl painted by 12-year-old Paula Zirpel. Jean sketched a nude woman who was drying her backside with a towel. After Gene complained about the towel covering too much of her derrière, Jean repositioned the woman's arms (and, consequently, the towel) exposing more. Jean also added a sketch of her uncle pulling the towel downward. Myra disliked the nude greatly and later covered it with a real towel when her granddaughters visited. It wasn't long before paintings covered the walls. Descriptions of the 250+ pieces of artwork would fill a book of its own.

Myra liked living at Craighead Station so well she purchased the Richard Reynolds Craighead house across the road for additional bedrooms and parking. Although Myra was very proper, she was also athletic and played golf at the country club as often as practical. Participating in the physical activities at Craighead posed no problem for her, although her bridge ladies were rather awkward getting into canoes in their finery.

In the 1930s, Gene left government employment to work as a salesman for a company that sprayed fruit trees. He was probably very successful because of his personality and knowledge of insects that harmed fruit trees. He returned to government work in 1941 when he took a position in the Bureau of Plant Pathology. He was working there and the family was living at 2742 North Second Street in Harrisburg when the Japanese bombed Pearl Harbor.

Eugene and Charles Craighead fish with the twins (Johnson Coyle)

Ruth Craighead at four (Barbara Gawthrop Hallowell)

7

Ruth Craighead Gawthrop

RUTH CRAIGHEAD WAS BORN at Craighead Station on April 19, 1895, only months before her father's older brother and business partner, Richard, died unexpectedly and the local iron furnaces closed forever. In spite of the family's reduced financial situation, Ruth had a happy childhood. With the Yellow Breeches Creek running by her back yard, she delighted in the many activities at hand she could do for free, such as canoeing, swimming, and fishing in the cool water. She had the freedom to explore the surrounding countryside, fields, and meadows; climbed in the barn; and loved learning about the plants and animals in her immediate environment. Besides playing the usual children's games like Ring Around the Rosie and London Bridge Is Falling Down, she loved to make "Witches' Fingers" by slipping flowers from her mother's trumpet vine onto her fingers and to fashion pocketbooks from mussel shells she found in the creek.

Her parents could afford only one inexpensive Christmas gift for each child. Ruth could not even dream of getting something as costly as a bicycle. But penury didn't dampen Yuletide spirits in their household. Ruth recalled having festive Christmases as a child even though impoverished. She wrote:

"My father went with horse and wagon two miles to the mountains to cut our tree. We popped popcorn and strung it. We also strung cranberries to decorate that tree. Little real candles were fastened to the branches with tiny tin clips and were actually lit for brief periods as family gathered about the tree (always a bucket of water on hand in case of fire). Many leaves to increase size of our table for Christmas dinner so it would become very long to accommodate all of the relatives. [We had] turkey, of course, but I remember my mother's fruit cakes, dark and light, baked well ahead and wrapped in brandied cloths to flavor them and keep them moist."

One Christmas present stood out above all others 63 years later:

"The doll—kid [skin] body, china head, lovely blonde curls—under that tree. My grandmother had dressed it for me and I can still enjoy every detail of the clothes [which were] all so beautifully hand sewn—panties, petticoat, white embroidered dress, grey silk coat with lace collar. How I loved and cherished that doll for many years!"

Ruth's daughter, Barbara, observed, "The doll sounds elegant in Ruth's description, but it is *not grand*, being only about seven inches tall. Even as an old lady, she treasured it, handling it with great care and obvious love, and through the many years had obviously taken meticulously good care of it."

Late in life, Ruth recalled her father's businesses: "I don't know who built the mill/ store. It had three floors. They used horse and mule power—on a treadmill—to lift grain high for storage, then loaded it into bags and onto the railroad cars for shipping." Although Ruth's father lost his money and businesses in her early years, her mother (possibly with help from her maternal grandmother Rebecca Miller) introduced Ruth to the Harrisburg social scene by taking her to children's birthday parties and other events when she still lived in the country.

Just two months before Ruth's eighth birthday, her 43-year-old mother gave birth to her baby brother, Charles Miller Craighead. When a little older, she served as his surrogate mother as she loved taking care of him, a fondness that continued throughout his life.

Ruth likely got her earliest education at the one-room schoolhouse down the road from Craighead Station, as had her older siblings. One incident in third grade impressed her forever. Brother Eugene's scarlet fever caused her to be quarantined at home and out of school for a protracted time. To let her know they were thinking of her, her teacher and classmates sent her a book of Longfellow's poems she treasured the rest of her life. She and Eugene lived with her maternal grandmother in 1907 to allow them to go to Harrisburg schools prior to her family's move to 1821 N. 2nd Street by 1908.

Ruth entered Harrisburg Central High School as a member of the Class of 1913. An excellent student, she made the Honor Roll in her freshman year. She received a $10 prize for winning the Junior Girl's Oratorical Contest sponsored by Harrisburg Civic Club. An alto, she sang in the Junior and Senior Girls' Glee Clubs and the Choir. Before her Senior year started, she was one of ten selected for the Demosthenian Literary Society. She also served as Secretary of her Senior class in the second term. She escaped with only minor wounds from the pundit's pen in her *Commencement Argus*.

Under Senior Police News, "The entire Senior Girl's Glee Club were found guilty of murdering harmony." And Turp N Tine had a little fun with her name:

"Turp: It seems as though this Facul_tea was a success. How were they arranged at the table?

"Tine: They put *Miss Craighead—*

"Turp: Oh, did they?"

An invocation credited to Ruth Craighead was also printed but may have been someone's idea of a joke:

"When I lie down on my bed,

It nearly makes me weep.

To think that I must close my eyes

Before I go to sleep."

After graduating in June 1913 with four years of Latin and three years of Greek under her belt, Ruth enrolled at Swarthmore College for the fall term, majoring in the classics. Agnes's close friend, Mrs. Fahnestock, may have influenced Agnes's choice. Mrs. Fahnestock had attended Swarthmore and recommended it highly. Also, her daughter and Ruth's friend, Dorothy Fahnestock, had enrolled at Swarthmore two years earlier.

Ruth made a splash right off the bat. Only a Freshman, she participated in the Women's Student Government Association, Pi Beta Phi social sorority,

Ruth Craighead at Swarthmore
(Barbara Gawthrop Hallowell)

Somerville Literary Society, Classical Club, and dined with the S. S. S. dining club. Dining clubs also sponsored social events called Table Parties. Those TPs figured prominently in social life at Swarthmore. A fast runner and strong swimmer, Ruth represented the college well in a meet in November 1913 against Bryn Mawr's student government delegates, winning both the Candle Race and Umbrella Race with times of 64 seconds and 1 minute, respectively. In January, she won the Tub Race in a Swarthmore-only meet. Specifics of these "races" are left to the reader's imagination.

Swarthmore yearbooks documented Ruth's activity in the above organizations throughout college, with a couple more added during her Junior year. She was one of six selected for induction into Pi Sigma Chi, "The honorary society for Senior women whose purpose is the furthering of student responsibility toward the best interests of the College. The members are chosen with reference to character, scholarship, and loyalty to Swarthmore." She was elected Vice President of the Women's Student Government Association for the fall semester and chosen to serve as Junior Delegate to the Student Government Convention. The short bio under her individual yearbook photograph read as follows:

"'Craigy' is one of those delightful surprises that occasionally drift into a college community. When first she came, we thought her the ordinary frivolous Co-ed, but here she is on Student Exec, and Y. W. C. A. Cabinet. Needless to say, we enjoy being surprised; but, best of all, her responsibilities have not spoiled her—she is still frivolous!"

By graduation, Ruth had studied eight years of Latin and seven years of Greek. The caption under her Senior listing was the first line of a Shakespeare quote from *The Rape of Lucrece*: "Beauty itself doth of itself persuade." Perhaps the yearbook staff found the second line, "The eyes of man without an orator," to be superfluous.

Financing four years of private college wasn't easy. Based on need, Swarthmore awarded Ruth a $75 per term work-study job to help with part of the $400 per term tuition. She made many of her clothes to keep expenses down. With no work-study job her Senior year, she took out loans to replace them.

Harold James Gawthrop, Class of 1916, a Phi Kappa Psi Mechanical Engineering major, and a friend stood at the bottom of the stairs in Parrish Hall, when a pretty freshman with a blue bow in her hair bounced down. He told his friend, "I want to meet that girl." And he did. That girl turned out to be Ruth. They dated throughout her college life.

In spite of her busy social life, she found time to return to Craighead Station to visit her family, particularly in the summer:

"I took the trolley from Harrisburg (First and Front Streets) to Boiling Springs many times, and many of those walked from Boiling Springs, lugging suitcases, to the Craighead house. Occasionally, I was met by a horse and buggy."

In the summer of 1914, Harold's father needed help in running the family coal, hay, feed, and lumber business in Kennett Square. Although he didn't enjoy academics as much as his classmates, he was in a quandary because not being on campus would put him at a considerable disadvantage in winning the heart of the fair Miss Craighead. He took the job with his father yet managed to pursue his courtship. He lived less than 25 miles from campus and had a car, something Swarthmore students were not allowed. He constantly tinkered on the revered internal combustion engine in his Elmore to ensure it would not fail to bring him to see his intended.

The United States entered WWI in the spring of 1917 and drafted young men into military service. Harold enlisted in the Navy on May 19, expecting to be sent to far off places to fight for his country, but the Navy had other ideas. Seeing he was a skilled mechanic, they assigned him to chauffeur an admiral at League Island Navy Yard, located conveniently in Philadelphia at the junction of the Schuylkill and Delaware Rivers about 35 miles from his home. Harold wasn't put on active duty until November 7, 1917 and served until January 18, 1919.

Harold Gawthrop with his 1916 automobile (Laurie Craighead Rudolph)

After graduating from college in 1917, Ruth couldn't wed Harold immediately because bringing debt into marriage would not have been honorable. A positive of the war was more job openings were available for inexperienced people. She took a teaching position at Alexis I. DuPont High School in Wilmington, Delaware. A nearby Quaker couple, Benjamin and Ida Smedley, accepted her into their home as a member of the family. Ruth remained friends with the Smedleys until they died. Her children called them Aunt Ida and Uncle Benjamin. Ruth taught a full program of Biology, Latin, and English classes each day for which she was paid $750 the first year and $900 the second. Her pay was not high but, with skillful management, she not only got by but paid off her student loans, too. A talented and gifted teacher, her former students still visited her at her home years later.

The proximity of Philadelphia Navy Yard to Wilmington enabled Harold to continue courting Ruth during the war. After being discharged from active duty, he returned to working with his father in Kennett Square and looked forward to the end of Ruth's teaching commitment. On July 29, 1919, Ruth married Harold in a simple service at Market Square Presbyterian Church, the Craighead family's religious home in Harrisburg, with only members of their immediate families attending and their pastor, Dr. George Edward Hawes, officiating. Ruth wore a gown made of taffeta and crêpe Georgette with a hat to match. The young couple took off for a two-week honeymoon in the New England states. Ruth later remarked, "Two greener young folks never set out on an auto trip!" Harold, then 26, hadn't gone to Wilmington until he was 16 and to Carlisle until he was engaged. Ruth was 24 and had been no farther west than Carlisle or east than Swarthmore and Wilmington.

When they returned to Kennett Square from their honeymoon, they had nowhere to stay. Harold's parents had given them half the cost of a brand new $10,000 two-story four-square house of Avondale stone in Kennett Square. But construction wasn't finished yet. Fortunately, the elder Gawthrops, who lived only five blocks away, were staying in their cabin on Lake Naomi in the Poconos at the time, so the newlyweds moved into their home. The two generations shared the house from the end of September until January 1920, when the new house on Lafayette Street was completed. Harold paid off his $5,000 half of the total for the house in which he and his new bride would spend the rest of their 47 years of married life.

Coming from different religious traditions—Quaker and Presbyterian—Harold and Ruth had to make some decisions regarding their spiritual life together. Not wanting to go to separate churches on Sunday mornings, they settled on the Kennett Square Presbyterian Church. Harold sometimes evoked his Quaker heritage by mischievously saying he was donning his "Sunday go-to-meetin'" suit.

Ruth set about turning their house into a home and planning for a family. The better part of a century later, her daughter, Barbara, observed,

"Mother excelled in housekeeping in an era when fine housekeeping was a virtue. A house in good order and a household working smoothly were goals among women. A major objective of marriage was to provide a relaxed, comfortable, loving home environment for husband and children—and therefore for self. I had not yet heard the old saying, 'It is more important to be a good homemaker than a good housekeeper,' but looking back, I give Mother A+—she had the art of being skilled in both."

Ruth strove for excellence in everything she did and expected good quality work from her daughters. One of her favorite sayings was, "If you're going to do it at all, do it well." This applied to everything she undertook, from academics to setting a table to arranging social events. She was a hostess par excellence. Punctuality was a sign of good manners; lack of it was considered rude. Since their circle of friends lived locally, they could time their arrivals precisely, often arriving simultaneously. During prohibition, a 6:00 dinner invitation meant arriving a few minutes before six and sitting down to eat at six exactly. "Fashionably late" was unthinkable. After prohibition ended, cocktails preceded dinner but, in this group, moderation was the byword. After dinner, guests would sometimes play bridge or another game. Ruth made life fun. She bubbled with enthusiasm and was creative. Harold preferred to watch, saying with a grin, "I don't make fun, I just enjoy it." He served in other very important ways. As one of the most trusted people in the community and, for his math skill, he was asked to serve as treasurer of several local organizations.

Barbara Gawthrop on privy path at Craighead House c1927 (Barbara Gawthrop Hallowell)

Having a family was important to both Harold and Ruth. They were blessed with a healthy baby girl, Nancy Craighead Gawthrop, on January 31, 1921. "Nance" was joined by a sister, Barbara Miller Gawthrop, on October 13, 1924. Barbie has fond memories of her parents:

"Mother and Dad enjoyed each other—and enjoyed us. They gave us guidelines, we followed them, and times together were happy. They showed love for each other openly, for us freely, and gave us attention generously, patiently, gently yet firmly. We were fortunate."

Barb also recalls her parents teaching them about nature:

"Both Mother and Dad enjoyed being outdoors in nature. They taught us to observe, and curiosity lured us into family projects. Dad loved to get outdoors and go camping. He went hunting because he loved the outdoors, not for the sport."

Harold enjoyed good health in spite of his dietary and exercise habits. He smoked several cigarettes each day, snacked on salted pretzels and nuts, ate few fruits or vegetables, ate red meat and cream, and drove his car the two-block commute between home and work, even for lunch. Ruth also enjoyed good health except for one major exception: terribly painful headaches, starting when her oldest daughter was a small child. She suffered from them for many years, experiencing excruciating pain whenever they afflicted her. She fought to function through the pain but often had to take to bed in agony. Ruth underwent several treatments, including having her teeth removed, to no avail. One summer, she taught nature at the summer camp Nance and Barb attended in the belief cool, clear Maine air would help. The cool air didn't help with her headaches, but many campers caught her enthusiasm for nature. Her case stumped specialists for years, but she soldiered on. When a relative asked how Ruth was faring, Barbie responded that, although she had been fighting gallantly, she was miserable with pain. He stated, "You know, she's one of the most outstanding people I've ever known. Her acceptance of what life doles out, her attitudes, her sense of joy is amazing. She is marvelous." Eventually, a specialist suggested she might be sensitive to abrupt temperature changes. This knowledge allowed Ruth to avoid situations which would bring on the headaches.

Nance and "Barbie" enjoyed family visits to Craighead Station to spend time with beloved aunts, uncles, and cousins. After marriage, Ruth no longer spent her summers at Craighead due to the Gawthrops having a camp of their own. She and Harold spent most of their vacations at Harold's family's cabin on Lake Naomi in the Poconos but visited Craighead on long holidays and special family events.

Harold and Ruth started their daughters' formal education at the Kennett public school on Mulberry Street, the same elementary school Harold had attended, then saw them enjoy school years in the new consolidated school. After Nance and Barb completed tenth and ninth grade, respectively, at Kennett, their parents sent them to George School, the Quaker prep school in Newtown, Pennsylvania to complete high school. A number of Kennett friends and Craighead cousins also attended George School with satisfaction.

Harold and Ruth wanted their daughters to follow in their footsteps and attend Swarthmore College after graduating from George School. Perhaps Ruth sent her daughters subliminal messages throughout their childhood when she called them with the Pi Beta Phi whistle she learned at Swarthmore. However, Nancy wanted to major in art and Swarthmore didn't offer it. So, she enrolled at Oberlin College in 1939.

By the time the Japanese bombed Pearl Harbor, Ruth and Harold had completed the bulk of their parenting and were about to enter a new stage of their lives together. If Barbie's feeling about their parenting is any indication, they were parents any child would be fortunate to have:

"As I hear others talk about trials or difficulties of their childhood years, I realize how stable, good, and easy mine were. Dad and Mother loved, enjoyed, and respected each other and treated us children with the same consistent love, enjoyment, and respect. At no time were we ever led to think we were a bother, an interference with their activities, an encumbrance, or anything except a wonderful, comfortable, and positive presence in their lives."

Harold & Ruth Gawthrop family 1933 (William Moore Craighead)

8

Charles Miller Craighead

CHARLES MILLER CRAIGHEAD WAS BORN on February 2, 1903 at the family home at Craighead Station. The almost eight year gap between him and Ruth, his mother's age, and the family's declining fortunes suggest he was not planned. That Ruth provided much of his care suggests that his mother, already unhappy over the family's financial slide, may not have fully welcomed another child at 43. The first few years of Charlie's life were spent at Craighead Station, but the family moved to Harrisburg before he was old enough to start school. However, they still summered in the country.

Charlie attended Harrisburg School District's Model School and made his stage debut in the Commencement program for the 1910 Harrisburg High School Teachers Training Class. Newspaper accounts gave him high marks, calling the seven-year-old's performance, "a distinct hit as the giant and his wild grabs from his far corner after the little pigs calmly feeding on acorns were truly thrilling." He attended elementary school in the Cameron Building where he was the school winner in the search for bag worm and tussock moth cocoons sponsored by the Civic Club. Collecting 358 cocoons at age nine was the first documented bit of Charlie's conservation work. That summer, he nearly drowned when his canoe overturned in the Yellow Breeches Creek. He supposedly swatted at a butterfly with such force with his paddle he flipped the canoe, landing him in the water.

Living in town gave Charles some opportunities his older siblings did not have. One was Boy Scouts. He joined Troop 11, with Edward Manser as Scoutmaster. The troop camped out for two weeks at his grandfather John Weakley Craighead's former farm in

Craighead Station, adjacent to his parents' summer home.

Based on the teasing he got in his high school's monthly magazine/yearbook, *The Argus*, Charlie must have been a popular guy on campus. At least one Argus staff member knew he spent time at his parents' home in the country:

"Charlie Craighead (boasting of how strong he had become working at his farm near Boiling Springs): 'Why, John, every morning before breakfast, I pull up 90 gallons of water for the stock.'

"John Fritchey: 'That's nothing, I go down to the boat-house every morning, get my canoe, and pull up the river.'"

And, in a later edition of *Argus*, poked more fun at him:

"Charles Craighead: 'There are several girls around here who intend never to marry.'

W. Stanford: 'How do you know?'

Charles: 'I have proposed to several.'"

Charlie was active in youth activities at Market Square Presbyterian Church, as well as on the school and local stages. He was a founding member of La Cercle Française under the direction of Miss Edith Philips, French Teacher at Central High.

The March 1920 edition of *Argus* included his page-and-a-half long short story, titled "The Mysterious Color," a murder mystery that required a chemist to solve. Perhaps he was hinting about what he intended to study in college.

Charlie graduated on Tuesday, June 15, 1920 at Central High School's 47th Commencement ceremony held in the Orpheum Theatre. His Commencement bio was short and sweet:

"'Charlie' is our famous botanist. If you find any blossom or flower, etc., just ask 'Charlie' what the name of it is and he is sure to give you the correct name for it."

After high school, Charlie attended Penn State College where he majored in chemistry and graduated with a B. S. degree as a member of the Class of 1925. Sadly, the Penn State yearbook, La Vie, no longer included gossipy quips about Seniors. So, all that can be gleaned from La Vie were his major, that he played in

Charles Miller Craighead college graduation photo (Ruth Craighead Muir)

the Mandolin Club, was a member of Omega Delta Epsilon academic fraternity, and was inducted into Phi Lambda Upsilon, the National Honor Society.

According to family lore, Charlie traveled to Russia on business and brought back a small oriental rug, a jewelry box, and a lovely perfume bottle as souvenirs from the trip. These artifacts continue to be family heirlooms. He probably took a job in the Pittsburgh area after graduation, quite possibly with Aluminum Company of America (Alcoa). The trip to Russia was surely done at the behest of his employer.

Charlie undertook graduate work at Penn State, while also working near Pittsburgh. He met Margaret Ellen "Peg" Lewis in a music store when he was looking for mandolin music. Peg put her considerable talent to use demonstrating new tunes to customers who were interested in buying sheet music. His older brother Frank's daughter, Jean, considered her Uncle Charlie to be the most romantic of the Craighead brothers. But all we can do is speculate on how he courted Peg, as nothing is known about that period in their lives. Charlie and Peg were married on September 4, 1928, while he was still working on his M. S. in Chemistry to better support himself and his new bride.

In November 1929, Charlie was voted into Sigma Gamma Epsilon, the Earth Sciences National Honor Society along with two other Penn State students. He completed his Master's Thesis in Chemistry in 1930. The title was: *The determination of aluminum and magnesium in zinc-base die-casting alloys.* By April 1930, these Craigheads were living at 447 Freeport Street, Parnassus (part of present-day New Kensington Borough) in Westmoreland County, Pennsylvania about 18 miles northeast of Pittsburgh along the Allegheny River. It's quite possible Charlie took employment somewhere while finishing his master's thesis. That would explain the possible overlap between working on his master's degree and living in Parnassus while employed as a chemist for Alcoa.

In 1936, Charlie and Peg adopted Ruth Ann as their first child. Shortly after she was born, Ruth Ann was placed in the hands of this loving couple through a private adoption

Margaret "Peg" Lewis engagement photo 1928
(Ruth Craighead Muir)

arranged by a respected physician.

His gentle and friendly demeanor made Charlie a favorite of his nieces and nephews. That he was the youngest of his generation and the only one born in the 20th century put him closer in age, both mentally and physically, to them. Only thirteen years older than the twins, he could participate in games and pranks with the younger generation more easily than his older brothers. Although he lived at Craighead Station only a few years, he was as emotionally tied to it as were his siblings. Ruth Ann recalled, "My Dad lived for his month of fishing in the Yellow Breeches Creek. He would tie flies all winter and make bamboo rods. He had made aluminum molds to form triangles of bamboo which then he fitted together to make the rods, tying the eyes on and shellacking all of it."

Sometime before May 6, 1940 the Charles Craigheads moved to 1711 Pleasant Street in New Kensington, just a few blocks from their previous home. Peg's widowed mother Vila Lewis, 72, lived with them at the time. In 1940, Alcoa gave Charlie the opportunity of a lifetime: the experience of working abroad. Charlie, Peg, and Ruth Ann sailed to Brazil so he could research bauxite fields in the mountains near Posas de Caldas. They lived in luxury at Palace Hotel for about a year before his assignment was cut short by the threat of war. They returned home in July 1941 on the S. S. *Argentina*, only five months before the U.S. entered WWII.

Charles & Peg Craighead wedding photo 1928 (Ruth Craighead Muir)

PART III

Focus on Education

CHARLES AND AGNES CRAIGHEAD'S GRANDCHILDREN have important stories of their own to tell, stories that in some cases began well before adulthood. This generation had several things in common: their Craighead parent had earned a bachelor's degree or greater, their fathers remained employed throughout the Great Depression, their mothers weren't forced into the labor market by necessity, none worked to support their parents and siblings, and their parents encouraged their curiosity. All found nature fascinating as half the blood in their veins was of the Craighead clan and the other half wasn't devoid of this interest, far from it in most cases.

Frank, Eugene, Ruth, and Charles M. Craighead differed from most other Depression-era parents. That they were far more educated than the vast majority of people may have factored into their parenting attitudes. They were not permissive and gave their children very clear guidelines to follow but used displeasure and disappointment rather than corporal punishment to discipline their children and held the children accountable when they misbehaved. When the children expressed an interest in something, the parents supported the interest, particularly when animals or plants were involved. They granted their children much freedom, provided they didn't abuse the privilege—too badly.

People's attitudes on mischief have changed considerably since the 1930s, even since the 1960s. Pranks were often viewed as "boys will be boys" then. Pranksters were punished when caught but weren't generally considered juvenile delinquents or criminals. Sometimes, adults joined in, especially at Halloween. For example, the father of the author's friend designed a scheme for the boys to use to embarrass the local auxiliary police in a small Illinois town and made the hardware necessary to pull it off. Such tricks might be considered vandalism or worse today in some cases. Children no longer have the freedom of movement that earlier generations had. Nor are tricks tolerated as much as they were before.

It is the author's belief that the freedom accorded this generation played a key role in them developing into the adults they eventually became. Youthful mistakes and successes gave them the confidence to try things not tried before and to undertake difficult, sometimes dangerous, tasks.

Craighead parents used evenings and weekends during the school year to model and pass along (sometimes Scots-Irish Presbyterian) values to their children and to teach them about nature. They also modeled how to perform as good neighbors and productive citizens. Although their fathers worked long hours as did many men of their generation and were sometimes away from home for extended periods, they figured prominently in their children's lives and provided positive role models.

In this part, the pre-WWII activities of Charles and Agnes's children's offspring will unfold in their parents' birth order: Frank, Eugene, Ruth, and Charles M. It tells their stories from birth until the Japanese attack on Pearl Harbor, except for the eleventh grandchild who was not born until WWII ended. His story begins later.

9

Frank Cooper Craighead, Jr. and John Johnson Craighead

With eugenics being all the rage at the time, particularly for scientists, Frank Cooper Craighead filed, revised, and refiled data on three generations of both his and his intended's families with the Carnegie Institute. After receiving their positive recommendation, he married Carolyn Johnson on October 12, 1915 at her parents' home in Alexandria, Virginia. The newlyweds settled in a house Frank built in East Falls Church, Virginia and set about starting a family. Carolyn gave birth to identical twin boys, Frank Jr. and John, on August 14, 1916 via breech birth. She was quite surprised, to say the least, because medical science had not yet progressed to the point of reliably predicting multiple births. Blonde like their mother, they were beautiful children. Bright, curious, active, and imaginative barely began to describe them. The boys were a handful. From the beginning, the twins posed quite a challenge for their mother in those days before labor-saving appliances.

In 1920, Frank took a temporary assignment away from the U. S. Department of Agriculture to work in Ottawa, Ontario. An early photo of

Twins at four or five (Barbara Gawthrop Hallowell)

the young twins "helpfully" washing their three-years-younger sister Jean's hair on the back porch at Craighead Station shows that Frank brought his family to visit his parents and his childhood home, even when they lived in Canada. When they returned to Washington in 1923, Frank and Carolyn bought a modest, story and a half, cedar-shake-sided bungalow at 5301 41st Street in the Chevy Chase section at the end of the trolley tracks, in what was then the outskirts of the rapidly expanding capital. With the city and Rock Creek on one side and woods and fields on the other, the children had a veritable playground just outside their door.

Virtually identical in all ways, Frank and John got the same childhood diseases at the same time. They thought much the same and would finish each other's sentences. They even referred to themselves as "I" when they meant "we" as if the two combined to make one person. When asked if he and Frank ever differed on anything, John, then 93, replied that they were always of one mind. Relatives and acquaintances remember otherwise. Lifelong friend David Masland described them arguing frequently about how things should be done. He even saw a disagreement escalate from verbal jabs to physical intimidation to hurling things. They threw larger and larger sticks, putting more and more distance between themselves until they were chucking firewood-sized logs at each other from opposite sides of the creek. Dave and the other kids present found the scene quite hilarious. Frank and John might not have considered that episode as being funny but they had well developed senses of humor, possibly overly developed.

The twins shone as students, starting with E.V. Brown School located near Chevy Chase Circle. They excelled at academics and athletics, attracting a gang of boys as their followers. One, Gates Slattery, met the twins during recess when he was in fifth grade and they were in seventh:

"They could do more chin ups and were always a step ahead of me in sports....They joined Boy Scout Troop 53 as soon as they could. They quickly became Eagles....They set higher goals. I couldn't reach what they did. Boy Scouts met at the Methodist church on Connecticut Avenue every Friday after school. We played King of the Hill and rough stuff like that. They were always on the top of the hill.... They were always tops at what they did, not satisfied with second class.

"They learned to use a sling with two strands above their head....It had a leather strap with a pocket half way in. They would whirl it around their head then let go of one end. The stone would let go with a lot of velocity and was hard to control. The stone flew across Connecticut Avenue and cracked the window of the confectionery.... I can still see the store across the street from E. V. Brown. It caused quite a stir."

Sister Jean concurred, "That is true. Yes, they made and used sling shots, but rarely after that. John smashed the candy store window and, instead of running away, he went to the owner and told him he did it and would work until he paid for it, which he did."

Gates valued the time he spent with the Craigheads on weekends: "Their father was a great outdoorsman. They picked up a lot from him." Frank Jr. elaborated on one such excursion:

"Back as far as my grade-school years, while hiking with my father, I recall the questions that, in one form or another, were repeated again and again: 'What's the name of that yellow flower?'

"'Dogtooth violet.'

"'Right. Do you remember the name of the bush beside it, the one with the tiny yellow flowers?' No reply. 'Here, try chewing the bark.'

"'Oh!' with no hesitation, 'spice bush.'

"'How about the little purple flower right at your feet?'

"'Violet.'

"'And the tree with the rough bark?'

"'Shagbark hickory.'

"'And the large tree with the hollow trunk?'

"'Basswood.'

"'Correct. The hollow is a result of a heart rot or fungus. These cavities often provide daytime re-treats for raccoons....'"

Besides Gates, other friends also participated in these hikes-turned-biology classes, learning about nature alongside the Craighead children. Not all of these outings were benign, though.

Gates kayaked with them once and only once. When his boat flipped over, he became the keel as it raced down the Potomac. One twin jumped into the water, righted the kayak, and saved Gates. That was his first and last kayak

Craighead twins with Eagle Scout medals
(Laurie Craighead Rudolph)

ride. However, he continued to hunt, fish, and camp with the Craigheads along the Potomac. While canoeing with the twins near Seneca Island, Gates found his first Indian arrowhead. That artifact ignited in him an interest in archaeology to last his lifetime, although he could only pursue it professionally after retiring from his first career as a management analyst.

In addition to their various friends, Frank Jr. and John had another constant companion to share in their exploits: Spike. Jean loved that hound whose bust one of her brothers painted on the kitchen wall:

"Spike was given to Dad by an old hunter on the Potomac River at Seneca. The 'old man' as we called him knew that pup would be a good hunter—and he was. Dad used to say 'Hunt raccoons' and he would hunt raccoons, not squirrels or rabbits but raccoons. He'd say 'Hunt rabbits' and he would go after them. He and Dad had a special relationship.

"With us kids in the summer he was just 'Spike.' While we were in school, he stayed home with Mother who was fond of him too. We didn't 'walk' dogs in those days, [we] just opened the door and they ran out to do who knows what doggies' secrets."

Gates had a bittersweet memory of Spike. While playing in the Craigheads' yard one day—he only lived a block away—he stepped on Spike's leg, breaking it. He felt terrible about hurting Spike, but the hardy hound recovered. Spike impressed him so much he made a point of acquiring a dog much like him in later life.

The twins, their friends, and ever-present Spike played in the small stream behind Connecticut Avenue that fed Rock Creek, in the woods west of Wisconsin Avenue near the streetcar garage by a grove of ironwood trees, and in the garage itself.

Gates recalled the twins jumping across creeks the others couldn't and swinging on grapevines like ape-men when playing Follow the Leader. When they were caught playing in old streetcars in the garage—where they weren't supposed to be—they escaped from the man who chased them by running into the woods.

A favorite trick of town boys of that generation was grabbing the rope hanging from the pole that connected the trolley car to the overhead electric wire. It was almost trivial to stop a trolley in its tracks by flipping the pole away from the power source, but very difficult for the conductor or driver to put back in place fourteen feet overhead. The Craighead twins pulled this prank regularly.

Ever fearless, the twins once rolled a lit cherry bomb toward a group of five larger boys standing on a Chevy Chase sidewalk. Even though the boys were older and larger, the twins and their gang escaped their targets by outrunning them. Gates reminisced about some of their more memorable stunts: "[We were] always faster than the other guys. Never got caught." One autumn, an old man was burning leaves (probably along the street as was common practice at that time). The boys threw firecrackers into the fire and ran. Leaves blew all over the street. Occasionally reckless, they swiped pigeons out of someone's coop and let a couple of them loose inside a movie theater. One pigeon even flew up to the screen.

Water often figured in their pranks. One of Gates' favorites was leaning large cans of water (about a gallon each) against someone's front door, then knocking on the door so the owner would open it and spill the water all over the porch. "We were gone before we could be caught. We were pretty swift on out feet." Even at 93, Gates didn't want to own up to the more outrageous tricks they pulled: "We did some bad things that I don't want to talk about. We were pretty reckless around Halloween."

Halloween was a prime time for pranks, but the Craigheads often celebrated it away from their Washington gang at Craighead Station, marking the end of the habitable season for the house because it lacked central heating. A major fixture in that little community was and still is, although scheduled for demolition, the one-lane iron bridge across the Yellow Breeches Creek built by the Pittsburgh Bridge Company in 1899. Heavy board planks, since replaced, served as decking to carry vehicle traffic. One dark Halloween night the twins removed the planks. An unwary driver, not noticing the planks were missing, attempted to drive across the bridge. His wheels dropped through the exposed openings, leaving the car perched precariously on its undercarriage. The boys didn't anticipate this outcome and re-thought pulling such a prank again. Like Gates, Jean and John wouldn't talk about some other tricks.

Frank Sr. and his siblings kept their childhood home, only four miles from Carlisle, as a vacation home after their parents died in the mid-1920s. Frank's job with the U.S. Department of Agriculture required him to inspect forests in the South and West in summers, so he ensconced Carolyn and the children at the house as soon as school was over. "We had glorious times," exclaimed Jean, chatting about their mostly unsupervised summers along the Yellow Breeches. She even described arriving at Craighead Station in her largely autobiographical book, *The Summer of the Falcon*:

"June burst through the big walnut doors and ran up the dark stairs to her room. With a hoot she pushed up the window, stood on one foot, and kicked back the shutters. Quickly, before it was all gone, she threw open the closet and smelled the mysterious scent of the bats which had been hanging upside down in the corners all winter. She slid open the bureau drawer and sniffed the too-sweet dust of the winter-working, wood-borer beetle. Then she closed her eyes and took in every musty smell, for they told her the routines of winter were done and the summer was beginning."

Eugene's family also stayed in the old house, whether he was working nearby or not. Myra, Sam, and Bill loved being there. The two boys and the twins slept on the upstairs porch, along with owls and other pets that happened by. Being the oldest and the leaders they were, the twins drew their cousins and neighbors in to participate in their adventures.

Carolyn required her children to nap for at least an hour after lunch long after other mothers had abandoned this routine. Forcing her early-rising sons to rest at an age at which other women had given up on years prior was probably done, in part, for them to have energy for evening activities. Keeping her very lively children quiet for an hour on summer days was anything but easy, for the Pennsylvania countryside constantly beckoned them to embark on new adventures.

Even in his mid-90s, John remembered her regime all too well, and not fondly, being forced to remain indoors for an entire hour each afternoon. "Naps! I hate 'em," he snapped more than eight decades after his last enforced siesta. David Masland recalled the Craighead children napping till they were nineteen, when he and the other kids had long been relieved of that indignity. Jean cautioned that it may have appeared that way, but her brothers were untethered from their beds when they were eleven or twelve. They feigned napping and read from the classics found in a bookcase in the attic. Jean explained, "We kept reading on and off during those hours when there wasn't something exciting going on—like Uncle Gene stirring up the bees under the bathroom window, or Windy, the barn owl chasing a croquet ball Frank rolled across the lawn." Helping their mother can peaches didn't draw them out of their rooms because Jean and her brothers agreed reading *Huckleberry Finn* was much more fun. Others thought quiet time in the middle of the day was a way for Carolyn to maintain her sanity amongst the chaos created by her children, their cousins, and friends. The only time the house was quiet was when the children were sleeping and the men weren't there, or the twins were out of earshot.

Naps finished and released from their bedrooms, off they'd go into the woods, across meadows and fields, or down to the creek. Afternoon activities included: shooting sparrows in the barn for hawk and owl food; exploring Bear Cave; watching the planing mill operate; avoiding trains on the railroad bridge; skinny-dipping, fishing, catching eels, fish bait and mussels; and pulling tricks on unsuspecting adults. The least interesting of these was far more exciting than a nap to the Craighead children and their willing accomplices.

Craighead summer evenings involved baseball games, horseshoes, and sitting on the railroad scale listening to the local men tell stories. The boys loved taunting Bill the blacksmith who lived nearby: "Buggedy Bill, never he worked and never he will." The blacksmith, who had arms like Popeye, grabbed the thigh closest to him, pinched it hard, and twisted it harder, leaving a large red welt. Never deterred, the boys found the pain a small price to pay for getting a rise out of him.

Friday night hymn sings along the creek with neighbors were special. Jean performed interpretative dances while her brothers occasionally walked among the singers and musicians with their hawks on their fists. Other evenings, especially those around the 4th of July, involved pyrotechnics—lots of them—even more so when Eugene and Frank were present. The adults were even more reckless with fireworks than were the children. One time, they battled friend and neighbor Mervin Coyle across the dry wheat field with rockets. It was a miracle they didn't set fire to the dry field between their houses.

One summer night, Charles, the youngest of the Craighead adults, retired early to spend the night with his new bride, Peg, in what had been his mother's sewing room at the top of the stairs. The twins crawled out onto the porch roof, lit a two-inch salute, carefully placed the explosive in Charles's open window, and climbed down a drain pipe to make their escape. "Bang!" Charles was not amused. He raced down the front stairs and across the lawn in hot pursuit of the boys. They escaped him only by climbing high up a tree.

Eugene played a bit of a joke of his own when, after cleaning the kitchen wall above the fireplace, he painted rats running into the open flue hole and a cat chasing after them. The children ached to try their hands and begged to be given the chance. Gene, who must have been the only adult present at the time, required them to clean six square feet of wall space first. John enthusiastically tackled the cleaning and painted his first piece of kitchen art: the large owl on the west wall. Over time, numerous others added drawings until few square inches remained bare. Frank Jr. and John contributed their artistic talents to the kitchen walls but not quite to the level of their sister Jean and first cousin on their mother's side, Paula Zirpel. Friends and visitors to the house tried their hands until the walls were covered with art of varying quality in every medium imaginable.

After Labor Day each summer, Frank Craighead reappeared from inspecting experiments in forests to return to Washington for the school year. The family went back to the regimented life they'd left in June. When their Pennsylvania friends went back to school, their summer was nearly over. Emily Coyle Jacoby remembered the time clearly: "We started school a week earlier than they did but didn't want to miss out on anything they were doing. So, after school, we ran from the school bus to their house."

Upon completing eighth grade at E. V. Brown School in 1931, Frank Jr. and John enrolled as freshmen at Western High School located at 35th and R Streets, NW. Western High produced numerous "stars" including a judge, four admirals, Gloria Steinem and two astronauts (Ed White and David Scott), plus the first Miss America, Margaret Gorman Cahill. Western operated in shifts due to overcrowding. In the summer of 1932 when the twins started training their first Cooper's hawks, they were most likely in or about to start their sophomore year. Western High fielded lightweight football and basketball teams in addition to the varsity. Although they were too small to make the regular team, their athleticism and strength helped them make the lightweight football squad which went undefeated in 1934 with victories over St. Albans, Episcopal, Washington-Lee, and again in a St. Albans rematch. They also played lightweight basketball in which their height was less of a disadvantage then.

The summer before they began their last year of high school, the twins and their close friend Steve Stevenson embarked on the trip of a lifetime. After leaving Ulysses, their peregrine falcon, with Morgan Berthrong for the summer, they were off. Frank Jr.'s son, Lance, told of his father's first trip west:

"In the summer of 1934, just after high school, Frank and John drove west in a 1928 Chevrolet with several of their friends, photographing and capturing hawks and falcons. They drove on dirt roads all the way, pulling over at night to camp. During this trip they first saw Jackson Hole, and they visited with naturalists Olaus and Mardy Murie. The spectacular beauty of Wyoming remained with them through subsequent travels, and they promised themselves they would return some day to live near the Tetons."

All too soon, it was time to for school to start again. The twins returned home in time to finish their senior year, loaded with photographs they took on the trip and birds they picked up along the way. They graduated in February 1935 with John as class President and Frank as Treasurer. Both were members of Phi Beta Rho, the school's academic honor society. Western did not join the National Honor Society because they would have had to lower the standards for membership below those for Phi Beta Rho. The twins also helped start the Biology Club.

Shortly after school was out for the summer for Morgan and Steve, the four embarked on an adventure in Canada seeking pigeon hawks (now known as Merlins). After being poisoned by uncountable mosquito bites and nearly drowning in freezing Lake Superior, they stopped at Craighead Station to visit with their sister, mother, aunts, uncles, cousins, and friends. The travelers told of their great adventures; Jean, Sam, Bill, Nancy, and Barbara wished they could have accompanied them. Maybe someday, but they were all getting older.

The fall of 1935 found Frank Jr. and John matriculated as freshmen at Penn State College, alma mater of their father and uncles. Jean revealed that her father remained a Pennsylvanian throughout his decades as a civil servant in Washington: he retained Craighead Station as his permanent address; he registered his car in Pennsylvania; he paid taxes to Pennsylvania; he voted there; and he enrolled his children as in-state residents when they attended college.

The twins made wrestling their sport of choice at Penn State. One of them (the *Collegian* apparently didn't realize a first initial was needed whenever a Craighead was mentioned) won the 118-pound weight class for the freshmen in the Interclass Meet at the start of the second semester. One of them had to have won the 126-pound weight class in the Intramural tournament, held in late February and early March, because they were the two finalists. The *Collegian* reported on March 20 that [sic] "Frank Grayhead '38" had won. On March 4, both wrestled and won in the Freshmen Team match at Mansfield State Teachers College. "Lions to pin their men were Frankie Craighead in the 118-pound class…" John won the 126-pound bout by points. This match illustrated the problem with both twins going out for wrestling as each team only competes one wrestler in each weight class. One had to grapple in a heavier class at a disadvantage if both were to participate in a match.

John pointed out another disadvantage: he and Frank hadn't wrestled in high school, where most of the grapplers they competed against had. They relied on their strength and agility to overcome their opponents' greater experience and skill. That didn't always work but both did well enough to "numeral"—earning embroidered 39s to sew onto their letter jackets or sweaters. The twins made the varsity their sophomore year but with one stipulation: they refused to wrestle each other to determine who would wrestle in a particular match. Wrestle-offs between the two would have been moot because John and Frank could substitute for each other when the one scheduled to wrestle was ill or had pressing school work, or just to drive Coach Charlie Speidel batty. It's quite likely records of the matches frequently attributed the win or loss to the wrong twin. John lettered for the 1937 season, but awards didn't mean much to either of them. In January, possibly to show off, John competed for the varsity gymnastics team against Temple, coming in third in the rope climb, an event in which several generations of Craigheads have excelled.

Frank and John spent their undergraduate summers in the Tetons much as they had first done in 1934. They gained much valuable experience as field biologists on those trips by putting theory to practical test. Their first *National Geographic* article, "Adventures with Birds of Prey," illustrated with 25 of their photos, was published in July 1937.

The twins wrestled varsity again in 1938 and John finished fourth in the NCAA Tournament. They both lettered in 1939, their senior year, but neither competed in the national championship tournament. They graduated in June 1939 from the school of Arts and Letters with honors. They were both awarded Phi Beta Kappa keys and John W. White Fellowships to help offset the cost of graduate school at the University of Michigan. However, they had much to do that summer before setting off for Ann Arbor.

In addition to publishing *Hawks in the Hand*, their book on falconry, that summer, they took another 10-week trip to the Tetons, this time with two younger boys in tow. David Masland, just fifteen and too young to drive, had been dying to go west with the twins since they made their first trip. The other boy, who shall remain nameless, was sent by his father to toughen him up. Dave later learned his industrialist and philanthropist father and the physician father of the other boy each paid the twins $100 to take them along. For Dave, it was the adventure of his life. They neither ate in restaurants nor slept in beds the entire trip. They brought along a tent but didn't need it: they slept under the stars every night. None of them called home during the trip but may have sent postcards.

While waiting by the gas pump at Jenny Lake in the Tetons as the others shopped in the general store for supplies, Dave met Margaret "Cony" Smith, the petite mountain-climbing daughter of a college professor who worked as a park ranger in the summer. After Dave introduced the twins to Margaret, the boys helped carry her purchases to her family's cabin twelve-miles away. (More on Margaret later.) Dave's one regret from the trip was not climbing the Tetons, but his father had ordered the twins not to let him do anything too dangerous.

Shortly after returning home, Frank and John hosted a distinguished visitor. After reading their *National Geographic* article, R. S. Dharmakumarsinhji (Bapa to his family and friends) of Bhavnagar, India wrote the twins to introduce himself as a fellow falconer. Their first clue to Bapa's station in life came when he wrote about a procedure for training a falcon, "Have your man hold the hawk while...." It turned out he was the Maharaja of Bhavnagar's youngest brother. He was a raja, a prince, a young man about the same age with the same interests as the twins. To make a long story short, Bapa arrived at Washington-Hoover Airport on September 1, 1939 to visit the Craigheads.

He came without servants as Frank and Carolyn requested due to limited room in their modest Chevy Chase home for guests. Bapa and the boys hit it off as well in person as they had in their exchange of letters. Communication was easy due to Bapa's British public school education. He did have to learn American slang such as OK and about such things as root beer floats and milk shakes. Of particular interest to him was the freedom and status American girls enjoyed relative to women in his country.

As soon as practical, the twins brought their guest to Craighead Station to show him the countryside, to fish, and to fly hawks. His arrival caused quite a stir among the young women in the hamlet because no dignitary approaching the status of a prince of marriageable age had ever visited the area. As they drove along the dirt road from the Holly Pike to the house, they passed Frank Masland's farm, Fallen Arches, where a polo match was underway. Frank Jr. found what happened that evening humorous:

"Bapa enjoyed this sport and his brother was on the all-India team, apparently the best in the world. Bapa just had to stop and try out the horses. So while the rest of the gang from Washington drove on to the house, Bapa rode the horses and discussed their merits with the owners. Soon a Ford coupe came streaking up the road and stopped with a jar at the polo field. [One of the blonde twins who lived next door] Lil jumped out and came running up greeting us as if she hadn't seen us for years, all the while looking over John's shoulder for Bapa. We vexed Lil for a few moments with conversation as she waited impatiently for an introduction. We finally allowed her a head start on the rest of the girls, for all the good it did her.

"The next day, while loafing on the lawn and listening to Bapa's tales of trapping methods and Indian shikar, Janette [Eshelman] appeared in a blue, skin-tight bathing suit. She was tall, dark, athletic, and moved with a grace that even a prince might admire. Janette was not one of our usual crowd and only the fact that a prince was visiting had caused her to come around. I noticed Bapa, who had barely registered the gorgeous reporter [at the airport] and appeared unmoved by Lily's practiced wiles, casting interested glances in Janette's direction. After a moment he turned and announced to our group on the lawn: 'Who is that girl? Do you not admire her? I should like to meet her.'"

No romance developed, but the vision of Janette in that blue bathing suit remained indelibly etched in John's and Bill's memories over 70 years later. Bapa enjoying fishing in the nearby creeks with Bill, Sam, and the twins is recorded on photographs taken of the fishermen and their catches. The weather still warm, Bapa slept on the sleeping porch with the other boys, something that was surely a new experience for him. Like other visitors to the house, he painted something on the kitchen wall—his family's coat of arms—which remains there still. The time with Bapa flew by too quickly. Soon, it was time for him to leave and for school to start.

Frank Jr., John, Ulysses, and Nancy, a recently acquired prairie falcon, headed west and north to start graduate work at the University of Michigan. The twins breezed through their master's program, with financial aid from scholarships, in a year without neglecting their raptor research. However, Frank and John had something even more exciting coming up that summer.

They spent June and July preparing for the trip of a lifetime: an adventure in pre-partition India that can never be repeated. On August 6, the twins picked up their steamship tickets, money, and film—color mind you, for both still and moving pictures—from *National Geographic* which sponsored their trip and, after leaving their tiercel Ulysses in the care of Morgan Berthrong and Larry Hufty and releasing their other birds, headed north in their 1934 Chevy. To fund the trip, they had $600 from the sale of an article to the *Saturday Evening Post*, $3,000 (mostly in tickets, film stock, and supplies) from *National Geographic,* and the Chevy. They spent the night at Craighead Station and headed west early the next morning. They slept in fields and pastures along the way, often stopping after dark, unaware of their surroundings until daybreak revealed "ghostly staring faces" of cattle looking at them. They bought newspapers along the way to monitor how England was faring in the Battle of Britain air war.

On August 11, they arrived at the Smiths' cabin in the Tetons and borrowed a tent to sleep in while there. They hiked and climbed mountains with Margaret Smith and her friend, Margaret Bedell, almost every day. Frank wrote about taking the Margarets out on the town:

"[On August 17] In the evening we drove to Jackson and danced most of the night at the Cowboy Bar. Lost 50 cents on the roulette wheel. Really got dancing after drinking my second Tom Collins. We danced every dance until 1:30 in the morning. Most of them were fast. It was the most fun I have ever had dancing....

"[August 21, Frank] In the evening, we drove to Jackson and took the girls to a movie and dancing. Mrs. Smith didn't approve of the Tom Collins, so we drank lemonade. I lost a silver dollar on the roulette wheel and then quit. I should have known better. I had a swell time dancing, even though my sore knee still troubled me. A fellow who had been watching came up to Margaret Bedell and me and said we were the best dancers on the floor. I almost keeled over, but I had a good time kidding John and Margaret Smith about it.

"[August 22, Frank] Margaret [Smith] is a swell girl, always happy....Margaret Bedell is a grand girl, a great hiker and has lots of pluck. She is getting her PH.D. in bacteriology at Wisconsin. I had a great time hiking with her, but she is getting a little too serious to suit me."

David Masland, Bill Shelley & Mike Masland head west in Mrs. Masland's new Ford station wagon
(Johnson Coyle)

When the author asked what Frank was better at than he was, John immediately responded, "Chasing girls!"

On the 22nd, the twins headed out for San Francisco, with stops along the way at Salt Lake City, Lake Tahoe, and Berkeley. Mostly, they focused on the flora, fauna, and geology, but they did visit Sally Rand's Nude Ranch on Treasure Island, most likely at the suggestion of the younger David Masland and Bill Coyle, who had visited it the previous year on their trip west. They sold the Chevy for $115 and boarded their ship, the SS *President Cleveland*, and, after some delays, pulled out of port on September 6 with a load of scrap iron and rubber headed for Japan.

They were finally underway to visit their friend Bapa. One could write a book about their trip. In fact they did better than that: they wrote an article for the February 1942 *National Geographic* and a heavily illustrated book, both titled *Life with an Indian Prince*.

On their first afternoon aboard, they received a steamer letter from the Zirpel children, mountain climbing pictures from Margaret Smith they took in the Tetons, and a painting by Jean done expressly for Bapa.

The first of their several stops was Hawaii, where the comely Abbey sisters (friends of friends) showed them around the island in grand style in a big Buick, wearing leis around their necks. This process repeated itself at several stops on their trip as they, or friends of theirs, had written ahead. Upon leaving Honolulu, they passed the rocky island of Nihoa at the southern end of the Northwestern Hawaiian Island chain about 250 miles west of Hawaii. Nine days later they sighted land again. They conversed with fellow passengers to break the boredom and, for two days when they were nearing Japan, experienced a typhoon firsthand. They spent September 21 sightseeing around Yokohama and Tokyo. The poverty of the people and the canals carrying raw sewage struck them. They observed how Japan's war machine was consuming most materials. The next day they sailed along the coast, reaching Kobe at 5:00 p.m. Three days later, after cargo was unloaded and machine oil loaded for delivery at Hong Kong, they pulled out for China. Disembarked passengers were replaced by new ones. A Lithuanian girl who had been in Manchuria when the Japanese took over told of the atrocities they committed. The twins noted, "We in America have been so little affected that it is difficult to imagine the magnitude of the changes taking place and the uncertainty and unsettled conditions affecting these people."

They spent the next evening in Hong Kong sightseeing before steaming off for Manila, where they spent five days before shifting to the SS *President Polk*. The ship was not as luxurious as the *Cleveland*. The passengers, however, were more interesting and included a number of young Indian girls who conversed freely with the twins, particularly about the unfair treatment Indians received from Britain, starting with preventing mass education. Four days of chugging through the China Sea landed them in Singapore eager to see the sights; however, the cocky Canadian chief of government detectives forbade them to take their cameras ashore, refusing to discuss the matter further.

The next stop was Penang, Malaysia where the twins astonished the native longshoremen by lifting 100-plus-pound tin ingots over their heads, a feat the dockworkers could not match. The Craigheads noticed the tropical paradise wasn't exactly as it seemed:

> "Towering over the houses were waving coconut palms that suggested a false peacefulness, shattered by the sight of camouflaged pillboxes and barbed wire entanglements. It was evident that Penang, now quietly sleeping under the tropical sun, is a potential hornets' nest, a potential theater of war."

While crossing the Indian Ocean, they heard Secretary of State Cordell Hull advise all Americans in Japan, China, Indochina, and Singapore to return home. They had an interesting talk about religion and the caste system with an Indian businessman, a Mr. Gopoldas, who told them he and Bapa both came from the soldier, or warrior, class. After seeing poverty and war preparations in the Far East, a twin noted, "The more I have seen of life and conditions in these foreign countries, the more I have come to appreciate what we have and take for granted in America." Their next port-of-call before arriving in India was Colombo, Ceylon (present day Sri Lanka).

Their voyage ended on October 21, 1940 in Bombay (present day Mumbai), where several of Bapa's men wearing colored turbans met their ship to handle their luggage. They dined at the Taj Mahal Hotel at something approaching a state dinner with the maharaja, Bapa, (his brother) Nanabhai, the state horticulturalist, and the state secretary. "We immediately felt a kinship with the brothers, conversing about hunting, hawking, riding, and photography, while we ate supper." While the maharaja conducted business in Bombay, the Craigheads attacked the unenviable task of processing their equipment through customs. Getting film through proved to be even more difficult than the cameras. Putting up a possibly refundable $100 deposit finally got it all released. On the evening of the 24th, they boarded a train for Bapa's home in Bhavnagar, an Indian state of about 3,000 square miles located on the Arabian Sea north of Bombay.

Frank and John spent the next 100 days enjoying a life of luxury they never before imagined or experienced ever again. They arrived to ceremonies celebrating the return of the maharaja, who rode in his personal railcar on the same train with the twins and Bapa. At one of the train's frequent stops, the maharaja, His Highness, addressed a group of his soldiers who were being sent abroad, to fight in WWII one assumes. The twins lived like princes with Bapa in pre-partition India. "Bapa saw us off the train and then left us at the state guest house (or hotel) that is to be our home while in Bhavnagar. We have a suite of four rooms with all modern conveniences. It seems like a dream."

They spent most days exploring nature, hunting with trained falcons and cheetahs, shooting game, sighting birds and animals previously unknown to them, capturing and training birds, and filming what they saw. Too many photos to count, over half in color, illustrate their book on the trip. The twins learned much about falconry from people who had been perfecting the sport for over a thousand years.

One day, they went on a hunt for a rare Asiatic lion that had wandered into Bhavnagar. The maharaja gave Zutshi, the man about to marry the sister of the maharani (the maharaja's wife), the honor of shooting the lion. Taking the fiancé on a hunt before the wedding was customary, but hunting a lion on elephants was spectacular. Zutshi shot late but six others, including His Highness, shot immediately after him. Since all the bullets were of the same .375 caliber, they gave Zutshi credit for the kill and the lion's skin.

The next evening, New Year's Eve, they watched a mongoose fight a cobra but not to the death because the snake charmer separated them before the mongoose could make the kill. An even more unexpected treat was in store for them when they steamed down the Ganges to Tripura with three maharajas, numerous princes, and Indian state officials aboard.

Bapa related that Prince Nanabhai's "first marriage had been a disappointment and ended in tragedy, so he was more cautious on his second attempt." Even with such caution, all he got to see of his future bride was a photograph, and only briefly. The twins found Indian customs to be very different from what they were used to:

"After her marriage, the bride must fashion herself a new life modeled around the existence of her husband. She must accept his customs, interests, desires, and peculiarities, and make them a part of herself. The wife is a mere satellite revolving around a sun, and the sun may or may not have a number of satellites. This, of course, explains why the husband is not too concerned about the attractiveness of his wife, as long as the dowry and family are good.

"All the elaborate marriage customs and rituals of Tripura [the bride's home state] were new to Nanabhai and he had little idea what to expect. Likewise, his bride returned, in seclusion, to Bhavnagar to take part in ceremonies which were foreign to her and conducted in a language she did not understand."

The wedding was a men-only affair with numerous processions of dignitaries in their finery, elephants, soldiers, native warriors, maharajas, and hundreds of variously dressed tribesmen in a moving rainbow of color. "My lasting impression will not be the silver elephant carriages, the trays of silks and jewels that were presented to the bride, or the gorgeously dressed groom and the attendants, but rather an image of a great color splash—a bubbling spring of pigments flowing as a long quilted ribbon from the old palace on the hill through the jungle growth, to the new palace by the lake," recalled one of the twins.

On February 1, 1941, their last full day with Bapa, the twins rushed to Palatani to see the famous Jain temples. Jainism prescribes nonviolence toward all living creatures. Orthodox Jains wear a fine light cloth over their mouths to prevent them from inadvertently inhaling small microscopic life and killing it. They boil all water before drinking it and readily admit they're killing bacteria when doing so, but consider it better to kill the bacteria outside the body rather than in it. The twins' purpose in coming was not anthropological; they came to see the beautiful temple. As state guests, they were seated on large cushions suspended on two poles and were carried by four men to the top of the sacred hill, where the palace was located. After a bit, they got down and walked the rest of the way on well-worn cobblestones to the 2,000 foot summit.

That evening back in Bhavnagar, the twins previewed their roughly edited movies.

His Highness and friends enjoyed seeing themselves, their hawks, and their cheetahs in action. The next morning they bid fond farewell to their host and the friends they made in Bhavnagar and caught a train to Bombay.

They spent the next five weeks touring other parts of India on their own. In reality, friends they made along the way often acted as hosts and tour guides for them. They hit the usual tourist spots but also sought out places of interest to naturalists. At Haldwani they met an English forester and leader in wildlife photography, F. W. "Freddie" Champion, and his wife, Judy. Freddie, the younger brother of the twins' father's friend, Harry Champion, was the first to photograph jungle animals, including tigers, at night. Freddie took them on a hunt for a man-eating tiger that had been terrorizing the district. They rode elephants for better visibility and safety. Not finding the tiger that day, they stayed up in a machan (observation platform) in the jungle all night hoping the beast would come, but it didn't. Instead, it killed a man in a village only a few miles away.

Champion pioneered remote photo-flash photography but had fallen behind technology somewhat because of the demands the war placed on him. The twins suggested he consider trying Kodachrome film, which was new at the time. The Champions took them boar hunting and bird shooting from elephants and on a trip to the Himalayas before depositing them at Haldwani on February 26.

The next day, they arrived at their last stop in India, Calcutta, with hopes of catching a ship for Hong Kong on March 1st. Delays in getting their film through government censors and newspaper headlines blaring "U.S. Warns Japan and Sends Flying Fortresses to Singapore" and "Australian Soldiers Land at Singapore" convinced them to book passage on a ship headed in the opposite direction. On March 12, 1941, they steamed out of Calcutta as "workaways" on the SS *Exemplar*, a fast new freighter headed ultimately to Boston. The captain put them in the hospital cabin at the stern but didn't work them, either by whim or to avoid friction with the union workers. After a two-day stop in Colombo, they sighted land a few times the rest of the way but didn't dock, even at San Fernando, the industrial city on Trinidad and Tobago, on April 11, when they took on oil for the last leg of the voyage to Boston.

Thinking their adventures were over, they reminisced about the adventure they had just taken. They also looked ahead to what they would do back in the States. They wrote letters to Professors Howard Wight and Samuel Graham at the University of Michigan, cajoling them to provide fellowships for their Ph.D. studies. "We thought they would be interested to know that we were offered junior biologist jobs at $2,000 a year. We must have done pretty well in the Federal Junior Biologist exam." Then the government intervened.

As the *Exemplar* steamed up the East Coast, the government requisitioned it for Navy service and truncated its trip. It landed in New York on April 17 before being recommissioned as the USS *Dorothea L Dix (AP-67)* and sent to England as part of Roosevelt's Lend-Lease Program.

Landing close to home in New York instead of Boston was convenient since they were (as always) short of money. They landed $500 student assistantships from the University of Michigan School of Forestry and Conservation to work on their Ph.D.s under Prof. Howard Marshall Wight, an early believer in the need to study the environment in which a plant or animal lives.

10

Falconry

WHEN THE TWINS WERE FIFTEEN, their carefree out-of-school lives changed forever. Life-long friend and co-conspirator Morgan Berthrong wrote 65 years after the fact about the pivotal event:

"Perhaps it was a chance encounter with an article in a 1920 *National Geographic*, 'Falconry, the Sport of Kings,' magnificently illustrated by Louis Agassiz Fuertes, that first aroused their curiosity. Then an aeronautical engineer and falconry enthusiast in Washington told them that, when his peregrine flew against a wind, it presented a silhouette ideal for an airplane, if only there was a motor powerful enough to take it airborne. And Captain Luff Meredith, an Army Air Corps pilot and falconer, further fanned their enthusiasm. He struck the spark that converted their enthusiasm into action when he suggested they attempt to train the Cooper's hawk, a fierce short-winged hawk (accipiter) found only in North America and therefore unknown and untrained by falconers of ancient times. This was the challenge they were waiting for."

The summer of 1932 was different from all the summers the Craigheads and their friends at Craighead Station had experienced previously, changing the tenor of those that followed. In prior years, the twins' morning chore was retrieving pitchers of drinking water from the well just across the dirt road. After completing their task, they were free to roam the fields and meadows until their mother called them for lunch. But keeping hawks brought much responsibility and required considerable attention. Trapping and shooting fresh food for them was just one of several tasks they had to accomplish every day. And training the birds was the most time consuming of all.

The hawks required a fair amount of fresh meat for feed, so the twins enlisted sister

Jean, cousins Sam and Bill, friends David Masland, Bill Coyle, Chet Eshelman, and others to shoot or catch sparrows, starlings, blackbirds, pigeons, rabbits, and mice. Their dog Spike stirred up rodents for them and the food collectors put the twins' trusty .22 to good use. Carolyn reserved a space in the left side of the ice box to store hawk food, provided it was wrapped in waxed paper. Jean admired her mother's support of her children's development: "She believed in children with projects and she put up with the difficulties such projects might involve."

The twins didn't completely make up their hawk-training regimen on the fly; they tried to follow the old texts they found. But not all the theory they found in the ancient book from the Library of Congress and the 1920 *National Geographic* article worked out in practice: many things weren't covered adequately. So the brothers developed techniques of their own, where they found none to follow or whenever the ones they followed failed. Frank Jr. and John put to practice the lessons from their scientist father by logging all pertinent data related to the health, growth, and training of their hawks. Periodically, they wrote to Morgan Berthrong to inform him of their progress.

At summer's end, the twins returned to Washington, where they not only applied themselves to their studies but also continued training their hawks. Morgan Berthrong joined them in flying their birds, but unfortunately his bird turned out not to be well-suited for falconry. Julian Griggs, Gates Slattery, and an older boy named Alva Nye also followed in their footsteps by training hawks of their own with Frank Jr., John, and Morgan. The twins and their friends attracted a good bit of attention, some of it unwanted. Frank's November 19, 1932 note observed:

"Today a reporter from the *Washington Star* took pictures of our hawks. Julian Griggs, Alva Nye, Morgan Berthrong, John, and I were in the photos. Gates Slattery was not able to get there on time. The pictures came out in the Sunday *Star* along with a story about our hawks and their training."

An article in the *Richmond Times-Dispatch* the next day headlined, "Game Wardens Puzzle Falconing Regulation," was more serious in tone, possibly a reaction to the *Star* piece. Maryland game wardens were in a quandary concerning falconry: there were no regulations covering the sport because it was virtually unpracticed in the U. S. prior to the Craigheads. All the wardens could think up was "stay with the bag limit of six rabbits daily."

The boys continued to fly their birds throughout the winter but less often due to demands of their school work and extra-curricular activities. Frank decided to keep Comet through her molt and fly her again the next year. They released John's bird and decided to get him another Cooper's hawk and to try their hands with sparrow hawks (kestrels). They took young birds from their nests in late spring and immediately began to train them. Their Pennsylvania friends also began training hawks. What began as an activity for identical twins a year earlier had spread to about ten boys in Pennsylvania and the District of Columbia plus their sister, counting only those who actually trained their own birds, not mere onlookers.

Soon, the Craighead yard was stocked with birds. However, one person in particular wasn't so fond of them. Mary Dunfee Campbell grew up in the house directly across from the Craigheads but didn't play with them much because she was even younger than the youngest Craighead who stayed the summer. Well into her eighties, Mary remembered the hawks clearly, but not happily. "They could get you," she said, her hand simulating a beak snapping shut. The twins soon learned some others weren't wild about them having these hawks and owls either:

"On July 14 [1933] two game wardens came and told us we had to let the screech owl and sparrow hawks loose as they are protected in Pennsylvania. They came again on the 17th and we flew the hawks for them. On the 18th we went to Harrisburg and got a permit to keep them. One thing that helped was the fact that Frank Masland [our neighbor] had taken some pictures [movies] the year before of Windy and the other hawks and owls. The state then used them in their educational programs."

The above log entry was the sanitized version. Jean and Bill recalled the encounter with the game wardens quite differently. In their versions of the story, the game wardens told the boys to release the birds because they had no licenses. The boys released the birds, which then flew off (probably perching in the tops of nearby trees). After the game wardens departed, the boys whistled and their birds returned.

The log didn't include an earlier encounter with game wardens. Frank, John, Sam, Bill, and Jean, each with a hawk on a fist, walked in a pet parade in Carlisle with other children who had cats and dogs and such. Upon seeing the birds, game wardens pulled the young Craigheads out of the parade to berate them. Jean still smarted from this encounter three-quarters of a century later:

"I can't remember what they said. I only remember that I didn't know why they were doing this and was frightened. No legal action threats. I guess they felt their reprimanding us was enough. I don't know why they did it. There were no Endangered Species laws or any other laws that said you couldn't have a bird of prey. Farmers shot them all the time."

The twins, their sister, and friends learned another life lesson one morning. Windy, their little screech owl pet, was extremely tame and feared nothing, neither man nor dog, cat, nor hawk, not even the larger ones that were his natural enemies. One day, he took his morning bath in the Cooper's hawks' basin rather than the sparrow hawks' as was his usual custom. Only a few feathers under the Cooper's hawk perch were all that remained of Windy.

When the Craigheads' summer ended, they loaded, with some difficulty, one Cooper's hawk, a goshawk, two sparrow hawks, and Spike into the car and headed back to Washington and school.

The next year, 1934, brought with it new goals and adventures. On March 30, the twins located a duck hawk nest in the gorge of the Potomac River at Cupids Bower, Maryland. The female duck hawk (peregrine falcon today) is the true falcon prized by practitioners for centuries. Its image was immortalized in the black statuette fought and died for in *The Maltese Falcon*. Three days later, they and buddy Robert "Steve" Stevenson lugged a camera and blind-making equipment to what they called Duck Hawk Cliff. John climbed 75 feet up a tree to get a close-up view of the eyrie, set up a camera about four feet from the duck hawk nest full of eggs, camouflaging the camera with burlap to keep the parent birds unaware. Meanwhile, Frank Jr. and Steve built a blind at the base of the cliff from which to trip the shutter to take photographs. John attached a long string to the shutter of the camera and dropped it down to Frank, who huddled in the blind waiting for the ideal opportunity to pull the string and get a good photo of an adult duck hawk returning to the nest. John climbed down the tree knowing his presence would deter the hawks from returning to their nest. He and Steve paddled the canoe across the river, where they were to signal Frank when the hawk flew back to the nest, but she passed them before they got into the canoe. John and Steve returned to the blind, thinking Frank had taken the picture. He hadn't because they hadn't signaled him. They wrongly assumed he'd seen the hawk return to the nest.

Cold and wet from lying on the ground, back and neck aching from crouching over and remaining motionless in the tiny blind, Frank was not pleased to hear he had missed an opportunity for a good shot. John missed seeing the hawk again on the second try but finally yelled to Frank because he thought the hawk must have returned to the nest. Frank pulled the cord. The duck hawk was on the eggs and flew off at the click of the shutter. They had taken their first falcon photo. All that was needed to take another was to climb up to the camera, remove the exposed glass plate, put in an unexposed one, climb down, and do it again. So started the Craigheads' careers as wildlife photographers. They honed their skills by repeating this process hundreds of times while teenagers.

Wildlife photography, especially as practiced in those days by teenaged novices, was a dangerous proposition. In addition to being attacked by hawks, owls, and eagles

Skinny Dipping at the Swirl Hole taken by John Craighead (William Moore Craighead)

protecting their nests, the boys faced greater risks climbing tall trees and rapelling cliffs. One lesson the twins learned early on was to use a rope long enough to reach to the ground, even when rapelling only part way down a cliff to a nest. The plan was for John, Julian, and Steve to lower Frank to the nest, where he would take photos, then pull him back up. But they loosened too many large rocks, one of which barely missed Frank, on the descent. Thinking pulling him back up unwise for fear of knocking another loose rock free and killing him, they lowered him down instead. When they realized the rope was fifteen feet too short, they threw Frank a piece of clothesline which he then tied to the larger rope. The clothesline broke when he was still 10 feet off the ground. A lesson learned the hard way.

Another time, they were rappelling in view of several spectators, one of whom, apparently expecting the worst, called an ambulance. Frank observed, "To heck with them. If we fall, a broom is what they need, not an ambulance."

Some of their photos were of a different type of wildlife—homo sapiens—at play. John's picture of cousin Bill fishing won a photography contest held by the Harrisburg *Evening News* and his shot of the "creek gang" skinny-dipping is priceless. He must have shot that photo several times to get exactly what he wanted—and for it to be acceptable to polite society.

By shooting and developing hundreds of photographs in their darkroom at home, the twins became skilled photographers, selling some of their works for publication. They used money from their first sale to buy a 1928 Chevrolet, an old and probably unreliable car for the time. That car expanded their range: they could then get farther up the Potomac after school and even farther on weekends.

That April, they gave a talk about falconry to the Carlisle Kiwanis Club, after which Julian and Morgan joined them on a trip to Spruce Creek in northern Pennsylvania where Harrisburg ornithologist Dick Rauch had told them about an unusual situation: a duck hawk nest and a raven nest in close proximity to each other. They easily found them: the two nests were only fifty yards apart.

On the nights of May 4 and 5, the twins, their father, and Steve camped across the river from the eyrie they'd previously discovered and photographed on Duck Hawk Cliff. The three young duck hawks were developed enough to be taken from their mother and were lowered down from their nest in a basket on the second night. Frank Jr. and John wanted to leave a pair of the birds behind, but two other boys had agreed not to disturb the nest while the twins observed and photographed the hatchlings. Frank Levy and Otho Williams each got a two-and-a-half pound falcon while the twins kept the pound-and-a-half tiercel. (The female peregrine falcon is larger and considered to be a better hunter than the male.) The twins took their tiercel home and began training him. Within a month, they had him flying tethered. They let him fly free on June 10. During those four flights, he earned his name, Ulysses, because of his propensity to wander. After two more weeks of training, summer vacation began and they continued his training at Craighead Station.

When school was out for the summer, Morgan and Steve joined the twins on a trip to Saganaga Lake, Ontario to photograph pigeon hawks and to capture birds to train. Two nights before their departure, a hit-and-run driver sideswiped the old Chevy, knocking off a back fender and wheel and pushing it against a tree, smashing the radiator. The twins spent most of the last two days patching up the car. Assuming it repaired, the four intrepid travelers drove off. Unfortunately, the Chevy had hidden damage: the drive shaft was bent, causing the universal joint to rattle. A proper repair would cost more than the car was worth, so they liberally lubricated the universal joint and continued on their way. The car carried them safely to Canada and back, but not without adventures along the way.

Ojibwe naturalist guides, Frank and Bill Powell, met them on the Boundary Waters about 40 miles northwest of Grand Marais, Minnesota and paddled them across the lake. The renowned guides quickly located pigeon hawk nests for them. In their few days with the Powells, they observed pigeon hawks hunting wily swallows, feeding their young, the male handing off food to the female in mid-air, and other behaviors not often seen by humans. They got all the still photos they needed, but the nests they found were unfavorably located for shooting movies. They departed mostly satisfied because they had captured four young pigeon hawks, a primary goal of the trip. On the way back, they found a nest well situated for taking movies. Sadly, the marsh in which they camped was infested with the most aggressive mosquitoes they had encountered in their young lives. After two nights in the camp, John could barely recognize Frank or Morgan, their faces swollen badly from insect bites. A twin reported, while the three others stood up to their chins in water:

"Steve very gallantly waded to shore and started preparing breakfast....A horde of these raptors trailed behind him trying to get under the netting hanging from his hat. Steve's hands, deep in his pockets, now and then flew into action when he turned over the bacon or put wood on the fire. Even more quickly he returned them, but not without paying a price....we decided to stay and fight mosquitoes for a few days longer. When we finally got our movies, we were sick from mosquito bites, but at the same time we did not realize that the swollen glands in our necks and the lazy doped feeling that crept over us was due to the mosquito poison injected into our blood. We imagined many terrible diseases."

All felt a good bit better by the time they got to Lake Superior, so they stopped for a swim. John knew Lake Superior was cold, even in mid-July, but didn't realize just how cold it was:

"Steve dived in, gasped for breath, turned around after swimming ten feet, and slowly dragged himself out. His arms and legs were too numb to function and his skin was red. He could hardly swim twenty feet...I followed Steve, and it was all I could do to crawl back out onto the sloping rocks. My limbs were as stiff as boards. We got back into 'Old Chevy' a little wiser from our experience."

The four also got a little wiser about birds when they tried to train their pigeon hawks. Once these birds became strong flyers, one by one, they'd catch a prey in full flight and, instead of returning with the kill, take off, never to be seen again, but not before the twins got several nice photos of these new-to-them falcons. John lamented, "With the loss of our pigeon hawks, we learned that we still had not mastered the art of teaching small falcons not to carry."

Soon after starting college, Frank and John made front page news in the November 12, 1935 *Penn State Collegian* article "Twin Brothers Revive Ancient Sport of Falconry on Campus." Apparently Ulysses caught a budding reporter's attention when the twins released him from his perch in the back-yard of their apartment. The tiercel was the

Ulysses's image adorned the cover of the twins' first book (Author)

only bird they brought with them; they had given away or released all the others. The article also mentioned they previously had articles published in *American Forests, Nature Magazine,* science bulletins, and newspapers before starting college. Anyone on campus who didn't know who they were before certainly knew after this.

Just before Christmas break, they took Ulysses out to the Penn State golf course for some exercise, but he gave two unlucky golfers exercise they hadn't expected when he dive-bombed them. Frank and John gave occasional lectures about falconry on campus because the sport was virtually unknown to American college students and faculty at that time.

After graduating in 1939 with A.B.s in Science, John and Frank had much to do before heading to Ann Arbor for graduate school. Houghton Mifflin had agreed to publish *Hawks in the Hand: Adventures in Photography and Falconry,* but much work was needed to get their manuscript and 57 photos ready for publication. Penn State Professors Edward Nichols and Gerald Stout gave them support, moral and otherwise, preparing their manuscript for publication.

The book put to press, Frank Jr., John, Ulysses, and Nancy (a recently acquired prairie falcon) headed west and then north to start graduate work at the University of Michigan. With financial aid from scholarships, the twins breezed through their master's program in Ecology and Wildlife Management in a year without neglecting their raptor research. They also wrote their second *National Geographic* article, "In Quest of the Golden Eagle," for the May 1940 issue. However, Frank and John had something even more exciting coming up that summer, a trip to India to visit Bapa. Before they left for India, they released all of their birds except Ulysses.

When they returned from their trip to India and enrolled in graduate school in the fall of 1941, they brought Ulysses with them and kept him in a cage in a biology lab, probably due to the harsh Michigan winter. A weasel owned by a fellow student escaped its cage and killed him in a sneak attack the same winter the Japanese conducted one of their own. It was all the twins could do to refrain from doing him—the student, not the weasel—bodily harm. On this sad note they ended their highly active years as falconers.

11

Jean Carolyn Craighead

O N JULY 2, 1919, CAROLYN CRAIGHEAD gave her extremely active sons a sister, blonde, curly-haired Jean Carolyn. She was the twins' first foil for pranks. When she was very young, they forced her to eat a poisonous elephant-ear plant that contained calcium oxalate crystals that give the throat a burning, stinging sensation. She survived because she couldn't stand to eat enough to harm her. Another time they locked her in a trunk, an experience she blotted from her memory. Not everyone thought their pranks were funny:

"The neighbors called them 'The Diablo Twins.' Who knows what other pranks the twins pulled to be labeled 'Diablo.' When I told Mother, she said, 'Humph, that's not true.' To her they were angels."

Jean wouldn't divulge the nature of the devilish pranks, but one may have had something to do with snaking a garden hose into a neighbor's mail slot. Jean tried one of their more benign pranks—once. She flipped the trolley pole off the wire easily enough, but her father was riding in the car right behind hers and saw her do it. He was not amused.

Like her older brothers, Jean excelled in school, but her talents lay in different directions: "I did go to E.V. Brown School. That's where a third grade teacher, when I couldn't do a math problem at the black board and wrote a poem, told me that it was very good and I should keep on writing." Buoyed by her teacher's compliment, Jean continued writing and also explored other avenues of expression.

Jean considered her summer days less exciting than her brothers' because her mother had her pull weeds and help with housework. To put it mildly, Jean found neither chore very interesting. She disliked making her bed so much she ran away from home at age three saying, "I'm tired of making my bed. I just mess it up again every night." However, she did enjoy going to the market house in Carlisle with her mother on Saturdays. They either caught the train just outside their door or rode in with Grace Goodyear, who owned a car. Jean enjoyed the sights and smells of the fresh fruits and vegetables. Her mother purchased healthy foods from favorite vendors decades before eating healthily came into vogue. Jean participated with the falconry along with the boys, or looked for wild flowers in the meadow and played girls' games with Emily Coyle when the boys weren't doing something that captured her imagination. The girls also skinny-dipped in the creek if the boys were off somewhere distant.

Starting in 1929, when Jean was ten, family members, friends, and visitors started painting on the kitchen walls of the Craighead summer home. Jean soon became one of the most creative and prolific artists. Paula Zirpel (first cousin on her mother's side) and Eugene's son Sam, who painted numerous airplanes on the north and west walls, may have been her greatest competition.

Jean still loved her bedroom over the kitchen at the head of the back stairs almost eighty years after the fact:

"My bedroom looked very much like it does today except that I had drawn elves climbing out of cracks in the wall and sliding down tears in the wallpaper." At age twelve, she painted the dressing table and chair in her bedroom overlooking the creek to use as a writing desk:

Jean at her vanity-turned-writing desk in 2011 (Author)

"While sitting at it, I could turn my head to the left and see the creek, the walnut and sycamore trees. If I leaned a little farther I could see my brothers on the railroad bridge having climbed down the rainspout when they were supposedly napping or reading….There was a narrow closet in the left hand corner of the room where Sam and I hid one day only to find it had no latch on the inside and we had to yell or scream and bang until someone heard us."

Writing at that desk paved the way for her numerous works that were published later. Jean discussed her childhood in *Journey Inward*, a reflective book some family members objected to because they thought it was too personal in nature:

"With two such brothers, a younger sister *had* to be a writer to find her niche and survive. The twins were sufficient unto themselves—although I lived in the same house with and followed them to rivers and cliffs, I was always an outsider—almost so as an only child. So, I dreamed up an imaginary companion for whom I began writing stories."

In Washington, maternal first cousins, Ellen Zirpel and her younger sisters Paula and Charlotte, lived around the corner from Jean. Jean's Aunt Polly (Pauline) and her daughters were warm and made Jean feel at home. The girl cousins spent much of their free time together drawing, making puppets, staging performances, keeping diaries, and sharing their deepest secrets. Carolyn and Pauline enrolled their daughters in the Carolyn McKinley School of Interpretative Dance, where they learned the style of Isadora Duncan. Like their idol, they danced barefoot. They tie-dyed their costumes, which always included long, flowing scarves reminiscent of the one that strangled Duncan. When class was over, they performed dances they invented on the Zirpels' lawn, interpreting music by Schubert, Ravel, and Debussey. Their mothers admonished them to dare to be different, to not follow the crowd.

When Jean was thirteen, her brothers gave her a young sparrow hawk. Referring to herself as June in *The Summer of the Falcon,* Jean wrote how he quickly earned his name:

"In the basket, braced on a stub of a tail, was a robin-sized sparrow hawk, North America's smallest falcon. Her hands cupped the screaming bird and she lifted it to her cheek. A blue talon dug her hand, the other clenched her shirt. The falcon was afraid, and he clung tighter and tighter. June held it close, for she knew that all young life is scared and unsure. Don gently pried the claws from the blouse, wrapped his palm around its feet, and presented her with the bird. She again took the screaming baby of the wild in her hands. The bird stopped fighting and chirped softly. June placed him deep in the basket, but as she released him, he shot out a blue foot, broke the skin of her hand, and screamed in rage."

For that, Jean named him Bad Boy. He reinforced her choice by pinching her with his claws whenever she caught him trying to get away. Jean's brothers had some reservations about giving her a hawk because she hadn't always been the most responsible. Her maternal grandmother told her that she had her head in the clouds. Frank Jr. nagged her, saying, "Get yourself in a work mood...training a falcon is tedious and demanding." Her father admonished her to let Bad Boy go if she weren't going to take good care of him. But Jean mustered the self-discipline to feed and train Bad Boy, a project that changed her young life and later provided her fodder for books.

Army brat Florence Kelton met Jean on the first day of school in the ninth grade at Alice Deal Junior High when her kindly teacher had Jean show Flo around at lunch "…and that was the start of our friendship." Flo and Jean were often in the same classes.

"Given the choice of History or Science, Jean and I chose Science, the only girls who did so. The teacher was Mr. Brian, if I remember correctly, and we picked up knowledge of biology, physics, and chemistry from him. Jean was of course smart and fun to sit next to, often thinking up entertaining things to do, e. g. once we surreptitiously drew pictures of the boys' haircuts, passed them to one another to 'guess who.'"

Jean and Flo attended Western High their sophomore year, riding the Wisconsin Street trolley home together, with "much cutting up, giggling and laughing, I recall." They shifted to newly constructed Woodrow Wilson High their junior year. It was built on the site of French's Woods in Tenleytown to serve the rapidly expanding Washington school population and accommodate overflow from overcrowded Western High. Seventy-six years later, Jean recalled entering Wilson High:

"I see myself walking the last bit of that mile from home. There is a water tower on the right and a large field. The steps are up ahead to the school door. I hurry. I enter the school's corridors to the smell of fresh paint. We were the first class, and the building was new and 'modern.' There were lockers, a gymnasium, art and music rooms, and a science lab. The teachers opened us up to new ideas; the science teacher taught biology by going on trips and physics by using objects to demonstrate— spinning Victrola records and falling balls. We took languages—I, German and Latin. The German teacher taught us by making us speak only German when we entered the class. When it was over, we carried the German chitchat to our lockers or gym classes. The English teacher had us read and act out Shakespeare for a better understanding of him. We read many other classics and some modern writers as well. She started us writing a school newspaper, *The Beacon*….We held proms and sports events and envied those who had cars or at least were able to borrow Dad's. Bobby socks were in, and saddle shoes. Mr. Nelson, the principal, was superior. I remember him as an open-minded person who entered into every school event, be it academic or social. He was a man who saw the potential in each one of us and sent us off well prepared for a new world."

Flo observed, "Here all Jean's talents came into play: she wrote, headed the yearbook, was artistic, danced, and was a truly outstanding member of the class." Jean's 1937 *Woodrow Wilson* lists her name on 11 pages and includes her full-page color drawings on four others. Perhaps her senior yearbook portrait encapsulates her high school best:

"JEAN CAROLYN CRAIGHEAD

Woodrow Wilson Players; German Club; Editor-in-Chief, Beacon; Swimming Team; Panel; Science Club; Honor Roll '35, '36; Year Book Staff.

A most outstanding person is Craigie. She always does her best in everything she undertakes and is sincere to the last ounce. She is talented, especially in writing and drawing, and hopes to become an author, illustrating her own books."

Jean working on the yearbook
(Wodrow Wilson High School)

Some of the entries deserve a bit of explanation. *Beacon* was, perhaps obviously, the school newspaper. She served as Art Director and the primary illustrator of the yearbook. In those pre-Title IX days, being on the swim team was a lot different than today:

"Approximately 60 girls met each Wednesday at Shoreham pool. Two meets were held, under the direction of Mrs. M. Steis and June Booth, student manager.... Because of graduation, the team will suffer the loss of some very good swimmers, among whom are Emma Shelton, Betty Flather, and Jean Craighead."

Jean and eight other girls lettered, one of whom, Eleanor Henderson, was considered a good candidate for the Olympic team.

Panel was "…the experimental Current Affairs Discussion Group, whose purpose is to have 'discussion in which all freely participate.'…This method of stimulating thought on today's questions proved so successful…our panel program is no longer an experiment…" Jean and five others discussed "Conservation of Natural Resources," a perfect topic for a Craighead. She also participated on the Special Panel which discussed "After High School, What?" at a dinner meeting of the Home and School Association. Jean's classmates also voted her "Most Versatile Girl" and "Girl Most Likely to Succeed."

Jean graduated in June 1937, looking forward to attending college. Flo sadly recalled, "I remember Jean coming to my house to say goodbye after graduation day. I never saw her again, I regret to say, but I followed her career, read some of the books, even got one autographed. She was a truly outstanding, amazingly talented woman. I'm so glad to say I knew her."

Jean's father gave her two choices: "You can go to George Washington University and live here at home or go to Penn State." Not about to live at home while going to college, she joined cousin Sam and the twins at Penn State where she roomed with friend Emily Coyle her freshman year.

*Jean made four full-page drawings for her high
school yearbook in her senior year*
(Wodrow Wilson High School)

Majoring in English and science, Jean established special relationships with Theodore Roethke, her poetry professor (who later won a Pulitzer Prize) and Clarence Ray Carpenter, a pioneer in the field of primatology. Roethke taught Jean what writing was all about: revising, working, and revising some more. One day, he told Jean about a poetry contest being held at prestigious Smith College: "Only one student can represent Penn State. I should send you—your delivery and personality would probably win." Putting his hand on her shoulder, he said, "But I think Maxine West is a better poet. I'm going to send her instead. Please don't be upset." But Jean was upset. Hearing Roethke say she wasn't the best cut her deeply; she was used to being the best and couldn't abide being less. She pondered her other writing classes, especially those for which she wrote short stories, deciding she was best at prose. She then shifted her focus accordingly.

Where her brothers aimed their talents and energies at their studies, birds, and wrestling, Jean participated in numerous extra-curricular activities as she had in high school. She wrote pieces for literary journals, danced in modern dance recitals, served as a class officer, and was involved in about every aspect of college life available to an undergraduate woman. As a result, she was voted Most Versatile Senior Woman by her classmates.

Jean excelled in her studies at Penn State, graduating in June 1941 with double majors in English and science alongside her cousin Sam. The *1941 LaVie* included in her activities: Junior Class Secretary; Cwens, "an honorary society for Sophomore girls… composed of girls who have shown outstanding ability in extra-curricular activities, leadership, and scholarship;" Penn State Players theatrical group; Pi Gamma Alpha fine arts fraternity; and Dance Club, its photograph on the last page of her Senior yearbook showing her beating a drum in a modern dance.

Jean along with several other students founded *Portfolio*, a literary magazine for which Jean served as the editor-in-chief. Missing the many lectures and cultural events she was accustomed to in Washington but lacking in State College at that time, Jean convinced the other *Portfolio* staff members to invite W. H. Auden, the renowned British poet who had moved to America, to spend a long weekend in Penn State's log cabin in the woods. He agreed to come—for free. She learned much from Auden and Roethke discussing poetry by remaining unusually quiet to absorb all they had to say.

The following fall, scholarship in hand, Jean enrolled in a graduate dance program at Louisiana State University in Baton Rouge. As in her undergraduate years, Jean didn't limit her energies to her studies; she applied her talents to extra-curricular activities as well. Early in the fall term, she and Alva Edwards put their artistic abilities to work designing the Queen's float, crown, and scepter for the homecoming parade held on November 1, 1941.

On November 17, as the Japanese prepared for their raid on Pearl Harbor, Jean and nine other members of the LSU Dance Center performed for the Louisiana Teachers' Association annual session in New Orleans at the invitation of the state health and physical education association. They presented four original dances:

Jean dancing with drum at Penn State recital
(Penn State University)

"Since the program is planned to illustrate certain types of character dances, the group selected will present varying shades of mood and tonal qualities." Two dances were danced by the entire group: "'Radiation,' a dance of pure design...and...'For Spacious Skies,' a spiritual also composed by the entire group." "Though spirited in feeling, the dance is of legato movement, depleting with dignity a combined gratitude, humility, and thoughtfulness." The two other dances were solos, one of which, "An Old Proverb," Jean danced to a poem of the same name she wrote. Miss Ruth Price, head of the LSU

Dance Center, recited the poem while Jean danced. "The dance has been composed to depict the varying moods of the notes." The caption under a still photo of her dancing "An Old Proverb" stated, "[she] is making a study coordinating art forms."

Frank and Carolyn's children were all away at graduate school when the Japanese bombed Pearl Harbor. Their lives would soon be changed immensely in different ways.

"Creek Gang" friends graduate together in 1941 (Penn State University)

12

Samuel Eby and William Moore Craighead

EUGENE CRAIGHEAD MARRIED MYRA EBY on August 6, 1918, but World War I raged, separating them. Fortunately, the war ended three months later, abruptly truncating Eugene's brief Navy career. Two years later on March 8, 1920, their first son, named Samuel Eby after Myra's father, was born in St. Petersburg, Florida, where Myra's parents vacationed. Being the shortest of a short family made his life difficult.

Sam's family lived with Myra's parents near Eugene's work for the Pennsylvania Department of Agriculture in Harrisburg. By 1923, they had moved to Guernsey, Pennsylvania, eight miles north of Gettysburg, probably because Gene was transferred to the Chambersburg office closer to the Adams County orchards he studied. Local newspapers noted Gene and Myra's frequent social and church activities. William Moore "Bill" Craighead joined older brother Sam on August 8, 1925 as his only sibling.

Gene's parents died the years before and after Bill was born, so Bill and Sam never really knew them. They left their house at Craighead Station to Gene and his siblings, who used it as a vacation and holiday home. Frank's and Gene's families spent their entire summers there into the 1940s.

By 1927, Eugene left the Commonwealth's employment, taking a job selling orchard equipment and spray, necessitating a move to Gettysburg. The boys attended public schools, first in Guernsey, then in Gettysburg. Myra joined the Mother's Club and the PTA and was quite active in both organizations. Typical of a Craighead, she argued that natural play originated by the child is superior to play organized and supervised by

adults. She lost the debate but still practiced
what she preached by giving her sons the
same freedom Frank's children enjoyed.
However, some of their play was structured.
Bill recalled spending time with his father:

"On weekends my father, Eugene, was
great. He often would take us [Bill and Sam]
and any of the neighborhood kids who
wanted to go fishing, hiking, hunting, and
ice fishing. Often we would go to the local
zoo. Perhaps one of the most outstanding
activities was when a carload of us kids
would go arrowhead hunting on the island
twenty miles north of Harrisburg in the
middle of the Susquehanna River. Years
later, I can remember ending up with a
half bushel full of Indian artifacts."

Bill Craighead at three
(William Moore Craighead)

In 1930 when they returned to Harrisburg, Bill and Sam attended grammar school
at Steele School and Camp Curtin Junior High for seventh, eighth and ninth grades.
Out of school, they had much fun; they didn't have to work like farm boys. Their home
was a gathering place for the neighborhood kids because they had a ping pong table and
a piano. Outdoors, the boys played mumblety-peg, shot marbles, and flipped baseball
cards. Bill remembered well flipping Babe Ruth and other notable players' card until
they were barely identifiable. Neighborhood boys also played team sports:

"There were pick-up games of baseball or (tag) football. Sometimes we would play
until it was too dark to see the ball. We would start playing just after nine o'clock,
take time out for lunch, come back about an hour later, and continue the same game
until it was time to go home for supper."

Sam and Bill also avidly collected stamps and coins. A physician across the street
from them would get them pennies from the bank to investigate. They completed their
penny collections, finding several Indian head pennies and a rare 1909 S VDB penny,
now worth seven to eight hundred dollars in good condition, much more if uncirculated.

Sam frequented area hospitals whether he was in Gettysburg, at Craighead Station, or
in Harrisburg. Accidents usually precipitated these visits. However, a tonsillectomy was
the reason he was at Gettysburg's Warner Hospital in 1928 and an appendectomy put
him in Harrisburg Hospital in early 1932. That summer, he spent a weekend in Carlisle

Hospital with his jaw wired shut after colliding with David Masland while playing baseball. Dave was much taller but self-described as uncoordinated. Sam out-jumped him to catch a fly ball and smashed his jaw when it struck the top of Dave's head. Cousin Jean described Sam as a grasshopper who hopped quickly and jumped high across the field.

Spelunking was another risky activity. Second cousin Dick Miller led the boys through the Harrisburg storm sewers, starting where they emptied into the Susquehanna River. Bill recalled, "We would go back the drains until when we looked back we couldn't see light any longer. Then it got spooky." They also scoured the city dump with Miller on Saturday afternoons, finding functional light bulbs and stamps.

To say Bill idolized his older brother would only be a slight exaggeration: "I feel even Jean, John and Frank might agree with me on this point. Sam was a genius in his own right. He knew the constellations in the heavens (sky) like a book and would comment on them from time to time." Sam cut out the shapes of the constellations using a jig saw, placed luminescent paint where the stars were located and tacked them on the ceiling above his bed. He would "…turn on the lights for a few minutes, then turn off the lights and you would see the constellations as they would appear in the sky. A marvelous work of art. You might think you were somewhere in a planetarium."

Bill also thought Sam was a genius in mathematics. "He loved statistics and invented a baseball game of his own which occupied a lot of his time as a teenager. It was during the mid to late 1930s when Monopoly became such a rage. Yes, he even sent his game to Parker Brothers for consideration to produce. A nice letter in return but no dice."

Jean sometimes played with Sam and observed his inventiveness and intelligence: "He had created a whole new language, complete with verbs, nouns, adjectives, adverbs…," Jean wrote in *The Summer of the Falcon*.

"Sammy was born to pick on girls. He loved to pick on me. In later years, he was a lovely man, just like his father," recalled cousin Barbara Hallowell. Mary Dunfee Campbell, who lived across the road at Craighead Station, recalled fighting Sam with switches and wouldn't have disagreed with Barbara's assessment. Jean considered Sam a troubled child or at least a child who didn't have a happy childhood. This may be why Jean modeled her hero in *My Side of the Mountain*, Sam Gribley, after him. Apparently, Sam and his mother didn't get along. Perhaps he thought Myra spent too much time with her society friends and organizations. Other children saying hurtful things about his small size may have bothered him, but he was far too tough to bully.

Bill said Sam and his mother shared one interest, music:

"He was a master musician. He learned to become a musician by learning to play a flute at an early age, with my mother playing the piano and Sam on the flute or piccolo [they] would play classical music as a duo."

Sam and Bill excelled at school, but summers freed them for more interesting pursuits:

"At Craighead there are still many things that could be reckoned. There was the old country store, [and] part of the mill or granary. Here is where we could get ice cream, especially on a hot summer day. The Popsicle sticks had 'free' on them. If you were lucky you might get a free one. In the evening the country store was a hubbub of activity. Many of the farmers would show up in the evening to play pinochle at the store or pitch horseshoes just across the road from the store. I remember many nights going to sleep hearing the clinging of horseshoes against the peg. I slept on the outside porch just across the road. Sometimes, so I've been told, I even went to bed with the clothes I had been wearing—too tired to change into pajamas. In the morning I would jump out of bed ready to go down to the creek to check the eel lines that were baited the night before.

"By the time we went to Craighead for the summer it was close to the 4th of July and some of the stores in nearby towns sold firecrackers. Well, there is nothing from a pyrotechnical standpoint that we didn't do. My favorite though, was to go down in the meadow and set a two-inch firecracker in a fresh cow pie and get away without being splattered with cow manure. Then to top it off, to treat some friends to the delicious persimmons from a tree that was also in the meadow. The green ones were bitter and would make your mouth pucker up. The ones that had color of red were delicious.

"On a rainy day a good time could be spent in climbing to the highest loft in the barn and jump in the hay below. Then too, occasionally we would go to the attic and rummage through old trunks or boxes with many kinds of stored items. Sometimes, in order to find food for the hawks and owls, we would go to the recently cut wheat shocks and hunt for mice. Or, go to the side of the mountain just above Mt. Holly Springs to the blackbird roost to shoot enough starlings for food for the owls and hawks.

"We hardly ever wore shoes while at Craighead. We took pride in toughening the soles of our feet. The real test was whether your feet were tough enough to run on the cinders of the railroad bed or on the hot macadam road in front of the house. Then when we had to go back to the city we wondered whether we could get into our shoes again."

Bill shared how he toughened the soles of his feet by smearing creosote from telephone poles on them and not washing it off. One wonders what his mother thought about what the creosote did to his bed sheets.

The youngest of the cousins at the time, Bill and Barbara Gawthrop often played together when she was there. Sam mostly hung out with the twins. Having the advantage of being at Craighead all summer, Bill learned a lot of things Barbara didn't know. He showed her how to use a long, skinny stick to catch the mussels that lived in the creek bottom below the dock. They would lie on their stomachs looking for air bubbles. Seeing one, they'd ease the stick into the opening between the mussel's shells, triggering the mussel to clamp down on it. They'd just raise the stick and drop the mussel into a bucket of water. They would repeat this process over and over until they tired of it. Then they'd dump the bucket of mussels back into the creek to be recaptured another day.

Bill and Barbara spent more time fishing for "minnies" (minnows) than doing anything else. Their angling expeditions began with a raid of Myra's sewing basket for black thread and straight pins. They bent the pins into wide Vs, forcing the sharp points into slight hooks. After tying the thread to the head end of their "fish hooks," all they needed was bait. A slice of Myra's Wonder bread with the crust removed, wetted and rolled on their pant legs to get the water out, served as bait to attract the unwitting tiny fish. Getting the dough the right consistency to stay on the hook was an art Bill mastered. They broke small branches from bushes along the railroad and tied their "fishing lines" to them. They often fished from the dock but the best spot was in the narrow part of the creek between the island and the opposite bank. There, they spent hours perfecting their skills. Barbara recalled, "Our business was riffle minnies, fall fish, sand minnies, and chubs or other names long forgotten. We didn't bother with pickerel, bass, and trout."

One day when Bill and Barbie were playing on the railroad bridge, a train approached unexpectedly. Barb saw it in time to race away to safety, but Bill saw it too late to dash or jump off the bridge. So, he lowered himself down between two ties and squatted on a concrete trestle as the train passed above him.

As if Myra didn't have enough actual concerns for her sons' safety, they manufactured some more for her. Another time Bill, Sam, and the twins found ripe cherries or red berries (versions of the story vary) at the edge of Masland's hay/polo field, the juice from which spawned an idea for a prank. They smeared Sam's visible parts with the red juice and headed home. When they got close, the twins carried Sam, who moaned for effect. Myra thought Sam had been mortally wounded. One can only guess what she thought when she learned the truth.

Dogs were significant characters in family lore. Bill fondly recalled his best friend:

"[Brownie] was a mutt, a cross between an Irish setter and a German police dog. Back in the days, during the 1930s, you could let your cat or dog roam the streets. He was always well fed and knew where to find the best to eat….dogs roamed the city streets, sometimes in packs, maybe fifteen to twenty dogs. Fights and all. During the

Railroad bridge across Yellow Breeches Creek
(Ruth Craighead Muir)

season when dogs were in heat Brownie sometimes would come home all chewed up. Eventually, he got rabies and died of the same disease."

Sam and Bill attended William Penn High School in Harrisburg for tenth grade. But then Myra enrolled them at George School in Newtown, Pennsylvania to complete high school. Thinking he was being farmed out for his mother's convenience or punished, Sam resented being there and tried (unsuccessfully) to blow up the chemistry lab but was not expelled.

He made friends and did well in spite of hating being at George School. In addition to his academic work, Sam played

Greatest flooding at Craighead House (William Moore Craighead)

woodwinds in the Classical Orchestra, was on the cub football and baseball teams, and joined hobby groups.

After graduating, Sam enrolled in the Chemical Engineering program at Penn State. The professor in his very first class told his students that only twenty-five percent of them would graduate. After three semesters, Sam transferred to the College of Arts and Sciences.

After turning eighteen, he applied for summer work with the U. S. Department of Agriculture Bureau of Entomology, probably at the urging and support of his father and his Uncle Frank. He was hired and worked his last three college summers as an Elm Scout, locating and sampling trees infected with Dutch Elm Disease.

Sam graduated from Penn State with a B. A. in Biology in June, 1941, along with first cousin Jean and good friend Emily Coyle. He was eligible for the peacetime draft instituted

in 1940, but was classified as 4-F, physically unfit for being too short and too light (5'2" tall, 100 pounds). Several months after graduation, likely after not finding something more aligned with his education and interests, he took an unCraighead-like job in cost accounting with the Harrisburg Machinery Corporation, where he was working when the U.S. entered WWII in the aftermath of the sneak attack on Pearl Harbor. Although still in school, Bill didn't escape the attention of the Selective Service Board.

John Craighead's prize-winning photo of Bill snagging his lure
(William Moore Craighead)

13

Nancy Craighead and Barbara Miller Gawthrop

RUTH CRAIGHEAD MARRIED HAROLD GAWTHROP on July 29, 1919 in her family's church in Harrisburg, then moved to Kennett Square, Pennsylvania, her husband's home town. Six months later when its construction was complete, the newlyweds moved into their mortgage-free stone four-square house at the corner of Lafayette and Magnolia Streets, where they lived their entire married life.

Ruth gave birth to Nancy "Nance" Craighead Gawthrop on January 31, 1921 at Delaware Hospital in nearby Wilmington. On October 13, 1924, Ruth gave birth to what was supposed to be Nance's little brother. Instead, Barbara Miller Gawthrop, arrived, completing the family.

As the first child, Nancy was always secure of her place in the family, but Barbara sometimes wondered if she was adopted when, all too frequently, people said, "Nance sure is a combination of Harold and Ruth, but who does Barbie look like?" often followed by "Who does she belong to?" Ruth satisfied Barb's concerns by answering those questions with "Barbie looks a lot like the pictures of Agnes's sister Aunt Annie when she was a girl."

Harold, like his father before him, was known for generosity, not just with money and goods but in service to others when needed. Ruth was no stranger to frugality either, due to her family's Calvinist background and impoverishment. Most people darned socks, turned off unneeded lights, saved string, and took good care of what they had those days. "Waste not, want not" was ingrained into most, but Harold turned recycling into an art form when he dismembered used envelopes with his well sharpened letter opener to save the clean backsides of the rectangular front panels for scrap paper. Frugality made generosity possible.

Barbara thought it no accident that she and Nancy were well-behaved children:

"We were disciplined, firmly, but not yelled at with angry words. We had disappointed our parents by improper behavior. Reprimands came to Nance and me with good reason. We'd done wrong; censure was justified. We behaved well not from fear, but to please. I recall 'being corrected' many times, but actual punishments were few. A spanking was merited at Pocono one time because, for some lost reason, I refused to put on overalls instead of a play suit. Maybe it was cold and Mother felt I should be more warmly dressed? Anyway, as she insisted I don them, I insisted otherwise, and quite properly, she took the upper hand with several meaningful swats. I put them on. Another quick spanking came when I was too old for such treatment, so I was highly embarrassed. I remember the embarrassment but not the cause!"

Harold and Ruth spent much time with their daughters teaching them, by example as much as explicitly. Social skills were as important to them as academics. Perhaps Ruth became more sensitive to such issues when she moved from rustic Craighead Station to the state capital. Overnight, she had to deal with issues that never arose in the country because people didn't live so close to one another. Harold and Ruth expected Nance and Barb to be considerate as most parents taught their children to be in those days and were disappointed when the girls misbehaved or acted without regard to others. Today, people might find keeping garage doors closed to give neighbors a more pleasing view than the inside of a garage and lowering all the shades and blinds to the same height for symmetry unusual. Choice of clothing had to be considerate of others as well, both in attractiveness and in care. Clothes must be pleasant for others to look at, not jolting to the eye.

When her twin nephews, Frank Jr. and John Craighead, stopped by on their way home from spending the summer in the Tetons, Ruth thought they'd appreciate sliding between clean, smooth sheets after sleeping on the ground under the stars while they roamed around the West. They astonished her by rejecting her offer. Barb observed, "They'd rather sleep on grubby old blankets under the apple tree."

Harold and Ruth supported their daughters' love of animals. His business supplied feeds, grains, straw, and hay to nourish their pets and lumber, nails, wire, and hinges for cages to house them. But their support had limits:

"Nance and I saw a Frank Buck movie that featured a thoroughly captivating baby elephant, and for awhile we desperately wanted a baby elephant. We could see no reason why they felt this impossible—our back yard was big enough, we'd feed the baby milk from buckets like in the movie and hay when it got older. It could be tied to the apple tree so it wouldn't get away, and it could go to the Philadelphia Zoo when it got too big. We were absolutely bewildered by their complete rejection of this wonderful idea. Nancy begged, I begged, but NO!"

Goats and piglets were also rejected as being too difficult and smelly to keep in town, but both girls had numerous pets from a variety of species, even though Nancy was much less interested in animals than her younger sister. Not surprisingly, Barbie claimed the puppy when it came along. Sam Goodyear, a friend and neighbor at Craighead Station, had a Boston Terrier with pups, the runt of which had odd markings and was unsalable. He offered it to Ruth and Harold. They accepted. On a day he had business in Philadelphia, Sam put the puppy in a box with holes in it and boarded the train for Philadelphia. When the train stopped at Coatesville, Sam handed the box down from the train to the platform where the girls waited. Not quite three at the time, Barbie said to Nance, "Maybe Mr. Goodyear will bring *you* a dog some day." Ruth named the pup Timmy, in remembrance of the pug she had as a child.

When writing her memoirs, Barbara didn't initially list Timmy with her pets:

"To me he was not a pet—he was my brother, a member of the family! Tim was

Timmy (Barbara Gawthrop Hallowell)

ugly. With white shoulders, legs, and chest, white head with a patch of black on top, and one ear black, one white, all else brindle, he could make no claim to beauty. He wasn't too bright, either. We didn't know or care and thought him wonderful.

"Tim became the epitome of canine devotion and good behavior. He loved to chase and retrieve balls, bark at rakes during leaf raking, and hunt frogs in the shallows at Pocono, though he detested water other than this special delight. His bulldog jaws would clamp down on the end of a rope, and he'd pull fiercely, growling happily. He possessed and protected us and ours and would take on any dog he came across, regardless of size and fighting ability. These battles netted him bloody cuts and rips—thank goodness Dr. Mancill lived next door—but never diminished his fighting spirit. Special enemies were Brownie and Spike at Craighead, an awkward situation."

Ruth and Harold didn't vacation at Craighead Station because Harold's family had cabins at Lake Naomi in the Poconos. But that didn't mean their children didn't enjoy the time they spent along the Yellow Breeches. When asked about spending entire summers at her mother's girlhood home, Barb replied, "That would have been the ultimate!" They did spend long weekends and warm-weather holidays there with their Craighead cousins, loving every second of it. Nancy and Jean, only a year and a half apart in age, often did "girly" things such as playing bride with old dresses and curtains in the attic. Barb and Bill, with a little over a year difference in ages, caught hellgrammites and minnows, "fished" for mussels, and played on the railroad bridge. Other times, they joined the twins in training hawks and owls. Nancy didn't generally participate in these activities as her interests lay elsewhere. Timmy was too timid to join Brownie and Spike in racing across the railroad bridge and only reluctantly got into a boat. The other dogs held him in contempt for his wimpiness and, had humans not been around to break them up, their fights would have been bloodier.

The Gawthrops stayed in the northwest bedroom overlooking Old York Road. Barbara recalls catching lightning bugs in a jar and bringing them or a flashlight to bed with her and watching them or reading under a blanket when she was supposed to be sleeping. Both girls participated in leaving their marks on the kitchen walls, but to considerably different degrees. Nance, being artistic, painted a large, colorful lady in a fancy gown high up on the west wall. Barb drew a rabbit hutch in pencil by the back door but later tried unsuccessfully to erase it.

Barb delighted in finger-snapping the screendoor to the sideporch overlooking the barn the other side of the tracks. She would laugh with delight as the thousands of flies perched on the screen scattered helter-skelter.

Nancy and Barbara began their formal education at Kennett Public School on Mulberry Street, an easy four-block walk from home. They sat in the same first grade classroom as had their father when he started school.

Summers for the Gawthrop sisters' were always more pleasant than those of children whose families suffered through the Great Depression. One stands out in Barbara's memory because it was so different from other summer vacations. Rather than spending most of the summer in the family's cottage in the Poconos, they undertook a much different adventure:

"The summer of 1933 we rented a cottage at Ocean City, New Jersey, for two months. The highlight of that period was Nance's study of seashore life as found on the beaches—for a Girl Scout badge. We both got really into it and learned a tremendous lot about seaweeds and a wide variety of shellfish and sand creatures. That 1933 summer I loved working on a bird book which had pictures of birds with perforated edges and glued backs. You found the write-up in the book, separated the picture from its place in the back, and glued it in place with its write-up. I spent hours on this, studying the birds, reading their write-ups, etc., and recall it as a wonderful activity, remembered with great pleasure."

Barbara remembers having more freedom than children have today. She explored the countryside on her bicycle and expanded her social life through dancing and music. She wrote about her youth:

"...self consciousness grew, and confidence grew. The days were ones of innocence and freedom. We didn't know the word 'stress.'...Perhaps most significantly, we lived unaware of sex. Among us it simply wasn't discussed, perhaps because most of us knew little about it, inconceivable by today's standards. We lived free of hard drugs—drugs were prescription items suggested by a doctor when one was sick. We could wander town and countryside without fear of muggings and rapes. It was a wonderful time to be adolescents....Several times at parties we were rash enough to play Post Office or Spin the Bottle. Much giggling. We felt so daring! I would never let anyone kiss me, though. I had resolved to be 'sweet 16' before I allowed it! (And I stuck to this!)"

Barbara remembered other, even more serious aspects of life so different for young people then than now:

"In the '20s and '30s, we children never heard the terms 'mugging,' 'rape,' 'drugs,' 'incest,' or 'child abuse.' But whooping cough, diphtheria, scarlet fever, infantile paralysis (polio), TB, and measles were not only familiar; we could name friends or relatives who had had them. Some we had ourselves. And we had great fear of blood poisoning. Even President Coolidge's 16-year-old son died of it....One of my playmates developed diphtheria, another TB. Measles, mumps, and chicken pox were routine. Most children had them. Nancy got scarlet fever, and Mother, tending her diligently, came down with it, too. We had to get nurses in to care for them. I had my baths in a galvanized tub in the middle of the kitchen floor and spent a lot of time at Grandfather's house. The presence of a contagious disease in a house meant that a quarantine sign was tacked to your front door to warn anyone coming there....We greeted quarantine signs with mixed emotions. At first, not having school seemed exciting, but one missed out on a lot of things, had to keep up on schoolwork as best as possible, and soon began to need friends. For me, animals substituted delightfully."

When Barb started eighth grade in 1937, she and Nancy no longer attended the same school because Nance transferred to George School for eleventh grade. Nancy began a successful career at the prep school along with her cousin, Sam Craighead.

Barbara's attention had already turned to birds. While visiting at Craighead Station over Memorial Day, 1936, at eleven and a half, her twin first cousins, Frank Jr. and John Craighead, gave her a sea gull chick, Snorky, to raise. "They knew I was interested in what they were doing. They were wonderful to me and I worshipped them." She diligently tended to Snorky and he soon grew to be independent. He disappeared at the end of summer without a trace.

Bill & Barbara feeding seagull chicks in 1933 (William Moore Craighead)

The next June, confident in Barb's ability to properly nurture a young bird, the twins shipped her a burrowing owl named Cactus from out West. Barb was at summer camp in Maine when the fuzzy ball of down with big, bright eyes and long straight legs arrived. Cackie, as Barb affectionately called him, soon grew to be a healthy, active, mischievous little owl. Taking a lesson from her older cousins, she logged all her activities with him. He died unexpectedly the Sunday after Thanksgiving a year and a half after he entered her life. Taking another page from her cousins, she wrote an article about Cactus and submitted it to *Nature Magazine*, which accepted it. *Nature* published "Cactus Was Not A Cactus: A western burrowing owl comes East to live" in their March 1940 edition.

Barbara shared another interest several with other Craigheads: music. When only five, Barbara mastered a simple two-handed waltz that Nancy, the one taking piano lessons at the time, had been assigned to learn. Her Sunday school teacher arranged for her to perform the piece as part of the Christmas program.

Nature Magazine cover

"I recall where the piano stood and how that sea of faces looked directly at me. They tell me I took the music book and solemnly set it on the piano rack—upside down! I couldn't read music anyway! Then, without even a glance at the notes, I raced through my waltz and escaped. Mother told the tale with great amusement, laughing at how the church folks chuckled freely at the curly-topped musician with upside down music."

Barbara began taking violin lessons at the suggestion of a music teacher cousin. "I had no idea what a violin was. Dismay struck when I learned it was one of those things that fits under the chin! [Before TV, children had little chance to see musical instruments.] But at so tender an age, one accepted parental decisions." Barbara practiced her violin diligently and played in the school's orchestra. She enjoyed orchestra so much she spent the first six weeks of the 1939 summer at Mansfield State Teachers College Band and Music School.

Afterwards, Harold drove the family to a

Barbara, 12, with violin (Barbara Gawthrop Hallowell)

favorite fishing spot in Ontario. The women saw it differently: "From his man's point of view, it seemed great. Not so from Mother's vantage…. But always the good sport, she got into the spirit of things and tolerated the miserable living conditions."

Barbara viewed the trip differently: "I reveled in this big venture, except when I, the ardent fisherman, dying to catch a big one, caught only small fish, whereas Nance, never enthused by the activity and engrossed in reading *The Scarlet Pimpernel*, heard her line zing out, reacted, and landed a whopper." At vacation's end, she left for George School.

Both Nancy and Barbara thrived at George School, though not there at the same time. Nancy graduated in the spring of 1939 after completing her last two years of high school. "To perfect diligence nothing is difficult" appeared adjacent to Nance's very serious picture in her Senior *Amphora*. She played field hockey on the varsity squad; worked backstage on the Junior Play; played a supporting character in the Senior Play, *Tovarich*; sewed costumes for the Fall Play; served on Religious Life Committee, Winter Sports Committee and Girls' Council; participated in Spring Festival; and worked on the yearbook staff. Rather than follow her mother's footsteps and attend Swarthmore, Nancy enrolled at Oberlin College as a member of the Class of 1943 as an art major.

Timmy died on July 2, 1941, two days after his fourteenth birthday. Harold buried him under the pink dogwood tree alongside several other beloved pets. Barbara missed him terribly. At summer's end, the girls returned to their studies at Oberlin and George School, respectively, where they were when the Japanese bombed Pearl Harbor. Their futures changed immediately.

14

Ruth Ann Craighead

After almost eight years of marriage, Charles and Peg Craighead didn't have a child although they badly wanted one. So, they chose a different route. They brought a baby girl into their home shortly after her birth on June 5, 1936 through a private adoption arranged by a respected local physician. They named their infant Ruth Ann, probably in honor of Charles's older sister, Ruth, who had helped raise him and remained close to him all his life. The new parents lived about 18 miles northeast of Pittsburgh in a neighborhood of New Kensington, Pennsylvania among other people who worked in the steel and aluminum industries. Ruth Ann's widowed maternal grandmother, Vila Lewis, lived with the family when Ruth Ann was young.

She tells of a major event in her young life that happened in 1940:

"My father and mother left Pittsburgh when I was four years old, spent a year or so in Brazil where we lived in a hotel while he did research in the Bauxite fields, his specialty in metallurgy being aluminum. He worked for the Aluminum Company of America in Pittsburgh. My parents often mentioned it was one of the highlights of their life, traveling on a lovely steamship down and back and being pampered in a lovely hotel.

"We lived in a lovely hotel called the Palace Hotel. My mother always talked about that wonderful stay where they drew your bath water, turned down your bed and had every meal cooked for you. Across the street from the hotel was a large park with a casino and in the park I often played with children; my mother said I even learned some Portuguese from them. They were to have stayed several years, but the war was on the horizon and one day my parents received a telegram that said war was inevitable and they should return to the U.S. on the next available sailing. So their wonderful adventure was cut short and they headed home."

In July 1941, Ruth Ann and her parents steamed north on the luxurious SS *Argentina* of the Moore McCormick Lines, enjoying all the ship had. In addition to lounging on the deck, they attended parties of various sorts, including a birthday party for another little girl on board.

For a fancy dress party, she and her mother came as Carmen Miranda lookalikes. For reasons long forgotten, her father disguised himself as a woman knitting.

She also recalled, "Then my father accepted a job with Battelle Memorial Institute in Columbus and from the age of five, I spent the next twenty-some years in the same house in Grandview, Ohio…" From her earliest memories, she and her parents spent a month each summer, generally July, at what her oldest cousins called their "ancestral home" along the Yellow Breeches. It was there as a toddler the twins had introduced her to hawks and owls and taught her to fish in the creek, as had generations of Craigheads before her. As a child with a father too old for the draft, Ruth Ann's life was changed less than others by the war.

Ruth Ann with the twins' owl
(Ruth Craighead Muir)

Peg and Ruth Ann Craighead on S.S. Argentina
(Ruth Craighead Muir)

PART IV

The War Years

THE FIRST TWO GENERATIONS of Craighead Naturalists, the focus of this book, have been brought from birth to Pearl Harbor separately in Parts II and III. This part follows the lives of both generations through World War II as adults (mostly) embarking on or pursuing their careers and making their marks on the world. U.S. involvement in the war announced itself to the Craigheads well before most other Americans were forced to deal with it.

Fearing an assault on the homeland when their troops were routed in France, British officials hurriedly put in place plans to evacuate children, mothers, and teachers from areas expected to be targets of aerial bombing to safer locations. About 1.5 million people were moved to sites unlikely to be targeted. As Dunkirk was falling in May 1940 and England braced for the onslaught of German bombing, a new program, the Childrens Overseas Reception Board (CORB), began signing up children to be sent to safety in Canada, the U. S., Australia, and New Zealand.

The quickly formed Yale Faculty Committee for Receiving Oxford and Cambridge University Children wrote Oxford and Cambridge offering to take in children of their faculties. Cambridge refused because, to them, it smacked of elitism. Oxford faculty, however, took them up on the offer. On July 8, a group of 105 Oxford faculty children and 22 mothers steamed out of Liverpool on the SS *Antonia* headed to Montreal. Among them were Jim and Heather Champion, the children of Oxford don and Frank Craighead's friend, Harry Champion. After six days of sailing and three of waiting in Montreal, the contingent continued their travel by train to New Haven. There, they split into a larger group to be settled in New England and a smaller party of 49 children and nine mothers, sponsored by Swarthmore College, who eventually went to Haverford, Pennsylvania.

Heather Champion Ashton, at 86, remembered well the trip during which most were seasick:

"I had my eleventh birthday on the ship; my brother was two and a half years older. We first stayed with the Craigheads in Virginia [sic] who were old friends of our parents and were very kind. My father and Mr. Craighead were both foresters. I think my father was 'sweet' on Mrs. Craighead when they were both young. He always referred to her with great affection. I remember their twin sons who wrote 'Hawks in the Hand'. Their sister Jean was also lovely and had a horse which she let me ride (I was horse-mad at the time). There may be a photo of me on the horse somewhere in the Craighead archives....

"The next ship carrying evacuated children from the UK to the US was torpedoed and sunk with much loss of life. I found out later that a torpedo missed our ship by six feet. A few feet nearer and that would have been the end of us, too. There were no more children on UK/US ships after that."

Heather and Jim Champion visited the Craigheads in their old Pennsylvania house where, on June 25, 1941, they were invited to leave their marks on the kitchen walls. Heather recalled:

"My brother and I were always fond of drawing and painting, but he was the much better artist. I mainly, and almost only, drew horses so that horse painting must be mine, drawn when I was just eleven. The cats must have been drawn by my brother who—sadly—has been dead for some years."

Heather's large, beautifully painted, black horse still rears high on the wall opposite the cellar door and Jim's two large, matching black cats chase rats above the fireplace to this day. The Champion children spent most of their six years in America farther east.

No one recalls Jean ever having a horse. However, the Maslands, close family friends of the Craigheads, maintained a stable of horses near their Pennsylvania home. Jean probably arranged for Heather to ride one of their horses. In addition to painting on the kitchen walls, the Champions likely participated in various adventures with Jean and the twins, who were back from India.

The Champions' permanent home in America, if anything about the sojourn could be considered permanent, was with the Marshall family. Shortly after the children's arrival, the family relocated to Chester County very near Brandywine Creek. Heather recollects:

"This was the site of the famous battle in the American Revolution, a battle which the American rebels won. A relic of the fight, an old cannon, was preserved in the garden of the house.

"'What was this cannon for?' I asked in my youthful ignorance.

"'To drive the British away,' was the answer.

"'Well, it wasn't very successful, was it?' said I, as I straddled the cannon with my American siblings."

15

The Home Front

WORLD WAR II AFFECTED EVERYONE'S LIFE to a greater or lesser extent. So it was with the Craigheads. Brothers Frank, Eugene, and Charles and brother-in-law Harold Gawthrop were too old to be drafted; however, their sons were of age. The women were impacted differently, largely by dealing with shortages and rationing on a daily basis and worrying about their children, particularly their draft-age sons and sons-in-law. The family home at Craighead Station was also impacted greatly by war-time rationing since gasoline and tires (two strictly controlled items) were absolutely necessary to transport Craighead families from their school-year homes to Craighead Station. Summers there were never again what they had been before the war, although the elder Craigheads tried to continue their traditions as much as possible, despite the severe constraints. Myra had purchased the former Richard R. Craighead house directly across the road at Craighead Station to provide additional bedrooms and parking space, both of which were in short supply as the family grew larger. During the war, she rented rooms in it to U. S. Army War College students.

Frank and Eugene continued to work for the federal and state Departments of Agriculture, respectively. Harold continued operating the Gawthrop family business in Kennett Square. In December 1941, Charles joined Battelle Institute in Columbus, Ohio after working ten years with Reynolds Aluminum, probably for the opportunity to do research. He, Peg, and Ruth Ann made their permanent home at 466 Mulford Road. Ruth Ann recalls living in that house:

"From the time we came to Columbus to the suburb of Grandview, we lived in the same house. I didn't leave it until my senior year in college when I lived in the [Pi Beta Phi] sorority house at OSU. My parents had many a friend with larger houses, and even

Charles & Peg at Craighead House (Ruth Craighead Muir)

though my dad had a very good job, he never felt the need to move on. He and Mom always seemed very content with things as they were."

Charlie quickly became a mainstay in Battelle's avocational activities. Thanks to *Battelle News*, we have reports on his hobbies at that time: elected President of Battelle Camera Club which went dormant, probably due to a wartime shortage of film and/or processing chemicals, and was revived in 1944; became champion horseshoe pitcher at the company picnic; and led the company fishing contest with a one-pound, fifteen ounce small mouth bass hooked on the Scioto River with a streamer fly he tied himself, only to better himself the next month with a two-pound, eight and three-quarter ouncer he caught at the same spot, again with his own fly.

Ruth Ann recalled her times during the war years:

"As a little girl, I remember going with him sometimes in the evenings to check on his experiments. It was a huge complex of underground tunnels and labs and large furnaces and complex equipment, and it all seemed to this young girl terribly important and mysterious. He would take readings on large thermometers and record and graph and chart things—my first introduction to real science. I remember later after the war hearing he went to Oak Ridge, Tennessee, and my mom said the FBI came to our neighbors to ask questions about him so he could get his security clearance to go there.

"I do remember that during the war we had a large victory garden down the hill from our house. We often worked there on the weekends and my dad loved being there. We also had a meat locker where my mom would order a side of beef to be packaged in individual cuts and sizes, and we would go there, put on a heavy coat and walk in this huge locker looking for our section. I can remember during some of the air raid practices, with blinds drawn, sitting on my dad's lap, somewhat anxious, and he would calm me down. We saved foil and had a huge ball that would be collected at certain sites.

"We never missed a summer at Craighead that I can remember, although I wonder how we got gas to go since gas rationing was a big concern. Perhaps his work enabled us to get more stamps. I really don't know. I thought the trip on the PA turnpike was just the most wonderful thing, and especially the long tunnels through the mountains and to be able to eat at Howard Johnson's. We had a Chevrolet car, as far as I can remember, and I know I learned on a stick shift Chevy with big fins.

"Usually in the early days, one or two and even sometimes three of my uncles and aunts and their families were there when we were. At least, we overlapped part of the time. There were John and Frank with birds, and I remember an owl Jean had there. There were always dogs in and out of the creek and under the table when we all sat down for dinner. There were three stoves (kerosene as I remember) and a big ice box that everyone shared. Sometimes, there were three women cooking their own menus at the same time! I particularly remember going with Mom and Aunt Carolyn on Saturday mornings to the great market in Carlisle. I can still picture it in my mind with stalls full of delicious smelling baked goods, shoofly pie, cheeses and peaches that still are my standard for excellence. The [Mennonite] ladies in their little white caps and, often, horses and carts parked outside."

The war years were a very different experience for Ruth Ann's first cousins who ranged from nine to twenty years older and were at very different stages of life than she was. Beginning with the youngest, Barbara Gawthrop was in her senior year at George School when the U.S. entered World War II. She graduated on schedule in the spring of 1942. Her senior yearbook entry summarized her time at George School:

"Music and nature are Barb's chief interests. She has played a violin for three years in the classical orchestra and is now in the throes of mastering the piano. She was an able right inner on the hockey team and spends lots of time in Retford taking care of her mice."

Immediately after graduation, Barb and four other George School girls answered the pleas of beleaguered upstate New York farmers to help pick their crops. The draft had decimated the available labor pool, leaving hard work-low pay jobs like crop-picking unfilled:

"After about two weeks of picking cherries and green beans and raspberries, which I found extremely interesting and informative, an arm got infected from an allergy shot. It had to be lanced, drained for days, and finally required more aid than I was able to give it. I had to return home, a *great disappointment*. But those several weeks on the land and up in the trees on ladders had great positive impact. I loved it—and learned a lot about different kinds of people as well as food production."

That fall, Barb matriculated at Swarthmore College as her mother had indoctrinated her to do:

"I majored in biology, absolutely loved most of my courses in that field, especially Embryology, Microscopic Anatomy, and Invertebrate Zoology, struggled with the miserable trio of physics/chemistry/math, and enjoyed a good assortment of liberal arts courses on the side."

A major frustration in college for Barb was that the Biology Department tried to make her into a laboratory scientist when she wanted to be a field person, a naturalist. "I managed to convince them that a graduate course in Plant Anatomy at Penn would be far more valuable than a blindingly impossible course in Organic Chemistry." She was most definitely a Craighead in that she knew her mind and stuck to it. Also typical of Craighead women, she was attractive to the men on campus:

"During all this, great numbers of young fellows were in Army and Navy programs in colleges—especially for pre-med and engineering. Swarthmore had a Navy Unit, and I had social times with these plus ones at Colgate and Penn. Social life at times was delightfully busy, at other times, nil. My spirits rose and fell accordingly, as having someone to date regularly being important. I had boy friends who became lifelong friends, even though not as married couples. They just weren't THE ONE for that."

The war weighed heavily on Barb during her college years, even though she wasn't directly involved in it:

"All through those struggling wartime years, I felt I should be doing something more for the war effort than studying. I was eager to do something active and discussed with the Dean the possibility of leaving college to do so. She woke me up to the fact that getting a degree was a productive contribution to the war effort, too. My college journals are full of the ups and downs of wartime, when friends and relatives, young fellows, my age and younger, were being killed in Europe and the Pacific. It was a terrible time, but our terrible was negligible compared to that of our youth in the services and of the people being bombed overseas."

At Oberlin College and Conservatory when war broke out, Nancy Gawthrop joined the YWCA and Modern Dance Group and, for two years, served as Social Chairman for her dorm. Nancy became acquainted with Gerald "Gerry" Sheppard Wilson, A.B. Pre-med Class of 1941, to whom she became engaged when she graduated in the spring of 1943 with an A.B. in Fine Arts. She moved home after graduation where she worked as a clerk for the Kennett Ration Board that summer.

On November 6, a summer-like sun shone on her parents' house when she married Gerald Wilson in a simple Presbyterian service conducted by the family minister in the living room. Planning the wedding was made difficult by shortages and rationing. For example, Nancy had to accumulate ration coupons for the refreshments. She became a full-time homemaker for six months while Gerry finished his M.D. degree at Western Reserve University. After his graduation from medical school and election into Alpha Omega Alpha, the honorary medical fraternity, on September 25, 1944, they moved from Cleveland to New York City for his internship at Bellevue Hospital. Nancy taught art at the Museum of Modern Art and worked as a commercial artist for Norcross Publishing Company in New York, where they lived for the remainder of the war. Gerry carried an even heavier than normal workload at that time due to the shortage of physicians created by so many being sent to treat wounded soldiers.

Nancy Gawthrop Wilson surely carried some of those Craighead Naturalist genes, although they manifested themselves in her eye for the artistic. Her younger sister Barbara observed:

"Nancy loved animals and plants as a child, but was never as 'bugged' on them as I was. She majored in art at Oberlin, took several biology and botany courses which

Nancy Gawthrop weds Gerald Wilson with Ruth Ann as flower girl. Jean Craighead & Barbara Gawthrop at far right (Ruth Craighead Muir)

she highly enjoyed, and might have had a side interest in botany had she not married Gerry, a surgeon totally oblivious to life in the outdoor world, though he loved sports and boating. They just did other things together. She'd go on a nature walk with me and be truly intensely interested. She excelled in observation, e.g. enjoying color patterns in rocks or of lichens on rocks or gradations of colors in a field, etc. She was an undeveloped naturalist—had the feel in there, just never had the opportunity to develop it because of so many other demands in the life of a surgeon's wife!"

However, Nancy did work one college summer as the nature counselor in the same job at the same camp in Maine where her mother had worked in 1934. Barbara worked there too in 1945, just before the war ended.

16

Different Paths for Bill and Sam

WHEN THE PEACETIME DRAFT STARTED IN 1940, Bill was at George School and Sam was at Penn State. Bill was underage and Sam was undersize, so neither was drafted at that time. Bill continued his studies and extra-curricular activities at George School as summarized in the Class of 1944's senior yearbook:

"Goal-kicking, swift-shooting Will Craighead is a scorer in any league. Soccer, basketball and baseball have filled up his time athletically. A lover of nature in all its forms, he likes birds, squirrels, and dancing."

Bill became eligible for the WWII draft the moment he turned eighteen on August 20, 1943, even though he still had a year of high school left. George Walton, George School principal, requested a deferment for Bill. To obtain the deferment, the school designed an accelerated program which allowed Bill to finish his coursework by February 1944. Even with the extra course load, he still competed on the varsity soccer and basketball teams and acted in *Arsenic and Old Lace*. He and three other senior boys replaced male teachers, who had been drafted, as dormitory proctors for the younger boys. "I was fortunate enough to have a girlfriend with whom I spent many pleasant hours my senior year. I especially remember dancing to the songs of the Big Bands of the '40s. All of this was part of growing up very fast. Then, like a bomb shell, it all came to an end when I graduated."

Bill reported to the induction center in Harrisburg at 9:00 a.m. March 11. After an hour, he reached the head of the long line to hear: "O.K. Mac, what will it be, the Army or the Navy?" At that time, inductees could choose to be what was euphemistically called "selective volunteers." Bill chose Navy because his dad had served in it briefly in WWI. Those bound for the Navy were herded onto buses bound for the Harrisburg Train

Station, where they boarded a sleeper train for Great Lakes Naval Training Station. "It was anything but comfortable. From Harrisburg to Chicago was about 800 miles, a good twenty-four-hour train ride. Our sleeping car on the train was no Pullman sleeper, that's for sure. The car was dark, dingy and without windows. There were interior lights and the sleeping bunks were four high, spaced like bookshelves in a library."

When Bill's company took its physical fitness test, Chief Howe gave them an incentive: the man with the highest score would stay at Great Lakes as an instructor. Bill set a bar too high for the others to match in the first two of the five tests that most of the others finished quickly while he endured. "I did a total of 30 chin-ups, over 200 sit-ups, and in the rope climb I had the fastest time in the company. I put so much physical energy into this test of endurance that I collapsed while performing the last of the five exercises. I quickly revived without any medication, but knew I had gone through quite an ordeal. I had taxed myself to the limit. To this day I have never exerted myself physically like I did during these endurance tests, even when I ran the mile and two mile in college."

When Bill met with the placement counselor—pretty much a formality at the time because most of his outfit were assigned to man landing crafts—Bill reminded him what Chief Howe promised. "The counselor took one look at me, all of 5 feet 6 inches and 122 pounds, and he knew, because of my size, boyish looks and age, that I would not be the man for the job. What a disappointment! I couldn't see myself becoming a war hero, so I thought being able to help the war effort stateside was good enough for me." The Navy thought differently.

With boot camp completed, Bill stopped in Harrisburg for a five-day leave before reporting to Little Creek, Virginia, for intensive training in amphibious landing. That break gave Bill the opportunity to graduate with his classmates. He was the sole graduate in a Navy uniform.

At Little Creek, he trained as a radio operator for duty on an LSM (landing ship medium), a ship designed to carry five or six medium tanks and a few other vehicles, as well as troops, and supplies from a larger ship to the beach. The forty-eight enlisted men and four officers assigned to USS *LSM 215*, a ship under construction, underwent six weeks of training to crew that very ship, but not without incident. Early in their training, the captain of their ship unexpectedly called the crew together:

"Evidently, he was upset about something in our day's performance. In the midst of his tirade he said, 'My initials are G. A. and that stands for God Almighty and as long as you are under my command you will do as I say.' We had no idea what had made him mad. We returned to our quarters in a very puzzled frame of mind. It was our first encounter with the true personality of the man that was Captain of our ship, the man responsible for directing us into combat. Was this a man who was a competent officer but occasionally lost his cool or was he a dangerous schizophrenic who can sometimes act sensibly? Almost from the beginning, we distrusted him. At times, he spoke with a snarling arrogance in his voice."

The crew especially disliked how he threw back his head and blurted out his comments and commands in a raspy, deep, guttural voice. According to Bill, "He was a man who let you know he enjoyed authority." Half way through their six weeks at Little Creek, just before their last liberty, thirty-five men went to the chaplain as a group to voice their concerns about the captain's mental stability. Rumors of the impending Normandy invasion increased their concerns, but they heard nothing further about the matter while at Little Creek. Soon it was time to pick up their ship at Philadelphia Naval Base.

The positive aspect of their time in Philadelphia was liberty every night. Bill's high point was meeting St. Louis Cardinals Ducky Medwick and Stan Musial. After watching a game between the Cardinals and the Phillies, Bill caught a trolley for Center City and found himself standing next to "Stan the Man," who became Bill's favorite player after Ducky Medwick retired.

Shortly after the ship's commissioning on July 23, Captain "G. A." threatened to throw overboard the gold-inscripted U.S. Navy Bible, a revered gift to the ship from Chaplain W. J. Lindemann. His action deepened the crew's concerns about his fitness to command. After a two-week shakedown cruise on the Chesapeake, the Little Creek Base Commander ordered a change in command without the usual fanfare. To the great relief of the crew, G. A. was gone and Lt. R. M. Donaldson was the new captain.

LSM 215 pulled out of Norfolk for its maiden voyage on August 30, 1944, traveling solo with no convoy. Their first foreign port of call was Colón in the Canal Zone. The highlight of the four days spent waiting for clearance to pass through the Panama Canal was visiting a bawdy house, an entirely new experience for the young crew. The oldest, and more experienced, sailor of the group plunked down twenty dollars for a girl for the day. The rest kept their money in their pockets.

Four days after exiting the canal, a typhoon struck. The ship either didn't receive the warning message or it was in Spanish, a language the radio operator didn't understand. Almost everyone aboard was seasick. After two days of rough seas, the crew found standing watch difficult and were unable to perform routine tasks such as painting. The captain became deathly ill and was unable to command the ship. Lt. (jg) C. E. Grandquist, Executive Officer, replaced the incapacitated captain. The pharmacist's mate saved Donaldson's life by diligently following procedures prescribed by a shore-based physician over the radio. After eleven days at sea, the ship docked at San Diego where an ambulance and doctor transported Lt. Donaldson to the base hospital for an emergency appendectomy.

They picked up six additional crew members and mostly practiced shore landings. The sailors got much liberty while in port. When they received two- or three-day passes, they generally headed to Los Angeles or Hollywood. Bill's favorite was Hollywood Canteen, where he talked with Angela Lansbury and saw Anne Sheridan dance with several servicemen. He also watched live radio shows with Jack Benny, Rochester, and other celebrities like Jimmie Durante.

Fearful she might never see her son again, Myra traveled to California before he shipped out. "As I look back, it was a real touching moment. At the time, however, I enjoyed seeing her. I told her not to worry, that there were millions of guys in my same situation. At least I didn't have a wife and kids to worry about. I had very little responsibility other than to love my parents, and fight for the protection of our freedom."

The crew received additional training, practicing hitting the beach at San Clemente Island five or six times a day as if they were in battle. As time neared to leave for San Francisco, the ship got its fourth captain, Lt. (jg) W. T. Mansfield. They spent nine days in the City by the Bay, the last two in Oakland loading pilings. Early morning November 17, 1944, they pulled away from the dock, passed by Alcatraz and under Golden Gate Bridge, with fog horns blowing every thirty seconds. Soon, the swells became very rough, the roughest they endured on their entire tour. The choppy waters lasted only a day, getting the entire crew seasick. But that wasn't all they had to endure:

"All of these pilings were treated with creosote and bore a penetrating and unbearable smell. We could taste it in our throats and nasal passages. It made our eyes smart and worse than that we had to endure all of this while in the sack at night in the crew's quarters just below the pilings on the well deck. The crew's compartments were so small and cramped they had to be constantly ventilated. The fans were located topside beside the gun tubs, just above the well deck. As the fumes from the pilings rose from the well deck, the electric fans pumped the acrid air emanating from the pilings right into the crew's quarters. When the sun came out and both the well deck and the pilings started to warm up, the smell became even more unbearable. We endured this, while at sea, for ten days until we were unloaded at the docks in Pearl Harbor, Hawaii."

At Pearl in January, 1945, the crew prepared for an invasion of an unnamed South Pacific island before pulling into drydock. All crew members below Petty Officer Third Class were detailed to scrape the hull of debris:

"We were almost 100 feet below ground level, in a drydock big enough to accommodate the largest ship afloat and at a temperature of 100 degrees or more. It was terrible. We scraped the entire hull of the ship below water line. Most of the debris would fall down on us, collecting on the concrete below. With paint scrapers in hand we wrapped towels over our heads like turbans and proceeded to scrape the bottom of the ship. We were in drydock only two days, but the smell of the dead and dying barnacles and algae stank beyond imagination."

The men were incensed the skipper had disappeared while they were forced to perform such a disagreeable task. Rumor had him at Waikiki Beach. The other officers questioned his competence after he backed over a mine cable and bent the propeller. A sailor had made some peach brandy, but it was far from enough for the whole crew. So, the pharmacist's mate and chief storekeeper chipped in some 190 proof medical alcohol. The crew started drinking when they finished scraping in early afternoon and continued until the captain returned that night:

"We decided to let the captain know we were pissed off that he had deserted us while we carried out this miserable task. Mickey was stationed at the head of the gangway to let the crew know when the Captain returned. It was well after dark, perhaps ten o'clock, when Mickey shouted, 'Hey, the captain is coming down the ladder into the drydock and should be aboard ship any minute.' With that, half a dozen guys, including Mickey, stood at the gangway beside the officer of the deck (an enlisted man) to greet the captain. Standing at attention, they saluted the O.D., then the flag, then the captain. The six crew members were stark naked."

The captain was humiliated by this insubordination and put the men on report. He declared he wouldn't go to sea with this "bunch of mad dogs" to the shore command. Meanwhile, the other officers voiced their concerns to Base Command. By the end of the day, the captain had cleaned out his belongings because he had been replaced by Lt. E. J. Percival.

Leaving drydock, they loaded the six Sherman tanks, two personnel carriers, and tank crews of the Fifth Marine Division for maneuvers and mock landings on the dark beaches at Hilo. After a week of landings, they took gunnery practice near Maui. On the way back to Pearl, vibration from the bent propeller shaft forced the ship back to drydock for repairs. The entire cargo was transferred to USS *LSM 49* which, a month later on February 19, 1945, participated in the invasion of Iwo Jima.

The ship had to wait a couple of weeks because the drydock was so heavily used. After straightening the propeller shaft, they sailed to Leyte in the Philippines, a thirty-three hundred-mile trip in twenty-two days, their longest continuous time at sea. From

March 7 to 27, they made practice landings for the invasion of Okinawa at Leyte and Samar. Most people on board, sailors and Army tankers alike, got seasick during the rough five-day voyage from Leyte to Okinawa. Fortunately, they recovered shortly after the seas calmed before the invasion started on April 1, 1945, Easter Sunday.

Bill took his first swig of hard liquor just before hitting the beach. "I felt that shot all the way down to my stomach. I was scared stiff, and so was everyone else." After the Army tanks and trucks rolled off onto the beach, the ship raised the ramp, closed the bow doors, and backed away to get another load from a large ship. They went about their jobs shuttling troops, equipment, and supplies from ship to shore in relative quiet for five days. The Allies landed unopposed, lulled into moving to places where they could easily be ambushed. On April 6, life changed dramatically:

"Then all hell broke loose. The enemy countered with a full-scale kamikaze attack. Shortly before dark, we were summoned to our battle stations. Almost before we had a chance to realize what was happening, Japanese suicide planes were plunging from the sky and hitting our ships. The troop ship which we were tied to, an APA, to take troops to shore, took a hit from a kamikaze, through the forward hatch. The bomb exploded at the water line, killing 27 men in the troop quarters. We immediately freed ourselves from the ship and took anchor elsewhere. We knew how many men were killed, because the next day we pulled up alongside again to take troops and supplies ashore. The dead were lying topside, covered in white mattress covers. That night seemed to go on forever. The sky was lit up with gunfire all night long. We must have seen nearly 100 Japanese planes shot down that night."

These attacks, by far the largest mass use of suicide bombers in the history of warfare, continued day and night for ten days. Attacks came so often crews ate and slept in their gun tubs. Over the next two weeks, attacks became more intense. One night, two seamen on Bill's ship were struck by shell fragments fired by their own ship. Both were treated by the pharmacists and transferred to the USS *Hope* for further treatment and transfer to the States. The kamikaze attacks were so successful during the first thirty days of the battle, the Navy lost more men than the Army and Marines combined. Although carriers, battleships and destroyers, in that order, were the primary targets, kamikazes sank twelve landing ships. No one was safe. After twenty-five days at Okinawa, Bill's ship received orders for Saipan in the Marianas for R and R. They saw no action after that. They shuttled parts and supplies from island to island and took more R and R until August 8, 1945, when they arrived at Guam to prepare for the invasion of Japan. They started overhauling the ship, thinking the invasion was only a month or two away, but the Japanese surrendered unconditionally on August 14, bringing the war to an end.

Bill reflected on the impact that historic event had on his life:

"I'm probably alive today because of the atomic bomb dropped on Hiroshima and Nagasaki. For this I am grateful but, on the other hand, I feel a great deal of remorse that so many died or were maimed for life."

Bill wasn't lucky enough to be discharged shortly after war's end; he was stuck on the decommissioning crew, a nasty job that left a bad taste in his mouth about the Navy and authority. USS *LSM 215* was decommissioned on April 17, 1946 after twenty-two months of active duty, including one hundred ninety-nine days at sea, and over fifty thousand miles traveled. The Navy delayed Bill's return to civilian life until decommissioning was complete several months after the war ended.

★ ★ ★

Sam Craighead's experience during the war was diametrically opposite of his younger brother's. This branch of the Craighead family tends to be short. At five feet two, Sam was the shortest, so short Selective Service rejected him from military service. Some men would have rejoiced to stay home. Sam did not. To the contrary, as Bill recalled:

"Being immediately subject to the military draft, he was required to report but was turned down, classified 4-F (physically unfit for military service). There wasn't anything further from the truth. He was in perfect physical condition but, according to military standards, he was too small, under the prescribed height and weight. His desire was to get in the Air Corps and be a tail-gunner on a B-17. If he knew then what I have learned since, I'm sure he would have thought otherwise. I don't know how true it is, but I have heard that the average life of a tail-gunner aboard a B-17 was 13 minutes.

"My brother tried different ways to get into the war. He was called up for seven of the eight drafts, every six months, but was turned down, to his immense disappointment. Finally, they didn't call him for the final draft.

"He told me on occasions the ridicule he had to endure because he was not in WWII which was most unpleasant. He hated it, and it was always a disappointment for him he had not served in the war."

Wanting outdoor work, Sam took a job with the U.S. Coast and Geodetic Survey in January 1943, working on a triangulation crew mapping the Southeast coast in the winter and Alaska in the summer. His summer 1943 ship pulled out of Seattle on June 30. In Alaska, Sam worked with a team to establish triangulation stations on mountains and ran traverse surveys to map transportation routes for war-time use. He encountered all sorts of wild animals, including grizzly bears and caribou, fish, and birds which he hunted, escaped from, or merely observed on this adventure. However, when bush pilot Sam White offered to teach Sam to be a pilot if he stayed in Alaska, as much as Sam wanted to fly, he reluctantly turned down the offer and headed south, arriving in Seattle on October 12.

His reason for not staying in Alaska soon became abundantly clear. He married Yvonne Nichols of Tuskegee, Alabama at her parents' home on November 22, 1943. Other than visiting his parents in Harrisburg shortly after the wedding, little is known about the bride except her full name was Mary Yvonne Nichols and she was about eighteen. How he met her is unknown. They set up housekeeping in Montgomery, Alabama, where his office was located.

But his wasn't an office job. Sam was usually out in the field somewhere in Alabama, Florida, Maryland, New York, or Vermont. He wrote, "In March 1944 I was working on the triangulation party of Lieutenant Commander John Bowie Jr. in Virginia. He had an assignment to go to Alaska in May…." On May 10, 1944, Sam boarded the SS *Denali* in Seattle bound for Alaska again.

Sam mentioned his bride just once in his memoir, after his party received its first mail for almost a month, around June 1: "We read and reread our letters; I know I wore the pages of my wife's letters thin reading them." However, when pulling into port in Seattle on November 4, he wrote, "I was thrilled at the thought of getting back to the good old U. S. A. after spending six long months in Alaska."

Shortly after returning from Alaska, in January 1945, Sam transferred to the U.S. Geological Survey (USGS) Montgomery, Alabama office. The reasons for his transfer are unclear as it could have been to obtain a more permanent government position or to save his marriage. Whether his marriage survived the war is unclear as he still had a Montgomery address when the war ended.

17

Jean and the Twins Fight the War in Unique Ways

JEAN CRAIGHEAD WAS ENROLLED in a graduate program majoring in art with a minor in dance at Louisiana State University at the time of the Japanese sneak attack on Pearl Harbor. Exactly how much longer she continued those studies is unclear. The April 26, 1942 edition of Jean's hometown paper, *The Washington Post*, included an article about her and her dance studies:

> "A new and simpler system of recording dance movements has been devised by a former Wilson High School graduate, Miss Jean Craighead of 5301 Forty-first Street Northwest. The system of notation consists of symbols for the head, shoulder, hip, knee, hands, and feet, placed upon ruled lines above the staves of accompanying piano music."

Two days later, *C. P. Phonephoto* ran an article with her photo across the country. It looked more like a lipstick ad than hard news, but it was. And it may have been the start of her professional career:

> "Miss Jean Craighead, of Washington, is shown holding a screw of the type used in the making of a snap fastener, lack of which caused delays on assembly lines of three American airplane plants, according to a charge by Asst. U. S. Attorney General Thurman Arnold. Miss Craighead holds a lipstick container at left to compare, for size. One of the plane companies mentioned, North American Aviation, denied Arnold's charge."

Whether she left LSU after the end of her first semester or after completing her first year isn't clear. Regardless, she returned home never to return to LSU or to study art and dance again; she embarked on a writing career, initially as a means of doing her part for the war effort. Living with her parents in Washington, D.C. gave Jean more than an inexpensive place to hang her hat; she was in the power center of world-changing events, and in a city that needed newspaper reporters because the men who formerly held those jobs were off fighting the war. As she sat in the office of the scowling bureau chief of the International News Service (INS), she wondered when the uncomfortable interview would be over. She thought she had the job but could see he was unhappy giving it to her.

"This is the end of the newspaper business," he said.

"What's wrong," she asked, thinking something like another Pearl Harbor must have happened.

"I just hired a woman," he said, looking her directly in the eyes.

"I beg your pardon?"

"You heard me. Women shouldn't be reporters. It's rough out there. A man's world. But this war doesn't leave me any choice."

Jean got out of his office thinking, "I'm going to have to show him."

In August of that year, 1942, Jean's pieces started appearing under her own byline. However, as a reporter just starting her career, she seldom got the above-the-fold-front-page stories to cover. In her first year as a newspaperwoman, she covered anything from Queen Wilhelmina of The Netherlands (in exile visiting the U.S.) holding the first press conference ever held by a reigning queen in Washington—to War Production Board (WPB) restrictions on the amount of cloth that was allowed to be used in women's skirts—to rationing of chewing gum and candy bars—to announcing that Santa will have more toys in his sack than in recent years—to scrapping plans for Victory Gardens to support our troops in North Africa. When the regular White House correspondent wasn't available, Jean sometimes even got the opportunity to cover presidential press conferences.

The new year brought more hard news stories for Jean. She kicked off 1943 by reporting on a new bill before Congress to reform how sentence lengths are determined in the federal penal system. Next up was covering the chaotic arrival of a newly-elected congresswoman, Clare Booth Luce (R-Connecticut), that Jean thought might better have been titled "Mrs. Luce Comes to Washington." Many of her articles for INS that year covered wage controls put in place by the War Labor Board and price controls placed on food items by the Office of Price Administration. Not exciting stuff but issues that had an impact on people every day.

"The Fall Fighters," an article about people who choose to go up the water falls at Difficult Run on the Potomac River rather than ride down them, appeared in the September 26, 1943 edition of *The Washington Post*. Jean had moved up from being a wire service staff correspondent to having her own byline for the largest newspaper in the nation's capital. A month later, Jean caused quite a stir on October 31 with her "Just an Atom-Smasher: He can't get a raise—hasn't accomplished anything" piece, ostensibly about the low wages paid to nuclear physicists.

The War Labor Board (WLB), the government agency which controlled salary increases during WWII, was one of Jean's beats. The WLB ruled on what everyone from Rosie the Riveter to nuclear physicists were paid based on the agency's perceived importance to the war effort. The WLB, in its infinite wisdom, didn't take the request for a pay raise from physicists seriously. In fact they thought it was humorous. Jean didn't share their sense of humor, though, and "remembered that in a physics class taken several years earlier the professor had said that the next war would very likely be won by technological superiority." She intuitively thought the physicists' work could lead to victory over the Germans and Japanese and set out to determine if she was right.

Jean first consulted her 1939-40 college text that included some information on nuclear fission (stripped from later editions). To make sure her information was up to date, she consulted with her friend Ruth Chew's kid brother, Geoffrey. He was an undergrad physics major at GWU, which was conveniently located near her home. The 19-year-old Chew was

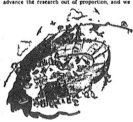

Just an Atom-Smasher
He Can't Get a Raise—Hasn't Accomplished Anything
By JEAN CRAIGHEAD

A young fellow who has been studying much of his life on the matter of blowing up nations with an atom would like to get a wage increase from the War Labor Board.

Preoccupied with discovering the formula for demolishing Berlin with a teaspoonful of dust,

An atom-smasher is just an atom-smasher

before the Berlin boys master this upsetting trick, he nevertheless needs a new pair of shoes and a winter overcoat.

In the laboratory where the young man lives, one seldom has such simple thoughts as the corner grocery and the Nation's wage stabilization policy.

The drift of the conversation usually tends toward bombarding isotopes, the effect of an alpha particle on the electric forces of an atom of uranium, and the explosive annihilation of Berlin.

So that it must have been with some bit of embarrassment that he found himself wondering about time and a half and incentive payments. Nevertheless, the very ordinary thought that he needed a wage increase for razors and cigarettes, outweighed the science of isotopes, and he took time to write to the War Labor Board to ask how it might be done in his case.

Why Not Another Job?

The letter stumped the WLB, and they looked through their directives and executive orders to see what could be done in the way of a pay adjustment for an atom smasher.

Teey suggested the Little Steel Formula, but the young man's natural inclinations run to bigger things, and 15 per cent of the amount he was receiving would hardly be enough to buy one new shirt for Wednesday evening forums, much less the latest textbook on extra-nuclear electrons.

The board then suggested that he be reclassified and given a raise on the basis of another job. But an atom smasher is an atom smasher, and after studying seven years to understand the trade, one would hardly want to make a shift.

On the other hand, the board stated, one can always obtain a merit increase.

In labor circles a merit increase means many things, but to a person occupied with the spontaneous desintegration of Axis cities and the Nazi war machine by bombarding an atom, a merit increase means only one thing: Finding the formula that will unlock uranium and with a dull roar of separating particles, buckle and rupture Berlin and Tokyo into fire and dust.

Don't Expect It Very Soon

Chances are slim that either side will have the formula before the next war, and that is a little long to wait for a merit increase.

Now this young man is no fictional character; he is very much alive, and very much kicking. But, because of the secret nature of his work, his name cannot be published.

In regards to the work he is doing, let me suggest that you keep on buying war bonds and turning out rifles. Although the dramatic effect of an atomic explosion in the Ruhr Valley is overwhelming, artillery is still a good thing in the absence of a formula.

Even the inspiration of a wage increase won't advance the research out of proportion, and we

A stadium around Germany, so we can see the show

can make use of the Flying Fortresses for some time to come.

When the young man with labor problems and his fellow genii do discover how to use the energy in an atom, it would be nice if they would throw up a stadium around Germany and invite the United Nations to the explosion of the Nazi war machine.

It would be a great spectacle—guns and war plants would spin apart under the violence of the impact, and erupt skyward in a fanfare of colors and electronic reactions.

Jean unknowingly spills the bean on the Manhattan Project
(The Washington Post)

taking a course on nuclear fission and its military potential given by George Gamow, a distinguished Russian theoretical physicist who was not allowed to participate in the Manhattan Project because U.S. military intelligence correctly believed him to be subject to pressure from the KGB. Chew recalled,

"Jean had stumbled on the (then amazing) military interest in nuclear physics and was told by my sister Ruth about the course I was taking. Jean quizzed me and I passed along Gamow's teaching."

He not only explained his understanding of how atoms work, he also conjectured about how Berlin could be annihilated by bombarding uranium isotopes to release the destructive power of the atom. Jean didn't just write about blowing up the enemy with such a weapon if the proper formula could be found; she drew a sketch of a stadium enclosing Germany where the United Nations could watch the explosion of the Nazi war machine from the bleachers.

The government's security apparatus was not amused. It seems that young Chew had come uncomfortably close to the truth. Early the next morning, Monday, November 1, 1943, a tall army officer appeared in Jean's newsroom, wanting to know where she got the information. Knowing that good reporters don't reveal their sources, she refused to tell him. Her editor told her she had to talk. After interviewing both reporter and budding physicist, the officer determined that neither was a spy: they'd just arrived at the same conclusions as had their more learned elders. But what to do about them? About all the government could do about the article was hope enemy spies hadn't noticed it. To lessen the chance, they stripped the article from every copy of the newspaper they could find.

But what could they do about young Mr. Chew? They couldn't legally lock him up. He later explained to the author,

"The article Jean wrote led to my being cross-examined by US Army Intelligence and may have led to my being sent to Los Alamos until the war was over. (Communication between Los Alamos and the world outside was strictly censored.) It is possible that my interaction with Jean was foundational for my career. The collective talent of the Los Alamos physics community has never been matched (before or since 1943-45)."

Thus, an innocent newspaper article by a young reporter jump-started the career of the preeminent theoretical physicist, Geoffrey Chew.

Jean's private life was also about to take a turn, but in a very different direction. Her brothers had told her much about their University of Michigan roommate, John Lothar George, but she had never met him. Until September 1943, that is.

"'That young man has come to marry you,' my ninety-year-old [maternal] grandmother said the night he arrived at our home in Washington. Later, when he slipped his arms around me and pressed me to him, I knew she was right. I was ready to marry—all of me except for that spark in the far right-hand corner that makes each one of us different from everyone else. In that far corner, my own belief in myself as a writer still held out. My solution would be to open up that corner and include John in it."

It's no surprise that Jean was taken by this dashing seaman with looks and personality often compared with John Wayne. Four months later, on January 28, 1944, Jean married Ensign John George, handsome in his Navy officer's uniform, at All Saints Episcopal Church with Rev. Charles Lowry officiating. John went to sea on the SS *Mervine*, a Gleaves-class destroyer on escort duty in the Atlantic and Mediterranean; Jean continued writing for the *Post* and soon moved to an apartment in Brooklyn Heights near the Brooklyn Navy Yard, his home port. She spent the duration of the war there drawing for *Pageant Magazine* and, later, as a reporter for Newspaper Enterprise Association.

For a time, Jean had a roommate. Margaret Smith was the young woman the twins had met at Jenny Lake on one of their trips to the Tetons and visited on their way west to catch the ship to India in 1940. Margaret stayed with Jean while attending the Art Students' League. As the daughter of a botanist father and an artist mother, Margaret had climbed all of the major peaks in Wyoming as a girl, learned all the wildflowers, and learned to paint. League teachers huddled around Margaret to learn the names of the wildflowers: glacier lily, starflower, dryad, and death camas. Jean mostly lived alone until the war ended. "[John and I] were more or less strangers and were separated most of the time by the war."

★ ★ ★

Jean's brothers, Frank Jr. and John, were working on their doctorates in wildlife management at the University of Michigan when the US entered WWII. They were awarded student assistantships to support themselves while pursuing their education. Financing schooling was always a Craighead concern.

The War Department had observed, to its chagrin, that draftees were not fit physically for military service and set about to change that by petitioning colleges and universities to institute physical fitness programs designed to prepare students for military service in the near future. U of M Regents responded by approving a compulsory physical conditioning program and allocating $11,000 to cover the 1942 summer term and the 1942-43 school year. The May 12 *Michigan Daily* reported, "In an all-out effort to adjust higher education to wartime exigencies, the University of Michigan, for the first time in its history, will open its doors June 15 for a full-length summer semester." After reconsidering his plan to join the Navy, athletic Director Fritz Crisler headed the new physical training program out of the Department of Physical Education and Athletics. However, not all of the courses fell completely under the auspices of the Phys. Ed. Department: PEM 39, Physical Conditioning and Field Practice, was offered jointly with the School of Forestry. That "[t]he field work consists of hiking, overcoming obstacles in field and stream and the techniques of roughing it in camp" created an opportunity for graduate students as comfortable in fields, creeks, woods, and rivers as in the classroom.

Not recorded is exactly how the twins landed the job of teaching PEM 39, referred to disparagingly by students as "the commando course." Perhaps they proposed it to the administration, or the administration, being well aware of their capabilities, approached them about designing and teaching this course. It might be that the School of Forestry and Conservation formed an unusual partnership for this one course only because it owned some of the facilities (if a bog is a facility) needed for the special nature of the training. Regardless of the reason, the summer session began on June 15, 1942:

"Two sections of 20 students each were signed up for the test course during the Summer Term under the supervision of Washington's well-known globe-trotting twins, Frank and John Craighead, who had gained their experience first-hand while traveling around the earth."

The twins put the prospective "Commandos," (the term used by *The Michigan Alumnus* for students taking their course):

"through as difficult a course as is offered by any branch of the service....The twins opened the program with instruction in wrestling and judo (Japanese art of dispatching an opponent as quickly as possible), as well as running, rope climbing, and obstacle racing. Then they took to the field for more rigorous phases of the program.

"In the outdoor phase of the instruction, the students were forced to find specified areas through the use of topographic maps and compasses, traveling across fields, swamps, and wooded areas to reach their destination. There was some trouble with poison sumac and ivy which was pointed out with instructions on how to avoid them."

Even though the students experienced "danger and discomfort," all passed the course. However, not everything came off without incident. During one overnight hike, an undergrad collecting useful plants wandered off by himself too close to a bog. He was up to his shoulders in muck before anyone heard his cries for help. After throwing the terrified student a rope and pulling him out, the twins added a bog-training phase to the program.

"The students soon learned the trick of swimming through swamps and improved

It's All Part of Michigan's 'Commando' Training Course For Students

"REPELLING" IS TOUGH ON THE HANDS AND ARMS

The art of climbing steep walls and cliffs with the aid of ropes, known as repelling, is a vital phase of the advanced training course, and mighty fatiguing work, as Clare Merritt, '43f, of Ann Arbor, left, and Leonard R. Martinek, '43f, of Hamtramck, right, found out after scaling this obstacle a dozen times. Classmates above and below watch their progress down the wall. The old cement kiln, used for the tests, is situated near Ann Arbor.

CROSSING SWAMPS IS STRENUOUS JOB

Swimming through murky water and wading through deep, muddy bogs is dangerous and strenuous business but its value is recognized. Richard W. Lapidos, '45e, of Fostoria, Ill., left, was more fortunate than Gordon T. Woods, '43f, of Newington, Conn., who sank to his neck in the muck. David F. Strifler, '44, of Pontiac, awaits the fate of Woods.

IT KEEPS MOSQUITOS AWAY

Sleeping in the outdoors is fun, if the mosquitos don't decide to keep you company from dusk until dawn. John A. Door, '44, of Detroit, was one of the fortunate few who brought along netting.

ORIENTATION WITH THE USE OF COMPASS

Russell J. Buster, '45, of Peoria, Ill., left, orients the topographical map to the terrain while Peter R. Sherman, '44e, of Saulte Ste. Marie, checks the location with a compass. This system helped the students locate unknown destinations and prevented them from wandering over new terrain aimlessly.

96

THE MICHIGAN ALUMNUS

Michigan Alumnus article on PEM 39 (University of Michigan)

quickly after gaining confidence and overcoming panic which tended to tense their muscles….[The twins observed] that courage is to a large extent self-confidence which is the product of training, accomplishment, testing, and acting. Crossing bogs, swimming rapids, scaling high walls and cliffs, hiking through strange country to an unknown destination, feeling one's way through the inky blackness of a dark woods, and encountering poisonous snakes and plants, when once experienced, furnish the individual with confidence."

They revamped the course for the fall semester, including such skills as skiing, camping, and cooking food in cold weather, building shelters, hunting, tracking, shooting, and trapping animals for food.

Realizing the value such a course might have for the military, they tried to market it to the government. The government saw no need to pay for something it could simply take from them through its power of conscription. Knowing they were about to be drafted, Frank Jr. and John prepared to join the Army's 10th Mountain Division, along with several Penn State friends. Meanwhile, the Navy, having no survival training facility, saw much value in their course and commissioned them as ensigns in the Naval Reserve with the assignment of creating a wilderness survival school for downed pilots.

Less than a year earlier, in April 1942, the Navy had opened its pre-flight training school at the University of North Carolina at Chapel Hill. Because the Navy's primary focus for the school was teaching budding pilots to get their planes off the ground safely, keep them in the air, and keep them in one piece when landing, surviving after being shot down or crashing in enemy or remote territory had been overlooked. The Navy saw in the Craighead twins a means to start up a wilderness survival school almost overnight and, in December 1942, commissioned them to do exactly that.

They soon had the school up and running, as documented in the September 27, 1943 issue of *Time* magazine, "Army & Navy—Navy in the Trees." The reporter observed:

"While the cadets watched, officers demonstrated some lore of survival. One found a swampy spot, dug up the edible roots of cattails. Another showed how to twist a fish line from tough inner bark, whittle a hook from a thorned twig. A third whacked out a four-foot section of wild grapevine which dripped a cupful of clear water, surprisingly sweet and cool to the taste."

He went on to discuss the students' final exam:

"Eventually, cadets will be tossed a 40-lb. pack. They will be trucked off 30 or 40 miles, given a compass and told to find their way home."

The twins attempted to have the Navy assign their cousin Bill to assist them in running the survival school. Higher ups refused. Bill was too young, too small, and enlisted: Junior officers wouldn't take directions from him.

Wedding Bells To 'Break Up' Twin Brothers

Wedding bells are breaking up the act. One twin deserts the other for a blue-eyed blonde, confetti and rice. Miss Esther Stevens of Wheaton, Ill., is crashing the long established twin team of Ensigns John and Frank Craighead of Washington.

The wedding, a hurry-up-before-orders-change-me affair, will be held in Wheaton, Ill., Tuesday at the home of Miss Stevens' parents, Mr. and Mrs. Chas. Stevens.

Both twins were in Wisconsin publishing a book for the Navy Preflight School when one of the life-long team decided to break up the act for wedding bells.

Miss Stevens attended Michigan University. Ensign Craighead, son of Dr. and Mrs. F. C. Craighead, graduated from Penn State and traveled to India with his inseparable brother, before taking graduate work at the University of Michigan.

Not unlike other classes, military or civilian, their survival course needed a text book. So, Frank and John wrote one. Part of their task was to get the book printed and that required a visit to the printer. Their route to the printer in Wisconsin brought them close to Chicago and to a more pleasant mission. The November 7, 1943 edition of *The Washington Post* blared a bit of news about the twins: "Wedding Bells to 'Break Up' Twin Brothers."

Two days later, Esther Melvin Stevens, the petite blonde sophomore Frank had dated at Michigan in the winter and spring of 1942, and he were married. Brother John served as best man. The twins looked dashing in their Navy officer's uniforms. When later asked how she told the identical twins apart, Esther replied, "I don't bother." After a much-too-brief honeymoon, Frank Jr. and John were reunited back at Chapel Hill where, one assumes, he and Ester eventually found an apartment of some sort during the war-time housing shortage.

Soon, the twins' book, *How to Survive on Land and Sea*, was in print and distributed to Airedales (slang for Naval airmen) for their use. Being a Navy manual, the authors' names didn't appear anywhere in or on it. However, their images appear in photographs on several pages. Later editions—the book was in print for over four decades—gave them attribution, though.

Other than making trips to a few remote places to gather information to improve their course, they stayed and worked at Chapel Hill. As the war wound down in 1945 and their workload decreased, Frank and John received a reward for what they had contributed to the war effort. Over fifty years later, Vince Devlin of *The Montanan* got John to recall his experience on a remote Pacific island:

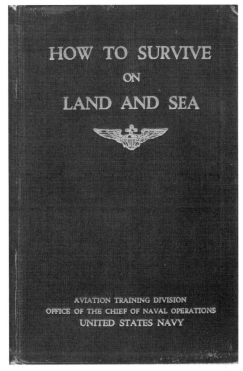

> "He stood somewhere between three and four feet tall. John Craighead, a small man himself, towered over the man. 'He was all sinuses and scars, and about as alone as a man could be,' Craighead says.
>
> "He met Antonio on Palawan, one of the 7,000 islands that make up the Philippine archipelago. In the Navy and assigned to write a survival guide for naval aviators, Craighead

Cover of first edition of Navy survival course text (Author)

traveled through South America and then into the Pacific doing research for the book.

"'Admiral Tom Hamilton had promised me he'd get me out in the Pacific after we'd written this book,' Craighead says. 'I was all ready to take off when the war ended. He told me he'd like me to go anyway and wrote out the orders. He wanted information on those who survived in that type of wilderness.'

"And so Craighead headed for Palawan, which he says was something of an 'open prison.' Antonio, he says, had been dumped on the island for killing a man who had stolen his wife. 'All he had was a bow and three arrows,' Craighead says. 'He'd kill monkeys and wild pigs to eat.'

"Using a Filipino translator, Craighead quizzed Antonio to uncover information on survival in the South Seas, struggling with parts of it. 'Monkey for lunch?' he says. 'It was like eating one of your own kids.' Antonio chased wild pigs and monkeys through the jungle and Craighead chased Antonio. 'I had a jungle hammock I put up over an old stream bed,' Craighead says. 'Antonio slept by the fire. If you've ever watched a dog sleep, where his feet move back and forth, well, that's what Antonio did. He was always running, even in his sleep.'

"When an American base on Palawan shut down with the end of the war, Craighead loaded a Jeep with K rations[3] and took them to Antonio. 'They were getting rid of everything,' he recalls. 'They had all these down sleeping bags, which were useless in the South Pacific anyway, a pile as big as a house they poured gasoline on and burned to get rid of. They were getting rid of the K rations too, so I took a load to Antonio. He opened them up, and he didn't eat the food, but he ate the cigarettes. I left him with enough K rations to feed a lot of people. But I don't know what he did with them.'

"Craighead made sketches of Antonio in the jungle and wrote poems about him. John Craighead has studied humans, too."

The twins also trained Office of Strategic Services (today's CIA) agents in survival techniques. Frank's son Lance shared,

"The only classified activities I know of were related to survival training after the war with the OSS. I believe they were preparing for some sort of infiltration into Siberia or somewhere so we could drop paratroopers into Russia to sabotage things if we had to go to war with Russia after WWII. I believe Dad and John would have had to go with them; luckily that didn't happen."

When their government service ended, Frank Jr. and John, their sister, and cousins, even some of their parents, were ready to embark on new adventures.

---

3 K rations came in three varieties: breakfast, dinner and supper, included such things as "canned meat product" (cheese for dinner units), biscuits, "powdered beverage," chewing gum, chocolate, toilet paper, cigarettes and matches.

PART V

Maturity

THE OLDER GENERATION OF CRAIGHEADS we have been following approaches retirement as the younger generation, after winning the war, embarks on careers well-suited to them by their wide and varied youthful experiences. The training they received from their parents, coupled with their unsupervised explorations as children, prepared them for careers they often created for themselves. Sprinkle on a good bit of formal education and these high achievers create extraordinary results. Their first real jobs during the war provided them additional experiences on which to build.

This part intertwines the lives of the two generations of Craigheads even further than did the previous part. All but the two youngest of the younger generation were adults when the war ended and were embarking on careers. The oldest of the older generation was rapidly approaching retirement, at least from his first career. But first we must complete the younger generation.

18

After the War

World War II formally ended on September 2, 1945 when the Foreign Minister of Japan signed surrender documents on the battleship USS *Missouri*. The next day, James Lewis Craighead was born and was immediately adopted by Charles and Margaret Craighead to start the post-war era and to complete the generation of Craigheads that began with the twins. It was no time for this generation to relax after a job well done; it was time to return to studies or careers or families long interrupted by the war. This chapter presents the activities of the two generations of Craigheads in the first post-war decade (give or take a few years), starting with the oldest of the younger generation (the twins), then proceeding to their parents' generation.

With the war ending, John undertook a new project. In late-November of 1944, he wedded Margaret Koep Smith, the mountain-climbing woman he'd met in the Tetons years earlier and visited on the trip west to catch the ship to India. When asked when they started dating decades later, Margaret replied, "I guess it was when he carried my skis for me." Their daughter Karen piped in, "I bet that was the last time."

The twins were eager to complete their education and start their families, but the Navy had more work for them to accomplish. The twins, two Navy officers, and Goniske, a Marshall Islander, spent seven months testing survival techniques and developing new ones on mid-Pacific islands, particularly a tiny uninhabited one in the Kwajalein Atoll. They documented their experiences in "We Survive on a Pacific Atoll" for the January 1948 *National Geographic*. Meanwhile, their brides waited for the twins in a log cabin on the Snake River. Once released by the Navy in late winter, Frank Jr. and John backpacked to their snow-covered cabin. They recorded their winter and early spring adventures in the mountains in "Cloud Gardens in the Tetons" for the June 1948 *National Geographic*.

While these articles were being prepared for publication, the twins returned to the Tetons they fell in love with years earlier, this time with wives. The Teton Range is part of the Rocky Mountains that lies on the border of Wyoming and Idaho just south of Yellowstone Park. French voyageurs called them *les trios Tétons*, the three teats, and the Shoshone are thought to have called them *Teewinot*, many pinnacles. Margaret "Cony" Craighead held the record time for climbing and descending the Grand Teton (the largest one) for both men and women. Using their mustering-out money, the twins and Margaret's mother jointly bought a 14-acre tract from John Moulton on Antelope Flats outside the then border of Grand Teton National Park. They built identical log cabins with short paths behind them to a common outhouse. On August 8, 1947, while living in those cabins their first children were born: Frank Lance to Frank Jr. and Esther and Karen Lynn to John and Margaret.

The twins moved their families to neighboring apartments in Ypsilanti for the fall semester to continue their graduate work at the University of Michigan. The infants

Twins, wives & firstborns watch 1947 Michigan-Stanford game at "The Big House"
(University of Michigan)

Johnson Coyle models Craighead-Masland backpack (Author)

made their first public appearance on October 4 at "The Big House" for the Michigan-Stanford football game. The infants didn't require tickets because they occupied no seats. They slept in backpacks their fathers had made from white oak staves they steam-bent and riveted to dowels. Family friend and neighbor near Craighead Station, Frank Masland, who had operated the world's largest supplier of canvas duck during WWII, provided them with the cloth part of the knapsacks. The twins continued making and giving away these backpacks for decades. Upon seeing a photo of a backpack Frank Jr. had given to Bill Coyle's son, Johnson, John Craighead's son, Johnny, responded:

"As far as the packs are concerned, they are ones that John and Frank made. I am pretty sure that the one Mr. Coyle has is from some they made in…the late fifties. I say that because I remember the red dye. We still have a supply of White Oak staves in the basement for making more. The frame pieces were steam-bent and fastened together with copper rivets. The pack was fastened to the frame with a system of dowels and eyebolts. While they were at school in Michigan and teaching their outdoor skills course, many of their students made these packs. I think the Maslands had a hand in sewing, or having sewn, the canvas packs. At any rate the Maslands got involved in producing a number of camping items for the boys, including my all time favorite, the tarp tent."

★ ★ ★

Like many war brides, Jean hardly knew her husband. Shortly after their marriage, Jean took John for an outing at "The Shack," her family's weekend house along the Potomac near Seneca, Maryland as a means of getting to know her new husband better. There, they listened to Buck Queen, a widowed outdoorsman who lived nearby, tell stories about life along the river. Enraptured by these nature stories, John made copious notes. Jean decided that some of these stories, particularly one about a red fox that loved to be chased nightly, would make great books for children. Already needing to do something more creative than writing news articles, Jean decided to write fiction, and Buck Queen had given her a subject.

About that time, a hunter gave Jean a red fox kit with a broken leg. She happily played with Fulva at night as she nursed her back to health. The little female made a perfect model for her drawings to illustrate the text she was writing. Not wanting to keep Fulva cooped up in an apartment when she moved to New York, Jean gave her to the National Zoo. In New York, the center of publishing in America, she approached Marguerite Vance, an editor with E. P. Dutton, a publisher that had recently published a book about a pigeon.

After perusing Jean's manuscript and illustrations, Vance looked up and said, "This is nice, but you know so much more about this fox. Go home and write about him from birth to death. Do it in about one hundred fifty pages, double-spaced." Undeterred—encouraged actually—Jean poured over John's notes and wrote the story Vance requested. However, she was concerned the book wouldn't succeed unless it was as accurate as humanly possible, so she waited for John's input until he returned from the war.

Released from the Navy, John George applied for graduate school at Michigan, as had Jean's brothers. Due to his being at sea for all but two months of their marriage, and barely knowing each other before their nuptials, they were almost strangers. Before moving to Ann Arbor, the newlyweds spent time in 1946 getting better acquainted at Craighead. There, they bought a male red fox from a farmer and named him Vulpes. John reviewed her manuscript, adding some ideas and paragraphs from his observations of birds and animals. He also painted a portrait of Vulpes over the kitchen door at Craighead, perhaps after the book was accepted for publication. Upon accepting it, the publisher, almost without thinking, put John's name in front of Jean's.

At Michigan, like her brothers, Jean and her husband set up housekeeping in Ypsilanti, except their "house" was a nine-by-nine-foot Army surplus tent pitched on the top of the highest knoll in an ancient beech-maple forest situated at the northern end of Olin and Cora Strang's farm. John, her brothers' former roommate, conducted fieldwork for his Ph.D. in ecology. He selected the site at the center of a one-square-mile section surrounded by tilled land because the land pattern attracted almost all wildlife species found in southern Michigan. Jean was exceedingly happy living in this tent among her many animal friends, several of whom she got to study up close and personal:

"Following her [Lotor] to the meadow and the stream, I learned how a raccoon pulls mussels ashore with its hands, not cracking them but leaving them out in the air to open. I learned how raccoons fish, by chasing minnows into the shallow water and flipping them ashore; how they find grubs in logs with their sensitive fingers, and how they sleep draped in the crotch of a tree on hot summer days."

John's research dragged on and on, which forced relocation into a tiny Ann Arbor apartment for the harshest Michigan winter months. Jean didn't mind not having all the modern conveniences, including canned goods with labels not removed by her wild pets. She wanted to start a family of her own—both of her brothers already had yellow-haired children—but John was far from finished. His prolonged doctoral work frustrated Jean a bit because her brothers had selected a site, split the work in half, and, after four seasons passed, had completed their research.

After *Vulpes, the Red Fox* was published in 1948, Jean took on some illustrating work to supplement John's G. I. Bill and meager graduate student pay. She started writing and illustrating a second book, *Vision the Mink*, again co-authored with her husband, and a third, *Masked Prowler: The Story of a Raccoon*, while he was still conducting his research. Over the Christmas 1949 holiday, while they were visiting her parents in Pennsylvania, Jean got pregnant. When they returned to the tent in March, John still hadn't finished his degree, without which he couldn't get a proper job and couldn't afford a proper house for their baby. Almost simultaneously that summer, he passed his oral exams and landed a temporary teaching job at Vassar College, just in time to provide a home for their child.

Looking at her tiny daughter born in Ann Arbor on September 18, 1950, Jean observed, "She isn't large enough to be a branch on the family tree. I will call her Twig." By this time, her brothers had each had a second child. Charles Stevens joined older brother Lance on December 6, 1949, and Derek Johnson had joined older sister Karen on July 29, 1949. Much relieved by John now having a paying job, Jean, Twig and John moved into a junior faculty apartment in a converted Victorian house on the Vassar Campus. Instead of pushing John to write his dissertation, Jean wrote *Meph, the Pet Skunk* and, again, published it under both their names.

Because they barely eked out an existence on his instructor's salary, Jean prodded John to complete his dissertation and become eligible for professors' pay. She set aside time in her schedule to work on it and typed it for him. About the time Jean became pregnant with their first son, John's Ph.D. was awarded and he was promoted to assistant professor, but still in a temporary position. John Craighead George was born on the first of November 1952. Rather than calling the baby by his first name (the same as his father, grandfather, and great grandfather), she called her son "Craig," her own father's nickname. Jean then wrote *Bubo, the Great Horned Owl*, which E. P. Dutton published in 1954.

Against Jean's strong advice, John George loaned his notes for the conservation course he taught to a woman Jean considered a "man-hater" with whom he was competing for a promotion. He exposed himself to an enemy who had already been publicly criticizing his work. Passed over for the promotion, he responded to her assaults on his competence by writing a scholarly paper on the water ouzel, aka American Ouzel, a bird that lives at higher altitudes and forages the bottoms of fast-flowing water for small animals to eat. Not much was known about these little birds that can submerge completely and swim underwater with their short wings. Jean and family spent the summer of 1955 researching this little dipper, so called because of the bobbing or dipping motion it makes while feeding.

One result of the research was *Dipper of Copper Canyon*, the sixth and last book Jean co-wrote with her husband. Another result was the American Library Association's Aurienne Award for 1958, the award's inaugural year.

Their second son and last child, Thomas Luke, was born on October 10, 1956, completing Frank and Carolyn Craighead's set of grandchildren. In the interim, Frank Jr. and John had each fathered his third child in 1954, Jana Catherine and John Willis, respectively. In 1956, Frank Jr. and Esther had a fourth child, Don Warren, who lived only two days.

Something the ouzel research did not accomplish was keeping John's job for him. Shortly after Luke was born, John was given notice his contract was not being renewed for the next school year. While he interviewed for new jobs, Jean wrote and illustrated *The Hole in the Tree* and *Snow Tracks*, books that were published under her name alone, all the while thinking about an important book about a boy named Sam who runs away from home to live off nature.

John was hired as Curator of Mammals at Bronx Zoo. While he settled into his new job, Jean and the kids adjusted to their new home in Chappaqua, New York in 1957. Jean was soon writing her most important work to date.

★ ★ ★

The twins' dissertation, *Hawks, Owls, and Wildlife: ecology of raptor predation*, "set a standard for the study of raptors" according to John Weaver, Carnivore Conservation Biologist with the Wildlife Conservation Society. After completing their doctorates, they found time to work together on government projects: being survival consultants for the Strategic Air Command in 1950 and organizing survival training schools for the Air Force in Idaho in 1951. In 1952, Frank Jr. and John went separate ways for the first time in their lives. John took a position as a professor of zoology and forestry with The University of Montana in Missoula and leader of the Montana Cooperative Wildlife Research Unit, making Missoula his permanent home. Frank Jr. worked outside of academia, first to do classified defense work, then to manage the Desert Game Range outside Las Vegas from 1955 to 1957 for the U. S. Fish and Wildlife Service. Family photos from that period show mushroom clouds looming in the background from nuclear tests in the desert. Frank attempted to measure radiation levels on the range, but the government, let us say, did not encourage his efforts in this direction. So, he headed east to take a job in Washington.

★ ★ ★

At war's end, Sam Craighead was in Montgomery, Alabama working for the U. S. Geological Service. Divorced by November 1945 when he transferred to the Harrisburg USGS office, Sam connected with former high school classmate Janet Crawford Strong, whose fiancé had died in the war. They were married at Covenant Presbyterian Church on August 24, 1946 with his younger brother, Bill, as best man. An only child, Janet had no siblings to participate in the ceremony. Their wedding reception was held at Penn-Harris Hotel and Convention Center, a large venue operating today as Radisson Harrisburg. Sam and Janet were less than two months apart in age. Prior to wedding Sam, Janet worked as a reporter for the Credit Bureau of Greater Harrisburg and, as was the custom of the day, lived at home with her mother and father, who was Superintendent of Harrisburg Steel Corporation. Sam demanded she quit her job to stay home with the children they planned to have.

Two years after their wedding, in August 1948, their first child, Robert, was born, sadly with severe birth defects. He died in September after living just a few days. Hospital personnel kept Janet from ever seeing the baby, but Sam saw him. A healthy daughter, Laura Jean "Laurie", was born on March 13, 1950. Five years later, on January

4, 1955, Patti Jane joined them to round out their family. They lived in a few different Harrisburg locations around the area where he grew up, while he continued to work for the USGS. Laurie and Patti spent summers at Craighead, as had their father's and grandparents' generations before them.

★ ★ ★

The Navy kept Bill Craighead on active duty until his ship was decommissioned in March 1946. His entrance into college was held up a year, being released well into the spring semester, far too late to enroll that school year. He entered Gettysburg College in the fall semester of 1946 where he involved himself fully in the college life he missed due to being drafted out of high school. He pledged with the social fraternity Phi Kappa Psi and played on the soccer team. Over the summer of 1947 using mustering-out money, Bill and partner Charlie Ridenhour bought a two-acre lot near the twins and built a shack on it. Bill's wife Betty described its best feature, "Wonderful view of the Tetons!" Bill's packing too much activity into too few hours to make up for time lost in the Navy took a toll on his studies, causing him to withdraw from college after the 1947-48 school year.

After sitting out a year, Bill transferred to Lebanon Valley College (LVC) in Annville, Pennsylvania where, having learned his lesson, he focused on academics. He earned his bachelor's degree in Zoology as a member of the Class of 1952. Bill was active at LVC, but this time with a focus toward the future. The *1953 Quittaphilla* reported him serving as President of the Biology Club, and Vice-President of his graduating class while working on his B. S. degree. Bill also took one last shot at participating in athletics at LVC:

"At that time I was 27 years old and went out for the college track team. You didn't have to qualify just get out there and run. I ran the 100-yard dash, the quarter mile, one mile, two mile and broad jump. In seven matches, I never won a point for the home team. In the two mile, I just tried to keep the winner from lapping me. Oh well!"

Bill was inducted into the Lebanon Valley College chapter of Beta Beta Beta, the honorary biological society, for having earned Bs in over 80% of biology courses he took and in over 50% of all subjects.

Bill left Lebanon Valley College with more than a degree. On a zoology class nature walk, he met a pretty co-ed named Betty June Bakley:

"He was so proficient with birds that when we went out on field trips he was forced to help all the rest of us who did not know what we were doing! The prof was very good, but seemed to think we knew more than we did. Bill was the expert. He had grown up with naturalists at Craighead and recognizing birds was a way of life.

"Then when we had Botany together is where we liked to say our relationship bloomed! I thought he was a very impressive guy and a very nice person. We were engaged our senior year. I was never impressed with the jocks on campus and here was this clean-living, little guy who had been in the war in the Navy and had fought at Okinawa. Very impressive!"

Miss Bakley was no ordinary co-ed as the *1952 Quittaphilla* explained:

"BETTY BAKLEY…Pitman, NJ English

La Vie Editor…diligent student

terrific personality…South Jersey's contribution

to South Hall…ready smile…L V's

Jinx Falkenburg[4] …did most for her college

always ready for a good time… 'Mel,

you joker, you!'"

Betty earned her AB degree in English with a minor in French in 1952 after playing leadership roles in what must have been every literary organization at LVC. She was also named Miss Lebanon Valley College and served as secretary of her junior class. She served as Senior Class Secretary as a senior when Bill was Vice-President and Secretary of the Biology Club when Bill was President. Both Betty and Bill took education classes to prepare them for teaching positions:

"I told Bill I needed some time at home with my folks before we got married. They had done so much to put me through school and it had been tough on them money-wise. So, I spent the year with them and worked that year at the Temple University Placement Bureau.

"We had a small wedding August 1 [1953] in the college chapel and a short honeymoon at Hershey Hotel and then on to George School. Bill was an intern in Biology; I was assistant librarian. Bill helped out in various sports, was in charge of Orton Hall with Mr. Larramore, coached wrestling with Stan Sutton, and helped with soccer and baseball. By the end of the year, he was teaching almost full time under John Carson. We lived on campus first in Orton Hall and then in half of a double house on campus, Twin House."

---

4 For the uninformed, such as the author, Jinx Falkenburg was an actress, expert swimmer, tennis star, radio and TV personality, movie star, and one of the first supermodels. Her legendary volunteer work with the USO during WWII earned her the Asiatic-Pacific Campaign Medal. After the war she entertained troops during the Berlin Airlift with Bob Hope. Betty maintains it was the similarity in their smiles that earned her the comparison.

In addition to their normal duties at George School, they also participated in extra-curricular activities with the students. An especially rewarding adventure was accompanying nine George School students to a German work camp in 1956. That year's trip was to a home for orphan boys in Wolfenbüttel, a charming medieval town mostly unscathed by the war, located eight miles from the East German border. There, they helped hand dig a root cellar that would eventually have a barn built over it.

Getting to Germany in 1956 was no easy matter. After the ten-day North Atlantic crossing, they landed in Bremerhaven. They went south by train, stopping overnight in Hamburg, to Düsseldorf, where they stayed a week before flying over part of the Soviet Zone to Berlin. A week's sightseeing included a bus trip into East Berlin where they saw still unrepaired, bombed-out buildings. From there they went to the work camp site. Betty recalled that the students performed wholeheartedly, even though the food was less than spectacular:

"The home was relatively poor. To give you an idea, dinner sometimes consisted of mashed potatoes with meat gravy. Salad was a quarter of a head of lettuce with a sugar and water dressing. We had shipped over powdered milk and cocoa, and in the evening we would share that with our hosts.

"[Bill] spent many afternoons at the bakery with Klaus Diederich, our German leader, talking about the war and Klaus's concern that Germans still did not understand or accept their guilt for the war and the Holocaust. One day they were invited to visit a local home; although the man had wartime and Nazi memorabilia on the walls, the visit was friendly."

The work completed, they took a three-week long, circuitous route through Oberammergau, Munich, Innsbruck, through the Brenner Pass to Bolzano, through Switzerland, to the Black Forest and Freiburg, down the Rhine to Cologne, on to Paris, and eventually to Le Havre, where they caught their ship home. Only two days out, they found themselves floating directionless in the Atlantic due to a broken turbine. They limped into port in the Azores for repairs, which took several days. They arrived five days late for the start of school. George School booked better ships, probably from Cunard Line, for later trips.

★ ★ ★

Nancy Gawthrop Wilson had accompanied her husband to New York City for his internship at Bellevue Hospital during the war. She resigned her position as an artist for Norcross Publishing Company to move to Cleveland, Ohio for Gerry's residency as a pathologist at Lakeside Hospital. In 1946, when that was completed, the army inducted him into the Medical Corps. Nancy moved home with her parents in preparation for the arrival of their son, Steven Craig, on May 2. Not long after that, the army sent Gerry to Korea, unaccompanied because of the chaos in that country at that time.

Nancy was heartsick at being separated from her husband but supported his army efforts by sending him medical books he requested. He needed them because the army had him performing surgeries of types he'd never previously performed. So, he boned up on them in order for his patients to have satisfactory outcomes. After he fulfilled his military obligation, he and Nancy made Michigan their permanent home when he took a surgical residency at Detroit Receiving Hospital from 1948 to 1953. Anne Gawthrop was born on April 16, 1949, and Barbara Jean (likely named after Nancy's sister and her cousin) on December 19, 1951 to complete the family. Nancy nurtured their family of pre-school-aged children. His residency completed, Dr. Wilson accepted the position of Director of Yates Memorial Clinic for the American Cancer Society.

★ ★ ★

Nancy's younger sister, Barbara Gawthrop, was still at Swarthmore College when the war ended. She was quite active in the college life she loved. An excellent student, Barbara still wanted to make a career of raising a family, a common goal of her generation. College was the traditional meeting ground for young people of her social class, but the war had depleted the dating pool.

Burned out from the pressures of the accelerated war schedule in spring 1946, Barbara chose to work for a while rather than begin the grind of medical school so soon after graduating. She taught second-grade reading and spelling to her home room and science to the elementary students at Shipley School in Bryn Mawr, Pennsylvania. Instead of returning to Shipley in fall 1947, Barb took a position teaching third grade boys at Landon School in suburban Washington, D.C. She chose not to return to Shipley because she did not appreciate the attitudes of what today are called helicopter parents.

In June 1947, while working a summer job as Junior Social Hostess coordinating teen activities at the Inn at Buck Hill Falls, a Quaker retreat in the Pocono Mountains, Barbara became seriously ill, with her temperature fluctuating between 96 and 106 degrees. Baffled at first, doctors at East Stroudsburg Hospital eventually diagnosed her illness as typhoid fever. "I don't recommend that for anyone," Barbara advised after many decades of good health. Streptomycin, a new antibiotic just emerging on the scene at the time, saved her young life. Barbara convalesced at her parents' home in Kennett

Square still too weak to teach in the fall . In January 1948, she felt strong enough to work two hours a day and taught sixth grade composition and grammar at Tower Hill School in nearby Wilmington, Delaware. She arrived home exhausted every afternoon due to typhoid's lingering effects.

Barbara was presented a difficult choice between two excellent opportunities for Fall 1948: teaching biology at Sidwell Friends School in Washington, D.C. or Germantown Friends School in Pennsylvania. The headmaster at Tower Hill School recommended Germantown as being a better fit for her. She happily taught high school biology and the natural history portion of ninth grade science for two years, shoehorning in a summer in Denmark inbetween.

In April 1950, Barbara contracted acute mononucleosis, truncating her teaching year. Worse yet, she had to cancel a long-anticipated summer and fall abroad where she would have taken a biology course on Arctic flora and fauna at the University of Oslo, followed by field studies in northern Norway. Afterward, she would have spent a month in The Netherlands before returning home. While convalescing with her family at the New Jersey shore that summer, a friend chided her for being less than perceptive of occasional date Tom Hallowell's good points.

One of Tom's first cousins was also Barbara's third cousin, who had suggested the Gawthrops put up Alban Thomas "Tom" Hallowell temporarily in August 1940, when he was starting his career with DuPont in Wilmington, Delaware. This temporary lodging lasted five years, during which Barbara and Tom seldom crossed paths. When they did, Barbara paid little serious attention to him. Being a petite, attractive young woman, as were most Craighead ladies of her generation, Barbara attracted young men. She even received proposals but didn't feel strongly about any of them. Tom periodically asked her out, but she was not attracted to him romantically and often turned him down. However, on those occasions she did accept, usually for nature walks or birding or photography, she enjoyed being with him, and so he persisted.

Tom had been an important figure on both the George School and Swarthmore campuses years before Barbara's arrival. His entry in the *1937 Halcyon* was quite informative:

"Tommy is Sandy Spring's contribution to facial serenity. All of the campus fame that has been directed at old 'Stone Face' hasn't changed his simplicity or love for the pleasant company of the old Quaker silence. A fast passing member of Pard's starring quintet and a varsity letterman in soccer and track besides, Tommy finds time to major in a stiff chemistry course and take time out for a lot of fun too. But be won't get excited about anything: during halfs [sic] and quarters, when everyone else is panting, Tommy lies back and looks at the ceiling of the locker room. It may be a sprite from Sandy Spring."

Not mentioned was that he was named to the All America soccer teams in 1935 and 1936 or that he was tapped for and initiated into Book and Key, Swarthmore's secret society that met in a smaller but windowless building inspired by Yale's Skull and Bones design. Tom then earned a Ph.D. in chemistry at MIT before taking the position at DuPont. Because the classified research he was doing was related to troop safety, he wasn't called to serve in the military during WWII. After the war, he worked primarily on photographic film products, mainly medical x-ray film.

In the fall of 1950, rather than return to teaching, Barbara enrolled in a year-long physical therapy program at Graduate Hospital, the University of Pennsylvania's teaching facility in Philadelphia. Barbara's instructors begged her to go to medical school, but she wanted marriage and family.

Chemistry didn't bring Tom and Barb together; it was their shared love of nature. Fun photographing terns, skimmers, and piping plovers together on Long Beach Island in New Jersey, in Barbara's opinion, topped off his many fine qualities. They became engaged in the fall of 1951 and married in a combined Quaker-Presbyterian ceremony in her parents' home on February 23, 1952. Tom gave Barbara an 8 mm movie camera for a wedding present. Barbara enjoyed their honeymoon in Bermuda. Unfortunately, Tom fell ill with flu the second day and was confined to bed four or five days. Upon their return, they split at New York's Penn Station: Tom to his job with DuPont in Parlin, New Jersey and Barb home to pack her belongings. Two days later, she loaded the blue Plymouth business coupe her father had given her when she was teaching in Germantown and drove off to Metuchen, New Jersey to set up housekeeping in a garden apartment.

After a first attempt to start their family, several doctors told Barbara she would never have children—a crushing blow to a woman who ached to be a mother. They stopped exploring adoption when they learned son John Francis was on his way. He was born on December 20, 1953. Three months later, they moved to a house in Little Silver, New Jersey where they lived seventeen years. Daughter Anne Craighead was born on September 6, 1955, and second son Charles "Charlie" Gawthrop on April 9, 1957. Tom and Barb gave their baby-boom children an enriched life similar to that her parents had given her and her sister. They lived on a quiet street in a heavily wooded development half-surrounded by a fruit and vegetable truck farm, just four miles from the ocean. They played kickball and basketball with the neighborhood children and explored the adjacent woods and fields. Family camping trips plus experiences at Outward Bound,

Teton Science School, and National Outdoor Leadership School expanded the children's knowledge of the outdoors.

★ ★ ★

Ruth Ann Craighead was attending elementary school in Columbus, Ohio when WWII ended and her brother James Lewis was born. Both continued their schooling in the early 1950s. Ruth Ann graduated from Grandview High in 1954 and enrolled at Ohio State University. Two things made college affordable for her after her father, Charles M., died unexpectedly: a Franklin County Scholarship because she was enrolled in a teacher

Ruth Ann and Jean on the Craighead House dock
(Ruth Craighead Muir)

Jim Craighead at Craighead House
(Ruth Craighead Muir)

education program and minimized educational expenses because she lived at home. Jim fondly recalled spending summers at Craighead. His mother, sister, and he would stay there all summer, even when his father was back in Columbus at work—until his father sold his share in the house to Eugene and Myra when Jim was eight years old. His earliest memory was playing in the dirt just outside the kitchen door. Although his was the only family living in the house those summers, he recalls other family members visiting the house frequently. Jim followed his father's and uncles' footsteps by fishing off the railroad bridge and jumping into the creek when a train approached—twice a day. He remembered the neighbor boy, Tim McCurdy, getting a rifle when he was too young to own one but didn't give the reason why. One can imagine.

Being nine years older than her brother, Ruth Ann became a teenager in 1949. Those years brought her very different experiences from those she'd had previously and which Jim was then having:

"When I was a teenager, I had several dates to the Allenberry Playhouse in Boiling Springs. I thought it was very special. I had a group of friends who lived up the road, and of course, teenagers find one another no matter what. Some of the names I remember were Bill Riggs (lived across from the lumber mill) and Jerry Davids whose family owned an orchard in the area. My parents often let me bring a friend for the month also and that increased our social life. We would spend hours in the creek, canoeing, pushing each other out of it, rowboating, swinging off the rope swing, and dropping into the swimming hole by the big willow tree next to Lil [Wilson] McCurdy's landing. We would walk the railroad tracks, and I would go with my dad fishing, wading, catching minnows in seines and worms on the dam for bait. A big treat was to walk over to the mill at Craighead Station and buy a cold Coke—a huge highlight of the day."

Jim was just nine years old when his father died but has fond memories of fishing with him and "helping" him fashion beautiful fly rods from scratch by first splitting the bamboo stalk into six equal length-wise slices. Ruth Ann reminisced about her father's hobby and other times:

"My dad lived for his month of fishing the Yellow Breeches Creek. He would tie flies all winter and make bamboo rods. He had aluminum molds to form triangles of bamboo which would then be fitted together to make the rods, tying the eyes on and shellacking all of it. People would give him feathers and he would try to make insect clones so the fish would be sure to bite. I remember when he first told me about Japanese beetles and he set to work to try to make a 'fly' that looked like the beetle. When he finally got to Craighead, he would go out to fish every morning very early and I can still hear the back door slam as he went down to the creek. My bedroom was right over the back door and looked out on the creek. I stayed in that room every summer.

"Aunt Ruth and Uncle Harold would come, usually briefly. They had me several times come and spend a night or two at their house with my friend from Columbus and would take us to Wanamaker's Department Store to shop and visit the Longwood

Ruth Ann lounges at the Maslands' pool with friends Lois and Barbara in 1951 (Ruth Craighead Muir)

Gardens in their town of Kennett Square. She always remembered my birthdays with a book when I was young, and a silver spoon each birthday as I grew older. I now have a beautiful set of twelve!"

In April 1955, Charles Craighead was on a business trip to Texas for his employer, Battelle Institute, when he collapsed on the Chicago airport tarmac while making a connection to another flight. He died on the way to the hospital of a heart attack at just 51 years of age. Life changed immediately for Peg, Ruth Ann, and Jim. Peg took a job with an adoption agency where she interviewed people who wanted to adopt babies. Ruth Ann and Jim focused on their studies.

For Ruth and Harold Gawthrop, the end of hostilities brought an end to war-time rationing and increased demand for the products they sold. Nancy was already married. Barbara was starting her last year of college and would soon start making her way in the world. It was a time for Ruth and Harold to enjoy themselves and prepare for the joys of grandparenthood. They didn't have to wait long: Nancy presented them with their first grandson in 1946. By 1957, their daughters had given them three grandsons and three granddaughters. Life was good.

★ ★ ★

A few months after war's end, Eugene and Myra welcomed older son Sam back to the area with a job transfer and, some months later, younger son Bill from duty with the U. S. Navy. Sam soon remarried and provided them with a granddaughter, Laurie.

Bill enrolled in college, graduated in 1952, started a teaching job the same year, and married the following year. Gene and Myra had to wait for more grandchildren. Sam and Janet provided them with a second daughter, Patti, in 1955, but Bill's would not come until later.

Gene and Myra were able to spend their free time on hobbies and interests. Myra, then sole owner of Craighead House, made several repairs and improvements, most notably rebuilding two fireplaces with Heatilator units and converting the pantry to a powder room. She spent time there as often as she could, even inviting her bridge group for outings. Nephew Jim Craighead vividly recalled seeing the well-dressed bridge ladies awkwardly canoeing, risking their finery as they climbed into the unstable watercraft, barely avoiding capsizing in the creek. Gene continued to work as an entomologist for the Commonwealth of Pennsylvania, fly fish, write articles for sporting magazines, and tie dry flies. He retired in 1956 from the state. In his third year of retirement, Gene suffered a stroke late the night of June 17 and died the next morning.

Myra continued being a grandmother and spent much time at the house. She

Eugene Craighead, master fly tier (William Moore Craighead)

Myra Eby Craighead in 1971 (William Moore Craighead)

lived until 1987, at which time she left Craighead House to her son Bill to prevent its destruction. "Dad said he'd bulldoze it and put a ranch house in its place, if it was his," recalled Sam's daughter Laurie. "He probably just said that to get his mother's goat."

★ ★ ★

Frank Craighead longed to return to his roots in Pennsylvania all those years he worked in Washington, D.C., but important work studies needed to be completed before he could rest. However, he purchased a run-down farm with an old limestone house and bank barn along the Yellow Breeches near the village of Boiling Springs in anticipation of his eventual retirement but not before making a study of a new pesticide.

DDT's value as an insecticide was first discovered in 1939 by Swiss chemist Paul Hermann Müller. It was used with great success to control malaria and typhus in the later years of WWII, leading to Müller receiving the Nobel Prize in Physiology and Medicine in 1948. Frank told Elwood R. Maunder of Forest History Society about his early experiences with DDT in a March 1977 interview:

"We got the first batch of DDT that came into this country and tested it. We found that, when spread on a log, DDT would keep the beetles from attacking, through the following year or even two years. On termite stakes, it's been proven to be effective as much as twenty-five years. But then we hadn't any idea how much to use in sprays, so we started out with heavy doses, as much as ten pounds per acre.

Frank Craighead fishes with David Masland Jr.
(David S. Masland)

"In cooperation with the Fish and Wildlife Service and the gypsy moth control in Pennsylvania, we killed every living creature in those forests; we even suspected some mortality in deer and birds. We came down to five pounds and that wasn't much better. Then we came down to a pound per acre, which killed the insects, with very little danger to other life, except in ponds and streams. There, the DDT killed eels, turtles, and all pond life. But that work was suppressed by the Department of Agriculture until Rachel Carson discovered it."

Frank left the Bureau of Forest Entomology in better condition than he had found it. When he took over as chief after returning from Ottawa decades earlier, the various units studying forests were not cooperating well with each other. "Looking back, many of those entomologists who headed up various divisions were brilliant, but very peculiar men. My wife has many stories." By reaching out to foresters, he was able to get problems solved that could only be solved by specialists working together toward a common goal. Prior to his tenure, they had common goals but didn't consider input from specialists outside their field. His article for the April 1924 *Journal of Forestry* helped to change these attitudes when he wrote:

"I have attempted to present these problems of the Dendroctonus bark-beetles in such a light that they can be more readily appreciated by foresters, and to show that they are not purely entomological but essentially problems of silviculture and management. Their solution is just as essential in the production of future timber as is that of other problems of forest research. Such complicated problems can be solved only by the cooperation of entomologists, foresters, and other specialists."

By reaching out an olive branch so openly, foresters who had previously been skeptical of entomologists' suggestions became more open to them: relations between the departments gradually improved, resulting in better outcomes for the forests under study. Ralph Hall, the head of the Central States Regional Forest Insect Laboratory at the Central States Forest Experiment Station in Columbus, Ohio described working under Frank:

"Dr. Frank C. Craighead was my boss. I always had a real favorable relationship with Craighead. I felt that he was a strict disciplinarian but a very fair person. I always respected him. I know that [Harvey John] MacAloney particularly had a deep regard for Craighead....I'd say he was a rather quiet individual, not in any way a forceful person. But once he made up his mind about something, it was pretty well made up. If you were of a different opinion, it took a bit of selling to convince him."

In 1949, after decades of his conducting studies, of writing numerous reports, articles and books, and of managing a government bureau, Frank and Carolyn Craighead sold their home in the Chevy Chase section of Washington, D.C. to artist Jean Plunket and her husband so they could retire to a country life raising beef cattle. Frank soon found the spacious old farmhouse a mile or so down the Yellow Breeches from his birthplace difficult to heat, but Carolyn later recalled, "I always felt at peace there." Regardless, he designed and built a small, modern cottage across the road from the stone house, handy to the barn. While lacking the charm of the stone house, it was more practical and Frank was a practical man. His niece Ruth liked the farm:

"When my Aunt Carolyn and Uncle Frank decided to buy the beautiful farm down the road, we would go there to ride the hay wagon and swing in the barn into the hayloft. A few times I got to eat the noon meal with the farm crew and had that huge spread made by Mennonite ladies that you always hear about. My Uncle Frank had a period when he tried an experiment with Brahman cattle, not sure how that worked out. He made the large pond down from the big house, and that was a pleasant addition. Several summers I got to ride on the tractor when they were bailing hay and the chance, once it was all stacked in the big barn, to swing on a huge rope swing and drop into a pile of loose hay. Can still remember the smell of freshly mowed hay."

Frank didn't live long in quiet domesticity: his close proximity to the state capitol and his international reputation as a forest entomologist soon brought a knock at his door. Oak wilt disease, a tree-deadly fungus-caused disease spread by insect vectors, had become a problem in Pennsylvania forest by the 1950s. He served on a team studying oak wilt in a forest near Blain in Perry County with Dr. Thomas L. Guyton, Chief of Pennsylvania's Entomology Division, Penn State pathologist William James Stambaugh, forester Jim Nelson, and Hugh Thompson, a freshly minted Cornell Ph. D. later hired to carry out the fieldwork designed by the team. Frank found conditions in Pennsylvania similar to those in Washington, D.C. in the 1920s:

"The unrest in Guyton's administration was obvious in the friction of objectives between the control unit under Jeffery and the research group. Nelson and I finally pulled away with the publication of a paper. This was later followed by a paper by Ibberson (forester)."

After disengaging himself as a consultant to Guyton, Frank teamed up with Joe Ibberson, with whom he had an excellent relationship. While searching for oak wilt trees in Fulton County one day, Joe spied a large rattlesnake and called to Frank. It took Frank some time to cover the distance between where he had been and where the rattlesnake was. So, by the time he arrived, the snake had crawled under a large boulder, leaving only its tail visible. Frank grabbed hold of the snake's tail, jerked it out of its hiding place, and flung it onto the ground. He quickly pinned the snake with his walking stick until he could grab it behind the head with one hand and by the tail with the other. Henry Gerhold retold the story as Joe had described to him:

"Now this was a very large snake and Craighead was a slightly built man. As the snake twisted and turned, Frank's body contorted violently in all directions. The snake appeared to be as strong as the man, and at times Ibberson thought the snake might be winning. Joe became very concerned as to what he might do if the elderly [60 year-old] man got bitten, and the struggle was so scary that he himself might even have a heart attack.

"After many anxious moments, Craighead somehow managed to kill the snake.

Frank skinned the snake in a matter of minutes and announced that he would send it to a friend in Florida who was skilled at making belts from rattlesnake skins.

"A week later, Ibberson again was startled by a rattlesnake while looking for trees infected by oak wilt, this time in Perry County. Craighead and a third companion had already walked past without seeing the snake just three feet off the trail. Joe asked them to stop and grabbed Frank's arm firmly with both hands. 'What's wrong?' asked Craighead. Ibberson blurted out that they had just passed a rattlesnake, and he couldn't survive another experience like the previous week's in Fulton County. Their companion found the snake and killed it, while Craighead just looked on with a big grin. As Frank skinned the snake, he marveled at the beautiful yellow and black pattern and remarked that the old skin probably had been shed recently. He sent the skin to his friend in Florida and had a belt made for Joe, who still has it in his possession."

Frank and Joe became close friends who hunted and fished together while continuing to work on oak wilt studies. On one field trip, they came across some cherry logs that Frank took to Coyle Lumber Company, a business his father had owned before losing his money a half-century earlier. Bill Coyle, who had returned home from flying as a fighter pilot during the war, had taken over the business from his father and Frank's friend, Mervin, and constructed a modern cement-block building across Old York Road from the old water-powered mill. Bill electrified the 19th century sash- and door-making machines that continue to be used well into the 21st century. He sawed and planed the cherry logs into wall paneling for the Craigheads' new cottage.

Freed from administrative duties after retiring, Frank began wintering in Florida. His first sojourn there had been in 1915 when he studied disease caused by beetles in pine trees that were destroyed by tornadoes. He had returned in 1917, this time to study deaths of Australian pine trees in Miami. After determining frost as the culprit, not insects, he performed a biological survey of Paradise (later renamed Royal Palm) Key in conjunction with the Smithsonian Institution. In the mid-1950s, after three retirement winters in the tropical paradise, he sold the fields and barn, retaining the old house and land south of the road along the creek for his children, and moved to Florida for a second retirement.

★ ★ ★

Summers at Craighead House didn't quite return to pre-war activity levels because the children had mostly grown up by then, and the adults' situations had changed as well. Frank and Carolyn no longer stayed there but visited often because they lived nearby. The twins summered in their cabins in the Tetons, and Jean couldn't spend entire summers at Craighead but did spend as much time there as she could. When she did, she invited friends, such as Ruth Chew, to visit her. Gene and Myra made the greatest use of the house due to living a convenient distance away. Sam lived and worked nearby. Bill could summer there even after he married because, as a teacher he had summers off. As a librarian, Betty had to work some, but far from all of the summer. Ruth and Harold never spent summers at Craighead but, with rationing relaxed, could more easily visit on long weekends and holidays. Nancy was married and living in Ohio (and later Michigan) and couldn't get there often. Barbara would have come with her parents until she married, but not on a regular basis. After her marriage, she vacationed elsewhere with her husband. Charles, Peg, Ruth Ann, and Jim spent their vacations at Craighead and continued to do so after Charles died. Ruth Ann has nice photos of the dock in the back yard from that period.

Informal social events flourished at Craighead House after WWII. People of the parents' generation had more free time, and travel was easier. In 1953, Donald Carpenter, apparently fond of the ancient spelling, wrote a song, *Memories of Craghead*[5], about life at the house. Friends and family would often huddle around the upright piano in the living room as someone, often Myra, pounded out the tune for *Ain't Gonna Rain No More* to accompany the singers who weren't always on key. Visitors also added considerably to the artwork on the kitchen walls. Examples are Ruth Chew's air castle (painted in 1946) and Robert Wingate's pencil drawing of cataract surgery (dated 1955). Myra kept the house in good condition, but family gatherings were fewer with the two generations scattered across the country. Although out of sight, it was not out of mind.

---

5 An ancient spelling of the family name.

19

Grizzlies, Wolves and Everglades

BY THE LATE 1950S, Frank was the only Craighead from his generation still active professionally. Brothers Eugene and Charles had died and Ruth had retired. The torch had been passed to the next generation, except for Frank Sr.'s vital work in Florida, which we will get to later.

Frank Jr. didn't break to harness well for desk work in a government bureaucracy. Accustomed to being extremely fit, in the spring of 1959, he found himself feeling not his normal self while living in Alexandria and working in Washington. So, he arranged to get a complete physical examination from his childhood friend Dr. David S. Masland at Dave's Carlisle, Pennsylvania office. Satisfied with the findings, Frank Jr. wrote Dave:

"I have realized that I must and should make a change but also know that I should be in good physical shape to do so. I feel relieved to know that I am O.K. physically. This Washington existence and organizational 'slavery' has had me constantly

Eugene Craighead holds Lance and Karen. (Barbara Gawthrop Hallowell)

Twins on a walk with their wives and first children. (William Moore Craighead)

doubting it. The necessary energy will come when the proper decision is made and action replaces frustration."

The opportunity for action happened later that year when Frank and Carolyn "retired" again, this time to South Florida. Frank Jr. and Esther then set up housekeeping in the old stone farmhouse outside of Boiling Springs and sent their kids to the Boiling Springs public schools. He resigned his Washington position in charge of Forest Recreation Research with the U. S. Forest Service when his superiors reneged on their agreement to transfer him back to the West. He remained in the East where he consulted with other agencies, but not in Washington. His family soon melded into the rural community. Mark Mullen, a childhood friend of Lance, Charlie, and Jana, recalls camping with them in a tent in their yard along the Yellow Breeches one night and being scared by grizzly bear growls Frank Jr. surreptitiously played from a recording he had made. No longer boys, the twins still enjoyed playing pranks.

In 1958, John learned grizzly bears were threatened and little was known about them. The only serious research conducted about the bears was done in 1944 by Olaus Murie. His cursory study was hampered by the inability to monitor grizzlies' nighttime activities:

"Practically nothing was known about it, its life history, and even less about grizzly populations. It was obvious if we were going to save the grizzly we had to know a lot more about its biology. At what age are females able to reproduce? How many young did they have in a litter? How long were the cubs kept before they weaned them? What was the mortality rate of the young, and what caused the mortality?

"It was obvious the grizzly needed a lot of wilderness habitat. So to protect the grizzly, we had to protect wilderness and increase designated areas classified as wilderness."

John applied for some grants and, in 1959, he and Frank Jr. began working together again, this time studying grizzly bears in Yellowstone Park. *National Geographic* and National Science Foundation grants funded the long-term grizzly bear research. So little was known about these mysterious creatures, almost every aspect of their lives had to be recorded and analyzed. Because the harsh winter weather at Yellowstone made fieldwork difficult and grizzlies hibernate throughout the winter, they conducted their research during warm weather. These seasonal cycles fit the twins' schedules almost perfectly. When temperatures broke in the spring, Frank Jr. headed out to Yellowstone to the Canyon Village lab they set up in an abandoned Civilian Conservation Corps (CCC) mess hall. John joined Frank at the end of spring semester. As soon as the Boiling Springs schools let out, Esther piled Lance, Charlie, and Jana and their equipment into and on top of the station wagon to make the long drive west to spend the summer in their then utility-free Moose, Wyoming cabin. Charlie recalled, "Mom was a good driver." However, she stopped and threatened not to move forward if he and Lance didn't stop fighting. Margaret brought Karen, Derek, and John Willis "Johnny" to live next door. On one summer visit, Jean observed:

"The two families of children moved easily from one set of parents to the other, eating where they landed, napping where they found a bed, returning to their own families in winter…I thought the children flowed between the parents because John and Frank were identical twins. Although to all six children they were Daddy John and Daddy Frank, as I watched I saw that they shifted parents because of Esther and Margaret. The two women were not competitive about their own children and genuinely loved the other's."

At summer's end, the women retraced their steps to get the kids home in time to start school each year. The men stayed in the West until the bears denned in late fall.

Each spring, Frank Jr. and John, along with several grad students (some of whom became assistants) and their own children (when they became old enough to help) assembled to do the physically demanding and sometimes hazardous work. Grizzlies do not welcome having their ears pierced and tags threaded through the holes, having their inner lips tattooed, giving urine samples, or having premolars extracted. As documented in *National Geographic* TV specials the twins filmed, an adult male grizzly bear dwarfed the four researchers who rushed to extract as much data from him as they could before he woke up from being tranquilized. In a frenzy to finish, they did to the sleeping bear what he would object to were he awake. When the anesthesia wore off too soon, he stumbled to his feet, roared, and charged them angrily. They raced to their red Ford station wagon, but not quickly enough to outrun a waking grizzly. He rammed the passenger door, then jumped onto the hood. Terrified, the driver threw the car into reverse and floored it, causing the bear to fall off, allowing the intrepid scientists to escape and tell the tale.

The twins responded to reporters' questions with the typical Craighead sense of humor when asked about the dangers of working with ill-tempered 1,000-pound animals. Frank wrote, "When releasing grizzlies, point them away from you." When a Yellowstone ranger asked if they were worried a bear might recognize them later and attack them, a twin replied, "Bob, we've got that all worked out. Each time we handle a grizzly, we slip into ranger jackets and put on ranger hats." Jean recalled meeting a trapped grizzly:

"Early the next evening we drove to Hayden Valley, where the grizzlies had been congregating in summer for a hundred years, feeding on the park dump on the garbage from the hotels and campgrounds.

"As we came over a rise, we saw a cylindrical trap made of a steel culvert with a drop-door. The trap had been sprung. A bear growled inside. He had come for the bait, stepped on the treadle and released the door.

"The cars came to a halt about twenty-five feet from the bear trap. Gingerly, Twig and I got out of the radio-equipped van and watched as John put an immobilization dart in a gun and shot it into the bear. Almost instantly he fell, unable to move. The anesthetic put him into a deep sleep. Frank opened the trap door; there, without bars to protect us, lay a wild grizzly bear. The assistants heaved him out of the trap into a cargo net and cranked him up to be weighed. I felt safe enough to slide down from the car roof, to which Twig and I had retreated, and walk closer to the stunning black animal."

One evening, John's daughter Karen complained, "We never get to do anything exciting." One wonders what she would have considered exciting.

Believing in keeping physically fit like their father, the twins made research team members demonstrate their fitness by climbing a rope before being allowed to eat. Johnny recalls his high school gym teacher requiring him to climb the rope in gym class a second time because he didn't think anyone could climb so quickly and didn't believe his stop watch. Johnny repeated the feat, showing that the stop watch, if not accurate, was consistent. More than once, these researchers put their rope-climbing skills to use escaping uncooperative bears.

Tracking and following grizzly bears were arduous tasks which absorbed incredible amounts of time and required considerable strength and stamina. Frank Jr. explained:

"Quite early in our work, it became evident that we needed a research technique that would permit us to readily locate and observe grizzlies at night, when they are most active, and to do so over extensive areas of timbered terrain. Similarly, to locate them in their daytime beds, secluded in dense timber and windfall, required something other than conventional methods of research. We turned to the field of electronics. In collaboration with engineers (Dick Davies and Joel Varney of Aeronutronic Ford Corporation [Philco], and Hoke Franciscus, a friend [from Carlisle, Pennsylvania] and ham [radio] operator), we drew up specifications for a system of tracking by the use of miniature radio transmitters. Step by step we tested prototype models, until the day came when, thanks to the technology of the space age, we succeeded in tracking a grizzly bear through her daily wanderings—and later to her winter den."

Through trial and error, the Craigheads pioneered the tracking of large mammals and developed methods used by other scientists to gather information not otherwise possible to record. And it wasn't a once-and-done operation: bears had to be refitted with transmitters each year because the collars holding the transmitters usually fell off each spring when the bears lost weight. Most of what is known about grizzly bears is a direct result of the Craigheads' efforts; they gathered the data or others used their methods.

Frank readily admitted it was a team effort; several others contributed greatly:

"Hoke Franciscus, who developed our system of telemetry, and Harry Reynolds, Jr., who helped us at first in his capacity as a park ranger, then served briefly as a field assistant after leaving the Park Service, and later publicly supported our work when it was under attack. Dr. Morgan Berthrong, a longtime friend and associate of John and me, worked closely with us in studying grizzly bear physiology and analyzing blood and tissue samples from bears we autopsied after they had been killed."

The grizzly bear research was conducted under agreements of understanding between the National Park Service, the Montana Cooperative Wildlife Research Unit at the University of Montana, and the Environmental Research Institute of Moose, Wyoming, the latter two organizations headed by John and Frank Jr., respectively. Beginning in 1967, Frank also worked as a Senior Research Associate and Adjunct Professor for the State University of New York at Albany at its Wyoming "branch campus." He described their collaboration with the Park Service as "close and amicable" for the first eight years of the study. Most park rangers welcomed the help when the brothers jumped out of bed in the middle of the night to help them deal with bear problems that occasionally erupted. However, some Park Service employees saw their involvement in bear management as intrusion by outsiders who were also researchers. Park personnel often view management as their bailiwick and resent researchers' prescriptions for improvement. Mutual distrust and blind self-interest often prevail. So it was for what became known as the Craighead Controversy.

Lacking a bear management policy beyond ad hoc problem solving, Yellowstone Park management inserted an unusual request for management recommendations in a 1962 memorandum of understanding with the Craigheads. A year later, ecologist A. Starker Leopold recommended "that the biotic associations within each park be maintained, or where necessary, recreated as nearly as possible in the condition that prevailed when the area was first visited by the white man" in a paper he produced as a committee head for Secretary of the Interior Stewart Udall. The Leopold Report, as the paper is often called, is often viewed as being the gospel for wildlife management. Unfortunately, the report recommended that parks each perform their own research, unintentionally removing the inherent checks and balances present when independent researchers conduct studies of their own design, creating a built-in conflict of interest. The next year, 1964, the requirement for management ideas was stricken from the memorandum of understanding. Not having read the fine print, John and Frank operated as before. Park Superintendents Lemuel Garrison (1956-64) and John McLaughlin (1964-67) welcomed their assistance but McLaughlin's successor didn't.

When Jack Anderson (not the columnist) took over in late 1967, he brought Glen Cole, a biologist, to serve in an influential capacity, the first to serve in such a way. As part of preparing for Yellowstone Park's centennial in 1972, Anderson started making changes, closing garbage dumps at which bears fed chief among them. Anderson closed the dumps cold turkey because Cole believed the grizzly population was much larger than the Craigheads had estimated and could well sustain the culling of bears that became a problem when they could no longer feed at park dumps. Cole also disagreed with the Craigheads in that he thought that two distinct sets of bears lived in the park: those that fed at the dumps and those that lived in the back-country on nuts and berries. The twins' research indicated otherwise. They warned that abruptly closing the dumps would result in undesired bear-human interactions and the untimely deaths of too many grizzlies.

Frank and John used the first major report on their research as a preemptive strike against Yellowstone's proposed policy change. Park staff were not amused with what they considered usurpation of their authority to manage the wildlife in the park. Famous by virtue of their books and TV specials, the twins had admirers who did not like to see them kicked around by government bureaucrats. Not unlike World War I, a seemingly unrelated event set off a firestorm.

One August night, grizzlies in Glacier Park mauled two young women in unconnected incidents. The killer bears were just two of many that had had lost their fear of humans from being hand fed in that park. However, the NPS absolved itself of any blame by stressing that both women were menstruating and were wearing perfume. A storm of indignation ensued, including a book by Jack Olsen titled *Night of the Grizzlies*. Park Service management feared they had a similar problem lurking on the horizon because they had numerous bears feeding at dumps. The Craigheads disagreed because Glacier's bears had been fed directly by people rather than browsing through dumps without humans present, as did Yellowstone bears. Terrified of lawsuits, the NPS dismissed the twins as being well-meaning but out of touch with reality and moved forward with their plan to close the dumps with all due haste.

In 1968, the NPS began separating edible garbage from the non-edible type at Yellowstone's largest dump, thus reducing the food supply for many bears. When the garbage wasn't separated, bears browsed through the dump searching for the edible food mixed among the trash. Food was more or less equally distributed among the bears. But when only edible food was present, alpha males easily located it and claimed it for themselves, leaving other bears with none. The underfed grizzlies looked elsewhere for food. Some bears wandered the eight miles from Trout Creek dump to Yellowstone Lake campground in search of nourishment.

For 1966 and 1967, the two years leading up to the food supply change, Frank Craighead noted the numbers of bears relocated or killed at that campground as thirty-three and nine, respectively. For 1968, eighty-four were moved or killed. Park Service official records only list twenty-four "control actions." Frank wrote, "according to rangers sympathetic to the bears' plight, the unofficial policy of the park superintendent was: get rid of the bears, just don't let anyone know." John added, "This was actually incorporated in an official inter-district memo which I saw. It has been authenticated by park personnel who also received the memo." However, the memo can't be found in Park Service archives. Park Service spokesmen do admit their record-keeping may have been poor at that time but insist there was no systematic campaign against the grizzlies. A scientific disagreement had morphed first into a philosophical dispute, then into all-out war.

The NPS bulldozed the CCC mess hall the Craigheads used for their headquarters in fall 1968, then burned the rubble. They claimed it was necessary to clean up the park for the 1972 celebration. The NPS didn't allow the Craigheads to use other vacant buildings in the park, so they were reduced to operating out of a house trailer owned by the U. S. Fish and Wildlife Service. Additionally, they were not allowed to handle or relocate bears.

Atomic Energy Commission officials, who had been funding the radio-tracking, were then denied access to the Trout Creek dump. In early 1969, Yellowstone Park Superintendent Anderson ordered removed all eyesores such as the colored ear tags and radio collars and forbade future marking and collaring as well as premolar extractions even though grizzly sightings by park visitors were unusual to rare.

The NPS claimed the Craigheads had provided no data to support their assertions. Of course they had no data, no one did. All conjectures about what would happen if the dumps were closed were speculation. But theirs were based on intimate knowledge of bear behavior; they thought themselves better qualified to make guesses than NPS personnel who knew a whole lot less about grizzly bears. Furthermore, Frank maintained that Superintendent Jack Anderson refused to accept reports and papers they tried to give him: he shoved them back, saying he didn't want to see them. Anderson closed the dumps at Rabbit Creek in October 1969 and Trout Creek in fall 1970.

The NPS introduced a new memorandum of understanding quite different from the ones in effect since 1959. Most egregious was the stipulation: "All oral and written statements, including but not limited to progress reports, popular and scientific articles and other publications, talks, and press releases prepared by the Montana Cooperative Wildlife Research Unit (and collaborators) concerning grizzly bear research within Yellowstone National Park shall be submitted to the Director, Bureau of Sport Fisheries and Wildlife, for approval prior to publication or otherwise disseminated [sic] to the public." John later recalled, "I showed that agreement to some of my professional colleagues at the University of Montana. They said in effect, 'John, if you accept that you can no longer call yourself a scientist.'" Unwilling to sign the agreement, the Craigheads' gathering of bear data came to an end.

The twins somehow had found time during their grizzly research to photograph and write *A Field Guide to Rocky Mountain Wildflowers* for Peterson, to publish articles for *National Geographic* on the techniques they were developing to track the grizzly, and to write what may turn out to be their greatest legacy: The Wild and Scenic Rivers Act. They still had mounds of data they had collected over the twelve years of their study and had much drama in their future.

★ ★ ★

"One day in late May, while John was in New York being interviewed for another job, I got up at six o'clock with the children. Last night's dinner dishes were still in the sink. Twig was cranky. Craig did not want to go to nursery school. I was tired. Three youngsters were taking more out of me than I imagined possible.

"'If I could just run away for a few hours,' I said, and I closed my eyes and went back to my childhood. I could see the falcons shooting across the sky like crossbows, could smell the wild garlic in the pot of mussel soup Dad was serving in a turtle shell. I could feel the crisp snap of a sagittaria tuber [arrowhead] between my teeth and hear John and Frank call from the river that they had a mess of catfish for dinner.

"That's how I get Sam Gribley out into the woods, I thought. He runs away as I am doing now. He even tells his father he is going to go, as I had told my mother when I was a kid and marched off into the night—only to turn around and come back. His father will expect him back...but Sam Gribley won't turn around. He'll make it."

Jean had been formulating her story line for a long time but now had the missing piece, the motivation for her protagonist, inspired by her first cousin, Sam Craighead. Writing could finally start:

"I am on my mountain in a tree home that people have passed without ever knowing that I am here," began Jean's new novel. "And so I ran away to the forest to survive—right in my own home."

Having landed a position very different from his previous work, John George spent long hours in New York City learning his new job as curator of animals at the Bronx Zoo. Jean devoted the extra time alone to writing and worrying about the future of her family. After *My Side of the Mountain* was written and illustrations drawn, she sent it to the publisher. While waiting for their answer, she anxiously anticipated her advance, "...that would pay for painting the woodwork and sanding the pine floors. Advances for children's books are small compared to those for adult books, but good children's books may sell for years and years. In the long run, they do better than most adult books....But more important than the money was the book itself. I had taken a major step forward. I was on my own."

Her publisher saw things differently. He didn't think they should publish a book

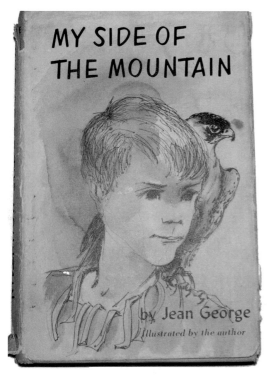

MY SIDE OF THE MOUNTAIN

by Jean George

Illustrated by the author

Cover of Johnson Coyle's well-read copy of My Side of the Mountain (Author)

in which a father encourages his son to run away. Jean whistled softly and replied, "But the father thinks Sam will be home that night." Shaken by the phone call, Jean sat at the kitchen table, head in hands. "I became frightened. A woman with young children is a fear box." It had become clear to Jean that John wasn't suited for the zoo job: he was an academician not "a stage manager for displaying animals." Seeing John's job evaporating even if he didn't, she called Eugene Lyons, her editor at *Pageant* magazine and now a senior editor at *Reader's Digest* a few miles down the road, and asked him for a job. He was interested and scheduled an interview.

Before the day arrived for the *Reader's Digest* interview, much happened. Jean's editor called, saying the publisher was going forward with *My Side of the Mountain*. "I breathed deeply and patted the walls of the house: it was still mine, I could make the next payment." Fear again gripped Jean when John was fired by the zoo, putting more financial pressure on Jean to support her family and weakening the ties between Jean and John: "What I couldn't do was support the family with John not working. I had been raised by a strong father and I needed a man who worked, who dominated and took care of us all."

The outcome of the interview was a commission to write a "nature detective" piece. John made suggestions; Jean did the writing. *Reader's Digest* bought it and two more articles. Looking for a job again, John received a letter from a friend and paced the floor. "The scientific community is criticizing me for popular writing." This criticism wasn't new to Jean; her brothers had received similar complaints about their "popular" articles and TV specials; she knew how petty academicians could be.

Stresses first appearing in Jean and John's marriage at Vassar got worse when he took the zoo job and brought their marriage to the breaking point when, against Jean's wishes, he took a job with Fish and Wildlife Service in Washington, D.C. She had established strong ties with the New York publishing industry and didn't want to lose them. Their marriage hung by a thread when he decided to commute to the job, only spending weekends at home with Jean and the kids.

One of his duties with the Fish and Wildlife Service was conducting research on pesticides at Patuxent River Naval Air Station. His DDT studies later served as the basis for Rachel Carson's *Silent Spring* and the eventual banning of DDT.

One bright spot in Jean's life came in January when *My Side of the Mountain* came in second for the Newbery Award for 1960. Jean danced through the house knowing that, although the award brought no honorarium, almost every library would buy a copy of her book. Her next book, the autobiographical *The Summer of the Falcon*, told the story of her summers growing up at Craighead Station, with a focus on the years her brothers trained falcons. This book didn't receive the critical acclaim her previous book had received because librarians found her family too unconventional. Her next books, *Red Robin, Fly Up!*, *Gull Number 737*, and *Marvels and Mysteries of Our Animal World* didn't raise reviewers' hackles fortunately for Jean because she needed good sales to help her support her family as she and John had separated.

Eight days before what would have been her twentieth anniversary on January 10, 1964, Jean divorced John in Mexico, a not uncommon custom because getting a divorce was then difficult in many states. Jean focused on writing enough books and articles to feed, clothe, house, and educate her children. She traveled frequently to research stories and took her children with her in the summer whenever possible. All learned much from these trips. The summer after her divorce was particularly fruitful. *Reader's Digest* underwrote their visit with her brothers in the Tetons. Her observations of the twins' grizzly research stoked what became one of the most popular articles the magazine ever published.

After the divorce, John L. George went on to a successful career teaching college at Penn State (1963-1981) and University of Pennsylvania (1981-2). Students considered him to be a charismatic, brilliant teacher.

Jean hired Mrs. Davidson, a grandmotherly woman who had raised eleven children of her own, to look after her kids when she was away on work assignments. Jean was appalled to learn Mrs. Davidson told stories about babies being born with pigs' heads, convinced the children to brush their teeth by taking out her false teeth and chomping her gums, and, perhaps worst of all, watched professional wrestling on TV, cheering animatedly for the wrestlers she liked. So, Jean hired a college girl who she thought would make a better role model. Her children didn't appreciate the change. They gobbled dog biscuits off plates, claiming their mother never fed them anything else. Craig barked to be more convincing. The girl never came back but, happily for the children, Mrs. Davidson did.

In June 1968, Penn State named Jean its Woman of the Year. During a ceremony held during its annual Alumni Reunion, Jean was awarded a medallion because she was a graduate whose "personal life, professional achievements, and community service best exemplify the objectives of her alma mater." Her old biology professor Clarence Ray Carpenter, a primatologist who on a visit had painted a rhesus monkey on the kitchen wall at Craighead, talked with her about the role alphas played in societies of Japanese macaques and asked Jean to write an article on them. Intrigued with the idea, she asked, "Aren't there any alphas closer than Japan?"

"Wolves," he responded. "Study the wolves."

Jean wrote about a book a year, except 1967 to 1969 when she wrote the thirteen volumes comprising The Thirteen Moons series. With that finished, she was free to study alphas. In 1970, she wrangled a *Reader's Digest* assignment to Alaska to learn about wolves. She took thirteen-year-old Luke with her for an experience that opened new windows to both of them. They traversed over a third of the globe to get to their destination in the Arctic Circle, the Naval Arctic Research Laboratory (NARL), which is located five miles down the Arctic Ocean beach from Barrow, the United States' northernmost town. In addition to learning about wolves from a researcher who was studying them, Jean was introduced to wolves and their social structure at Sanctuary River by Gordy Haber. Jean made a bond with wolves that lasted the rest of her life. At Barrow, she also became acquainted with an Inuit Shaman named Julie Sebevan, who had seen a ten-legged bear. Julie made Jean a parka of red velvet trimmed with a white wolf ruff and decorated with white and silver kimono trim from Japan.

Shortly after returning home, Jean got a call from her *Reader's Digest* editor:

"Stop working on the wolf piece. While you were away some yo-yo bought an article on the wolves. It's going into the magazine. Yours is out."

"My generosity about the mistake did not last. I was devastated and—as usual after a rejection—overwhelmed with worries. There were college bills to be paid… And there was my obligation to the scientists who had given me so much of their time; had it been for nothing?"

After much commiseration about the unfairness of it all, Twig suggested, "Well, then, write a children's book about wolves."

"Best idea yet. Pat Allen called earlier this week. She once worked with Elizabeth Riley and is now at Harper Row. She wanted to know if I would write for Ursula Nordstrom now that Elizabeth is retired."

"The Ursula Nordstrom who was E. B. White's editor for *Stuart Little* and *Charlotte's Web*?" I asked.

"And for Maurice Sendak, Shel Silverstein, Arnold Lobel, Charlotte Zolotov and on into the night."

The next day, Jean met with Ursula Nordstrom. "I want to write a book about an Eskimo girl who is lost on the Arctic tundra. She survives by communicating with a pack of wolves in their own language."

"Will it be accurate?"

"Yes."

"I'll write up your contract and advance now. Who is your agent?"

"Never before had I been offered a contract and advance before a word had been written. But I, like the alpha wolf of Sanctuary River, worked best when kissed under the chin. I went home and began writing *Julie of the Wolves*. The book was finished before the spring thaw…"

Jean had wanted to write a book about nature with a female protagonist akin to Sam Gribley for years and, finally having her chance, succeeded. *Julie of the Wolves* won the Newbery Medal for 1973 but, even after reaching such lofty heights, Jean was far from finished writing.

★ ★ ★

In 1915 when Frank Craighead first came to Florida to study pine bark beetle damage, turpentine from these trees was the state's major money crop. Two years later, the government sent Frank back, this time to study deaths of Australian pines. Intrigued by the new and still undeveloped areas of South Florida, and after completing his government and Smithsonian projects, he crossed the state at Lake Okeechobee, traveling from Belle Glade to Moore Haven in a fisherman's gas boat, and then walked thirty miles to LaBelle. Much later he recalled that trip:

"It was lovely, the custard apple groves were still intact around the lake, but there were no roads, just cattle trails, and they were largely under water. I still have vivid memories of the beautiful Caloosahatchee River with winding curve after curve as we went across by paddlewheel steamboat to Fort Myers, two days for twenty-one miles.

"There was an abundance of wildlife, quail, and turkeys everywhere, and it was nothing to catch a meal of them. Cattle ranches depended on wild game for food."

Well aware of the changes to Florida since his studies in the teens from wintering there the previous three years, Frank and Carolyn moved to a warmer clime in Homestead, Florida around 1956. Settling on a permanent location apparently posed a challenge as they lived like gypsies, shifting from place to place for quite a while before deciding on a site. His retirement work was no less controversial than before:

"At the same time, I became interested in the ecological problems which had also been a hobby of mine during the days of forest insects. I lost confidence in control work that was being carried on against bark beetles and suggested more elaborate research, much to the dislike of the old timers. It was through my efforts in hiring pathologists and physiologists that we finally determined that the bark beetles were acting in symbiotic relationship with the bluestains in killing the various trees they attacked. I was even accused of favoring the forest pathologists instead of backing up the entomologists on insect losses."

Frank's second retirement was far more active than many people's primary careers. He served as Park Collaborator and Research Consultant for the Everglades National Park. He collected the plants of the park for the museum as well as advised on management of water and wildlife. He identified at least twenty previously unknown species of insects and sent specimens to Washington for registration. He even worked on a study for Disney for three years until the travel became too much of a problem for him, particularly since he wasn't being paid:

"Possibly I am a bit old-fashioned, but my service during my forty years with USDA always seemed to be more of a hobby than work. On retirement and coming to Florida, it was apparent that my past experience was in reality a preparation for what I might do here and felt that my services should be given freely to Federal and State agencies."

Frank traveled extensively across South Florida by foot, canoe, skiff, airboat, and glade buggy. He paddled to the sources of all the major rivers in South Florida. He visited every key in Florida Bay and listed the plants and usual features, cored many of the mud flats to determine stratigraphy of the calcareous deposits and the geological age of several strata. For twelve years, at twenty stations, he kept weekly to monthly records from Homestead to Flamingo of water levels, direction of flow, food fishes and wildlife abundance. He wrote scholarly papers about a variety of subjects, including: three trees not previously identified as being found in the Everglades; effects of Hurricane Donna on the vegetation of South Florida; impacts of closing culverts along Flamingo Highway; vegetation and sedimentation of the Whitewater Bay drainage system; the role of the alligator in shaping plant communities and maintaining wildlife; and the impact of a jetport. In addition to writing fourteen articles, Frank found time to write two books: *Orchids and Other Airplants of the Everglades National Park* and *The Trees of South Florida, Volume 1*.

Dr. Robert Krear, who left Penn State's ski team for combat with the 10th Mountain

Division in WWII and, as of this writing, a director of The Murie Center, worked with Frank on the orchid book and recalled how physically fit he was for a man his age (early seventies at that time):

"It has been a long time—1960-61, I believe—when Dr. Frank Craighead Sr. asked me to photograph some orchids for him. Frankly, I did a poor job for him, and I do not remember that he used many or any of my photographs.

"I had spent several days with him fighting our way through the mangroves, and collecting orchids, and I remember the tremendous admiration I had for the energy being displayed by a man of his age. If you have tried to walk through a mangrove swamp, you know what I mean. He was a dedicated man, and it was easy to see where his children—Jean, John, and Frank Jr.—got their inspiration for the great contributions they all have made.

"We did not attempt to photograph any orchids in the mangroves but, rather, brought them back to his place of residence, and I took the photos there....I admired him greatly."

An October 31, 1966 letter from the U. S. Department of the Interior gave Frank the satisfaction of knowing all his work had not been in vain. The letter began: "As a result of your report and recommendation, Big Cypress Bend was proposed to Secretary Udall's Advisory Board at their meeting in April for Registered Natural Landmark eligibility....Big Cypress Bend is now a Registered Natural Landmark." Frank's work led to the protection of the 729,000 acres of swampland adjacent to the Everglades whose freshwaters are essential to the health of the Everglades.

Carolyn, who had started painting landscapes in Pennsylvania, continued her new hobby in Florida but switched to tropical scenes. Instead of having occasional visitors for short periods of time as they did in Pennsylvania, Frank and Carolyn then started having numerous visitors for weeks at a time. Their guests included philanthropist friends Joe Ibberson and Frank Masland, who canoed through the Everglades with Frank for two weeks. Ibberson continued the rattlesnake theme when he told Henry Gerhold of his trips to visit Frank in Florida:

"Encounters with rattlesnakes continued at Homestead. One day, Craighead returned from the Everglades with a diamondback in the station wagon. He forgot to remove it or tell his wife about it. Imagine her reaction when she got into the car and heard the rattle of the diamondback! Another time, he picked up a huge rattler coiled in front of his daughter Jean in a hammock. On yet another occasion, he left a bag containing a rattlesnake in an attached garage. The snake escaped and surprised his wife in the bedroom. That could not have fostered matrimonial harmony either.

"Craighead became a consultant for several influential groups and moved to Naples, Florida, which was more convenient for these activities. He also wanted to be on higher ground at Naples, having studied the destructive force of hurricanes and lived through Diane [in Pennsylvania]. He believed the Homestead area was due for another hurricane, and he was high and dry at Naples when the killer storm Andrew demolished Homestead. His command of all the disciplines involved in environmental issues, along with his ability to analyze and find solutions, made him very effective. Craighead tried to persuade Ibberson to become involved in the environmental groups, but Joe was too deeply rooted in Pennsylvania to consider such a change."

Employing what Jean called "Dad's uncanny insight into nature," he and Carolyn moved to Naples on Florida's Gulf Coast, settling in at 87 East Avenue off Pine Ridge Road in April 1972. Although his geography changed and he was rapidly approaching eighty-two, his interests and energy didn't. He was far from finished as a naturalist. If anything, he was more dedicated than ever.

20

Waters Flow and Families Grow

S AM CRAIGHEAD CONTINUED TO WORK at the Harrisburg USGS office measuring water flow in local streams. An outdoorsman, he disliked desk jobs almost as much as his boss, the head of the office, Robert Steacy, always preferring to work in the field. Dr. Michael Stoner, a former co-worker, immediately recognized Sam's wading breeches—pants with legs tapered to fit into his boots—upon seeing the tiny pair. Mike still remembered him fifty years later:

"Sammy was a great guy with a big heart. He was also a practical joker who would annoy the secretary/office manager by changing the office thermostat when she wasn't looking. Sammy reminded everyone of the cartoon character Popeye, especially when he was smoking his pipe. We went stream gauging together several times and I remember always being concerned Sammy would get tipped over in the stronger currents. I thought, perhaps, he carried extra weights in his waders."

Like most Craigheads, Sam passed along his love of nature to his children, and Craighead Station was the perfect place to do it. Laurie recalled:

"He taught me how to fish and I remember catching my first rock bass at the dam at Craighead. My father taught me how to swim at Craighead. When I was nine, my father had me swim from the dock at Craighead to the iron bridge. Mom and Dad taught me how to love and care for wild animals. We raised ducks, squirrels, raccoons, opossums, birds, owls, and even skunks. Some we took back to Harrisburg with us when we went home after the summer, but most were let go in the meadow at Craighead. I remember the rope and swinging off the tree into the water. I remember baseball games. Friends from Harrisburg would come to visit and we would have picnics. The old home 'Craighead' was a paradise for me. Another memory was when the train would come through Craighead with its shrill whistle, and I was scared for a few years. The engineer of the train lived in Harrisburg and was close friends with my parents, so one summer he would pick us up when he came through Craighead, whistle blowing, and my sister and I would ride into Carlisle and come back to Craighead. We had the privilege of using the whistle. At times when we would come to the Craighead homestead in the winter, my dad would be out there testing the ice so we could ice skate."

In 1962, when Laurie was eleven and Patti was five-going-on-six, Sam and Janet bought a house almost next door to the clan's summer home. The girls were just old enough to capitalize fully on what their new home's location offered:

"When we moved two doors away from the Craighead house, next to the iron bridge, that did not stop us from spending a lot of time at my grandmother and grandfather's summer house. There was something about that old house that just drew me in. My grandmother would have bridge parties during the summer and she would let my sister and me come and visit with her friends. I had my sixteenth birthday at the homestead. A local band was there. People I didn't even know came to Craighead for that event. My husband and I spent part of our honeymoon at Craighead. Before my husband left for Vietnam in 1969, my grandmother held a dinner at Craighead. It was in November so we had to light fireplaces to keep warm. It was sad because he was leaving, but the place was so cozy we just relaxed and took it easy that day. During this time, we did have an opossum visit us as it was cold and he wanted the warmth of our old homestead. During the 1970s, we spent time at Craighead with our children where they also learned about taking care of small wildlife and all types of adventures."

Sam left the Geological Survey to work for the Susquehanna River Basin after he retired from the government around 1977. Unusual for a man who lived, worked, and fished in water all his life is that he eschewed boats. He had a good reason for that. Patti and Laurie recalled him going on a boat deep-sea fishing during a family vacation in Florida. They laughed when he returned, green from seasickness. It wasn't funny to him, though.

Younger daughter Patti was married at Craighead on June 24, 1978. Laurie remembers the affair well:

"That was such an exciting event. My dad sang *Daddy's Little Girl* at the wedding for my sister. I remember my son who was the ring bearer tripped in a hole as he walked with the rings on the pillow and went down to the ground."

Janet had problems breathing for as long as the girls could remember. Extremely thin although she ate like a horse, Janet smoked, likely exacerbating her problems. Patti remembers her mother being short of breath and asking her to slow down as they made preparations for her wedding. Janet died at home six weeks later on August 6, 1978 just fifty-eight years old. With his wife gone and his daughters married, Sam moved out of his house along the creek and into a double-house in nearby Boiling Springs where he remained involved in the community. A consummate musician, Sam played several instruments. After the Boiling Springs Tavern reopened as an upscale restaurant, Sam joined a local band that played in the Tavern on weekend nights. When attorney Tony DeLuca needed to have the flow of water from the springs in Boiling Springs Lake measured for the lake trust, Sam jumped into the water and showed him how to do it.

Sam gave Tony's son, Anthony, lessons before school each morning when he wanted to learn how to fly fish. Sam was a heretic within his family when it came to fishing. His father had taught him how to fly fish, but he preferred to angle another way, and not with a cane pole as was his Uncle Frank's preference. Sam cast for trout with a rod and reel without using a dry fly. Instead, he used worms or, his favorite, Velveeta cheese and bread. He taught Laurie and Patti his chosen method.

Disturbed by parishioners' hypocrisy, Sam stopped attending church when his daughters were young but allowed them to participate fully. He never stopped believing, he just couldn't stomach the contradiction between several members' out-of-church behavior and their supposed piety in church. In later years, he attended services again, but with a different congregation.

Sam retired from the Susquehanna River Basin in March 1985, when he turned sixty-five, and died unexpectedly in his sleep on August 19, just six months later.

★ ★ ★

Bill Craighead continued teaching biology at George School. Betty resigned her librarian position in 1960 to start their family. John Bakley Craighead was born on October 30, 1961, and William Clay Craighead on October 22, 1965. In 1961, Bill took a sabbatical to earn his master's degree in Fisheries Management at Penn State. He remained active in community service by chairing the Fish and Wildlife Committee of the Neshaminy Valley Watershed Association. He left George School in 1967 to work for the Delaware River Basin Commission, where he made a study of the low oxygen level in the tidal portion of the river. After that, he worked as Biological Consultant to Public Service Electric and Gas Company in Newark, New Jersey, for three years. He wanted to return to teaching but, being over fifty, schools and other employers were reluctant to hire him. He worked at Geerling's Florist just outside of Newtown for ten years until he retired.

In 1968, Bill used the money from selling the Antelope Flat lot to purchase a beekeeping business from Glen and Helen Kline of Idaville, Pennsylvania as a side business he ran out of Craighead. He located his hives on farms and orchards whose owners paid him to pollinate their crops. Unfortunately, his attempts to breed a strain of bees resistant to a prevalent disease that decimated hives failed, ultimately causing him to sell his less and less profitable business in 1983.

Tragedy struck Bill and Betty in 1993 when their oldest son, John, died at just thirty-two years of age. His untimely death left behind his wife, Melissa, and daughters, Mary Catherine "Katie" and Sarah Elizabeth, five and three and a half years old, respectively. John was Grounds Supervisor at Pennswood Village and was enrolled in an Ornamental Horticulture program at Delaware Valley College in Doylestown at that time.

Younger son, William Clay, graduated from George School in 1983 and from his parents' alma mater, Lebanon Valley College, with a B. A. in History in 1987. He lived at Craighead while he worked at Gettysburg National Military Park for a short time after graduation. He then took a position at Washington Crossing State Park in New Jersey as a Resource Interpretative Specialist. His summer work on the Pennsylvania side of the park during his student days surely helped him land this position on the New Jersey side. After ten years at the park, Clay was promoted to the head museum position, which he currently holds.

Betty returned to George School in 1977 as a part-time librarian in McFeely Library. She shifted to full-time in 1980 and continued in that capacity until 2005. Then seventy-five, she cut back to part-time until she retired in 2012 at age eighty-two.

In retirement, Bill wrote two books, *As You Were: Memoirs of World War II* and *All Ahead Full: World War II Memoirs of an LSM 215 Veteran*. Bill and Betty attended the grand opening of the National World War II Museum in New Orleans in 2009, where he was one of 250 veterans who represented each of the branches of the armed forces. He was escorted on the red carpet by an active duty person for the dedication ceremony which featured celebrities Tom Hanks and Tom Brokaw. Because he had written about the Hollywood Canteen, Bill was driven by limousine to New York City for the filming of a documentary about it. There, he encountered Angela Lansbury again. "When I met her, it was like greeting a long lost friend. She wouldn't remember me from Adam. It was just delightful to see her firsthand. They photographed us together. As a celebrity she appears to me to be very outgoing and so responsive to conversation. She's a very attractive woman, and for eighty-four, she's exceptionally so, I might say."

Bill was still involved with ecological projects at George School in his late eighties. He died on January 1, 2016 at age 90. Betty puts her English major to good use writing articles for *Craighead House Chronicles*.

★ ★ ★

Nancy Gawthrop Wilson and family lived in the Detroit area where Gerry's father, also a surgeon, lived and practiced. They attended the same Baptist church Gerry's parents attended, but the theology didn't suit Nancy's family. So, they shifted to a Presbyterian church and stayed there.

Nancy's daughter, Barbara Wilson, summarized her mother's adult life:

"Rather than pursue a career in art after graduating from Oberlin College, Mother chose to focus on being a full-time, at-home mother to three children and wife to a metropolitan surgeon/hospital administrator.

"Mother shared with us her love of the outdoor world. She had a reverence for the fragility, magnificence, and *process* in nature. Mother was keenly observant, always alert to tiny sounds, odors, the tactile variety and richness of the natural world, and tastes—munching wintergreen from the woods, making flower salads or tea from roots or bark, slurping fresh water from leaves. She encouraged art projects using found objects from sea, lake, pond, woods, and fields and science projects relating to weather, use of natural resources, and animal behavior. Mother adored animals, and many (some unusual for a typical suburban setting) enjoyed nurture in our home. In designing a cottage in northern Michigan, Mother altered the architect's plans so that three huge pines would continue to live—by growing through holes cut in the deck. The spiral staircase was homage to nature's bendable and cyclical patterns as well as creative use of space.

"'Let's go for a walk' was an invitation to adventure—not simply the physical exercise, but a natural one as well—what might we see?! My brother, who loved birds and study of bird habitat in his boyhood, grew up to be an avid birder. In her later years, Mother, still curious and delighted to observe and learn, continued to revel in outings with Steve. Mother explored principles of *beauty* and *function* in natural art with my sister—countless museum and art gallery outings, drawing and pressing flowers, tracing wave patterns on clay or sand, sketching rock formations, or examining the fineness and versatility of a seashell (inhabited or not!). Anne is a professional artist. I had an early love of reading and, like my siblings, was brought up on Jean George's books, but Mother introduced me to a host of authors who wrote

215

of the natural world and creative endeavors. I have a graduate degree in English literature and have just finished rehabbing an old house on the ocean.

"Nancy Gawthrop Wilson was not a naturalist, per se, but an artist with a tremendous and lifelong reverence for, appreciation of, and fascination with the natural world that was evident in her artwork. Originally an oil painter and graphic designer, Nancy returned to her passion for making art after her children left home.

"She moved on to watercolor as well as mixed media designs of paper, ink, paint, and chalks, and her work became more conceptual than concrete. Nancy loved color and appreciated nuances of color. She focused on the layering of materials that enhanced or obscured objects' visibility, with literal and suggested traceries. She liked the sense of costume in both the natural and social worlds and played with these themes. Nancy was inspired by Asian art and its subtleties of line and balance. Waves, fish, shells, reeds, sea fans, seaweed, mountains, rocks, and the textures, shapes, and proportions of these fascinated her. She integrated Flemish geometric block, Native American and ancient Greek symbols, and pattern-on-pattern techniques with a looser, more fluid perspective of a watercolorist."

★ ★ ★

In the 1950s and 60s, Tom Hallowell worked at DuPont while Barbara Gawthrop Hallowell managed the household and raised their children. Tom devoted most of his leisure time to the Boy Scouts and his family. Their children played outdoors much of the time, catching tadpoles in the neighboring farm pond in warm weather and skating on it in the winter. They paddled around the pond in a tub they named "Old Plasticsides" and played kickball in the dead-end street with neighborhood children. Barbara recalled, "The children learned how corn grows and when strawberries ripen, watched spring plowings and summer-fall harvests, and witnessed the results of drought and deluge on a farmer's crops. The moods of the woods and life of the pond were everyday experiences." She drove them the four miles to the Jersey Shore, where she taught them about birds and sea life and collected driftwood the kids used to build tree houses. "The house welcomed a clutter of beach combings and defunct hornets' nests, baseball gear, and roller skates. Snakes and turtles, injured birds and baby raccoons, infant cottontails and developing toads, even creeping creatures from mantids to monarch larvae, found care and eventual release from our home," remembered Barbara fondly.

The possibility of a transfer had hung ominously over Barbara and Tom Hallowell's comfortable lives the first nineteen years of their marriage. In March 1971, DuPont sent

Tom to a job near Hendersonville, North Carolina, with no advance notice. Barbara's family move wasn't just a geographical shift from North to South; it was more of a cultural shift from northeastern coolness to southern hospitality; it was from a densely populated part of the most densely populated state to a rural area.

Unable to find an old farmhouse that hadn't crumbled years ago or had been "modernized" out of recognition, they settled on a rambling modern house on four acres that lay in a hollow bordered by a stream. Its shed and small meadow enthused horse-loving daughter Anne; however, its views of white pines surrounding the house was the trade for the desired mountain vista. Although comfortable and practical, the new home just didn't have the spirit of mountain living.

The local public school provided a bit of culture shock for Anne and Charlie. They "were astonished and pleased to find that if they left a sweater or book lying somewhere at high school by mistake, they would find it when they returned to hunt it." Academic standards were also different. After a year, Anne, who had previously attended an acclaimed private school, pleaded with her parents to send brother Charlie to Asheville School, a private boarding school on 300 acres where the academics were more challenging, for his last two years, even though she chose to finish at the local public school.

The Hallowells did not easily surrender their dream of a house with a mountain view. Instead, they modified the dream to something more likely to be found—like a few acres with a view of the mountains, a bit of woods, some open land, a stream or a pond, perhaps a shack. Eventually, Tom and Barbara found a worn-out farm with a comparable log house housing an elderly couple. They also got a half dozen or so automobiles that hadn't been drivable in recent memory.

A repairman suggested they demolish the house and start over, while an architect advised them to disassemble it, saw off the logs' bad ends, and build a new cabin from the shortened logs using plans he drew up for them. They discarded aspects of his design not in harmony with vernacular Appalachian architecture and hired a contractor who had wanted to build a log house. A year later, it was finished. It served as a great place for weekends, a place to hold nature and writing classes, and as a gathering place for the Hallowell children and friends when they were home.

With their children away at school, they traveled more and pursued their interests more fully, which included lots of observing nature. After Tom retired from DuPont on February 28, 1979, they had even more free time. Travel played a major part of the Hallowells' retirement and provided fodder for the talks they had begun in a small way in the late 1950s. Two days after Tom retired, they set off for a trip across the southwestern

United States. Later destinations included: Iceland, the Norwegian archipelago Spitsbergen, the Galapagos Islands, monarch butterfly wintering sites in Mexico, the Okefenokee Swamp in Georgia, East Africa, repeated trips to the Canadian Arctic (a favorite region), and multiple trips to the British Isles to study birds in Scotland, on the Shetlands, and Fair Isle plus an archaeological dig in Yorkshire.

Tom and Barbara put together nature and adventure travel talks from their mountains of 35 mm slides. Audiences included scouts, clubs, nature and botanical groups, museums, libraries, and schools. They presented featured programs for three consecutive years at the annual National Wildlife Federation's Blue Ridge Summit in Black Mountain, North Carolina. Both were on the teaching staff for five years in the 1980s: Tom leading bird walks and Barb teaching native fern classes. They presented programs in New York, New Jersey, Pennsylvania, Delaware, and Maryland, as well as North Carolina.

Some years they taught continuing education courses at the local junior college and they helped students develop skills of observation. For one exercise, Tom set up items out of place for students to identify along the quarter-mile lane that led to their cabin, such as white pine cones hanging on a hemlock tree or a large whelk shell nestled in a clump of hair-cap moss.

In 1980, Barbara was asked to write a field guide for identifying ferns of the Northeastern U. S. and Eastern Canada but didn't have the time to take on such a large undertaking. However, daughter Anne was looking for an interesting project between teaching assignments. When she heard about this project, she exclaimed, "*I'd* like to work with you on that." Anne lived and worked with her mother, co-writing and illustrating the book. Tom "test drove" their guide in the field and at home, providing valuable feedback which improved the book. *Fern Finder: A Guide to Native Ferns of Central and Northeastern United States and Eastern Canada* was released in 1981 and sold well. By 2000 DNA testing had reclassified several ferns, so Barbara produced a revised edition in 2001. *Fern Finders* continues to be popular.

For four years beginning in 1985, Barbara and Tom wrote a weekly 700-word column, "Nature Notes," that ran in the *Hendersonville Times-News*. Barbara wrote about acquiring and rebuilding the farm in *Cabin: A Mountain Adventure* published in 1986. She also authored *Mountain Year: A Southern Appalachian Nature Notebook* in 1998, discussing the plants, animals, and birds as found in that part of the country each month. This, her third book, won *ForeWord Magazine's* Book of the Year Award.

She spent time in 1988 and 1989 writing *Growing Up in Kennett: My First Fourteen Years*, an autobiographical essay about life and times in the 1920s and 30s and comparisons with life for children today. She also wrote a biography of her husband's father and a book about pets, both wild and domestic, that she and her children had had, all unpublished.

In October 1973, Barbara's mother, Ruth Craighead Gawthrop, moved to Kendal, a brand new continuing care retirement community adjacent to Longwood Gardens and Kennett Square. Tom and Barbara moved in on July 1, 1994, four months after Ruth died, when he was seventy-eight. He died from effects of Parkinson's Disease and Alzheimer's in 2009 at ninety-four. Barbara continues to work on putting his autobiography in book form and occasionally gives nature and travel programs at Kendal.

★ ★ ★

Peg Craighead continued to work for the adoption agency in Columbus, interviewing prospective parents, but quit when they started sending her around the state. She then worked as a librarian in Upper Arlington, Ohio until she died in 1979. Library staff planted a tree in her honor and held a balloon release for her.

Ruth Ann Craighead graduated from Ohio State University in 1958 with a bachelor's degree in elementary education. While on a skiing trip in Michigan during her first year out of college, Ruth met Richard Dale Muir. A graduate of Miami University of Ohio, he had finished his obligation to the Navy and was working for Minneapolis Honeywell in Columbus. The next year they married. Richard's relationship with the Muir naturalists, if any, has not been traced. Ruth and Richard set about raising a family in 1961 when son Scot Alan Muir was born. The year John Charles Muir was born, 1963, Ruth tucked a sheet of postage stamps commemorating the naturalist John Muir that came out that year into his baby book, where they remain. Sarah, their only daughter, arrived in 1967. Richard and Ruth didn't take the easiest route. She recalled a particularly stressful time:

"In 1983, we had four of us in school: Richard working on Doctorate at Hartford, Ruth at Boston College, Scot at Ohio Wesleyan, and John at Santa Cruz! To this day I don't know how we did it so can really relate with the Craigheads and all their struggles going through school."

Living far from Craighead, Ruth didn't go back there often, nor was she able to bring her children there with any regularity. In spite of this, her son John wrote a paper about Craighead Station and had his marriage blessing at Craighead.

Jim Craighead graduated from Grandview High School in 1963 and from Case Institute of Technology (known as Case Western Reserve University today) in Cleveland, Ohio in 1968. His graduation with a degree in applied mathematics marked the completion of undergraduate degrees by two complete generations of Craigheads. All five of Charles and Agnes's children graduated from college and all eleven grandchildren did, too. Few families can make that claim, particularly those of ordinary means. Jim married Carol Gabrielle Snyder, who graduated from Ohio State in 1967, and worked briefly for Proctor and Gamble in Cincinnati. They moved to Canada, making it their permanent home. Their two sons, Allan Eugene and Theodore Jack, were born in 1970 and 1971, respectively. Jim made his career working in the computer field, not with nature like so many other Craigheads, as his company designed software for the automotive design and film industries. However, when Bill Craighead needed help maintaining the old house in the 1980s, Jim and Carol stepped forward, became half-owners of the property, and paid to have maintenance performed. They also used it for a vacation home and brought their kids here. Their children and friends lent a Canadian flavor to the artwork on the kitchen walls.

One winter when Tom and Barbara Hallowell were staying on Sanibel Island in Florida, they took a nature walk along the two-mile-long boardwalk through Corkscrew Swamp near Naples. They came across a woman wearing a large sun hat sitting in a chair situated perfectly at a bend in the walk with her tripod-mounted telescope to focus on a barred owl about twenty feet away. When Barbara got closer, the woman shouted, "Barbie!" Barbara hadn't recognized the woman with close-cropped white hair as her next-to-youngest first cousin, Ruth Craighead Muir, because they hadn't seen in each other in some time.

In retirement in Lake Forest, Illinois, Ruth wrote, "I still carry a lot of curiosity within me and a love for nature. My husband and I monitor seventy-eight plus bluebird boxes at the moment and have a team of three others helping us. I am continually reading and learning and gardening—all three my favorite 'hobbies.'"

21

From Career to Legacy

I N NAPLES, FLORIDA, FRANK CRAIGHEAD CONTINUED some, but not all, of the work he'd started in Homestead and took on some new projects. Disney World was one of the projects he jettisoned due to the amount of driving it required. Horace Marden Albright, co-founder of the National Park Service, asked him to reconsider, "You were the ablest of the group, and we on the committee depended on you for advice more than on the Disney people." He also said committee members were full of remorse that Frank's needs had been overlooked and were willing to make amends and to provide him with any and all facilities he would need in the future.

Frank replied, "One phrase in your letter struck home with me, 'Nobody listens to me.' I left the E. N. P. [Everglades National Park] for that reason but am still getting in a few good licks as I publish my notes on over twenty years study....This gov't bureaucracy is destroying our parks and if it is not curtailed will destroy our nation."

Frank didn't slow down much. He loved to tell much younger reporters who were assigned to cover him in the field, "It's not my fault that I am 82, 83, or 84 plus. I can't help it if you can't keep up." He didn't let up on politicians, either. In a letter to Senator Lawton Chiles regarding pending legislation to shift control of the Florida Barge Canal to the Florida cabinet and governor, he wrote:

"This project, in my opinion, is one of the many costly adventures of the Army Corps [of Engineers] that will destroy one of the most scenic rivers in Florida. It is of questionable economic value and may prove to endanger the natural water system of the area.

"I also hope you can support President Carter's effort to curtail many of these Army projects throughout the United States.

"I have lived in Florida since 1950, and have spent these 26 years studying and writing about the destruction of the area's remarkable environment. Over 50% of my time during these years was spent in actual field work in the marshes, mangroves, and rivers of the area. During my 20 years as a collaborator of the Everglades National Park, I watched the progress of several projects that were costly and useless."

Even a cracked vertebra in his lower spine in 1973 didn't keep Frank down for long.

"When I think of my father, I see him standing in his canoe poling among the glistening blades of saw grass in the Florida Everglades. His trousers are wet from wading and he wears the expression of a man fulfilling his dreams," Jean wrote twenty years after his death.

As he aged, Frank's activities narrowed to tightly focus on those projects in which he was interested, paying little attention to anything else. In 1974, he wrote, "I have not been out of Florida since settling here over twenty years ago but once to visit Frank and John and their gang at Moose, Wyoming." Visitors not as keenly interested in his projects sometimes felt ignored or slighted. However, his children's interests often aligned with his: "This frequently brings them [his children] to Washington and hardly a month goes by that one or more of them doesn't stop in to discuss common problems." David Southall, Curator of Education at Collier County Museum in Naples, worked closely with Frank on several projects, recalling that Frank "had little patience for stupid or destructive people." His neighbors called him "Frank the Crank."

Around the same time, he wrote Jim Buckner, a grad student at the University of Florida, about dealing with the younger generation. "Having nine hippie grandchildren of our own, we are somewhat sympathetic to their problems in growing up, even though they are vastly different from our day."

Frank became an early authority on Collier County's freshwater supply and was among the first to take on what he called the "ridiculous" man-made over-draining of Golden Gate to allow development of that land. He tutored government planners about better water management techniques and the need to preserve native habitats to mixed results.

Frank and Carolyn bought a home in Estero Woods Village in nearby Estero, Florida. He thought the place would be more ethically managed because it was operated by a religious organization. A few months later, Jean got a call from her mother.

"Your dad thinks this place is corrupt," Carolyn said. "We are getting none of the services we were promised. There's no infirmary, no nurse, no dining room. Instead, we have a tennis court. And me and Dad almost eighty-four and the other people all over seventy."

Frank got on the phone. "Something is seriously wrong here," he said. "The manager of the village owns the construction company and landscaping company. He sells bonds to religious people all over the country and has a mansion of a place in Canada."

Carolyn took the phone. "Your dad is not well."

"I'll be down."

Estero Woods Village was soon in bankruptcy, forcing them to hustle to find a new place to live. With Frank's health failing and her mother aging, Jean helped them move into a condominium in Naples. When they left Estero, Frank donated the small building he had used for a lab to Collier County Museum where it remains, as does an orchid house, named after Carolyn because of her love of the beautiful flowers. Unfortunately, orchid thieves have picked the collection clean and Hurricane Wilma nearly destroyed the structure.

Frank received a number of awards during his "retirement:"

1957   The Pennsylvania State University School of Forestry—Forestry Achievement Award

1962   Gamma Sigma Delta, The Honor Society of Agriculture—For High Scholarship and Outstanding Achievement

1968   United States Department of the Interior—Conservation Service Award

1973   National Park Service—Honorary Park Ranger, Letter, Shield, and Plaque

1976   Proclamation by Governor Reubin Askew naming Frank Craighead as Scholar of the Everglades

1976   Collier County Board of Commissioners—Dr. Frank C. Craighead Day

Frank died on May 14, 1982 at the age of 91. Carolyn lived over a decade longer, enjoying good health. She died on April 12, 1993 at 103 years of age.

"Where he saw greed, stupidity, avarice and bureaucratic bungling, he fought them vigorously." Hal Scott, Florida Audubon Society Executive Director.

★ ★ ★

The twins' research on grizzlies continued in spite of their eviction from Yellowstone Park; they had tremendous amounts of data to analyze and numerous reports yet to write. However, as much writing was done about them as by them in the early 1970s. These laid-back naturalists had become minor celebrities—but celebrities with a mission. Syndicated columnist and a father of investigative journalism Jack Anderson and animal rights activists took up their cause, presenting them as well-meaning scientists being persecuted by the government. Soon *The New York Times* and *Washington Post* ran pieces about the dispute. Then members of Congress interceded by putting pressure on the Park Service's parent agency, the Department of the Interior.

While all this was going on back East, bears were dying in Yellowstone. Frank Jr. claimed, "In the years 1969 through 1972, there were a total of one hundred sixty known [grizzly bear] deaths, an average of thirty-two bears per year, with highs of forty-six and forty-five in 1970 and 1971, respectively." An accurate count of illegal kills during this time, although substantial, was unknown. He cited the bear-proofing of the West Yellowstone, Montana dump in 1971 as a gruesome reminder of the impact of closing a dump to bears. Nineteen grizzlies were relocated from that site, but all of them died before spring of the following year. Frank also pointed out an additional twelve known and four probable grizzly fatalities in West Yellowstone, just in 1971. The total number of bears killed in that year alone ranged from 43 to 48 (depending on the source) including Marian, their first radio-collared grizzly, and seventeen other bears they had tagged.

Feeling the heat from conservationists in 1973, the Secretary of the Interior requested the National Academy of Sciences to form a committee to sort out the mess. Ecologist Ian McTaggart Cowan, considered by most to be a disinterested observer of the fight, headed the committee. Instead of conducting new research, the committee gathered up all available information about the controversy from all sources they could find, noodled over it a good while, then issued their findings. Although gently stated, the report hammered the NPS, especially regarding the assumptions on which they based their bear management policies. Particularly troubling was that the NPS completely ignored the decade's worth of data the Craigheads had gathered and the conclusions they had drawn from it. The language used to admonish the NPS for the manner in which it conducted its own research was damning: "The research program carried out by the National Park Service administration since 1970 has been inadequate to provide the data essential for devising sound management policies for the grizzly bears of the Yellowstone ecosystem."

Cowan's committee supported the Craigheads' conclusion: there existed a single population of bears in Yellowstone, not two as the NPS claimed and accepted the twins' contention that their censuses had counted three-quarters of the population. It also supported their conservative policy on bear removal and insisted that marking was essential to conduct proper research. They did criticize some of the Craigheads' conclusions for having insufficient data—data they would have had if they had been allowed to continue their research.

In 1975, Cowan's committee reversed itself on the estimate of the bear population, this time accepting the NPS contention that only fifty-nine per cent of the bear population were found in dump censuses conducted by the Craigheads and that a significant number of bears that didn't frequent the dumps existed in the back-country. The report concluded with the recommendation that further research be conducted but by truly independent scientists. Because rangers had killed so many bears, grizzlies had to be placed on the Threatened Species List.

The new research committee was fraught with dissension from the first day. Its head, the headstrong and irascible Dick Knight, was renowned for being the opposite of diplomatic:

"Of *course* the agencies *all* say they want to save the grizzly bear. Every winter I sit through meetings with the Fish and Wildlife Service, the Forest Service, the Park Service, the states—I sit there till I'm sick of them, listening to everybody tell each other how great they're doing, saying, 'By God, I'm for the bear!' And they are, as long as it's easy. But let them come up against something that's difficult from a public-pressure standpoint—well, then the bear takes it. They doze him away."

With the dumps closed, the remaining grizzlies scattered to the far corners of the park. Without tagging and radio-tracking, taking a census was impossible, and Knight knew it. So, he didn't give population figures; he just gave trends. Eventually, officials demanded a number; he gave them 350.

In 1977, the NPS opened a new front by trying to force the twins to sell their land to the expanded Grand Teton National Park. Cousin Bill Craighead's property on Antelope Flats was also condemned under the façade of eminent domain and was eventually taken. Park Superintendent Bob Kerr's actions marked a departure from the previous willing-seller/willing-buyer policy. He justified his action by saying, "This is a national policy." Only public outcry prevented the passage of HR 5306, a bill that would have mandated the acquisition of all privately owned land within national parks in a three-year period. The revised bill deleted the mandated land purchase and passed but included an appropriation to buy private land. Kerr maintained that any development of unimproved land or expansion of living area of existing structures by what the Park Service called "inholders" would not be permitted. Local residents were concerned the NPS's action would increase already high land prices and taxes because less than three per cent of Teton County land was privately owned. Over ninety-seven percent was owned by various state and federal agencies and, as such, paid no taxes to support community services.

"We first purchased our land here 30 years ago when it wasn't even in the park,"

Frank said. "The land around us was made a park without even so much as a public hearing." Of the approximately 300,000 acres encircled by Grand Teton National Park boundaries at that time, about 300 acres of land within the expanded park boundaries were small parcels owned by a number of individuals; another 1,200 acres were owned by the State of Wyoming; and 3,000 acres were owned by John D. Rockefeller. It was the 300 acres of small parcels owned by ordinary citizens the NPS was most interested in controlling.

When Frank met with Kerr at park headquarters, he told him he had firm offers for his land in the $50,000 per acre range. NPS bureaucrats conducted their own "analysis" and came up with a price of $25,000 an acre. The NPS made a practice of finding a few inholders who could be intimidated into taking lower-than-market prices for their land and then claiming these low prices were the true market values of the properties. Frank called the government 'socialist' for its interfering ways; supposedly conservative Senator Clifford Hansen of Wyoming, Energy Committee chair, approved the lower price.

The National Park Inholders Association (NPIA) was formed to represent people in the Craigheads' situation across the country. Frank's wife, Esther, served on the Advisory Board as a representative for Grand Teton National Park inholders. One of the purposes of the NPIA's newsletter was to inform inholders of government abuses to inholders:

"Harassment

Grand Teton: *Newsweek* quotes park residents as saying the Park Service deliberately did not remove snow from the roads as a penalty for the citizens of Kelly signing a petition to withdraw from Grand Teton. In addition, the Park Service has been accused of blocking access to people's property and of intimidating real estate brokers who wanted to list property by threatening future buyers with condemnation."

"Waste and Mismanagement

Grand Teton, Olympic and many other parks: The Park Service condemns or pressures people into selling because their property is 'desecrating' the public land and at the same time built new housing subdivisions for employees, many times only a mile or two from the park boundary. Clearly, as stated in the Congressional Record by Senator Stevens, this is a double standard."

"Tactics

Buffalo and Grand Teton: held down prices by intimidating local real estate sales people."

The newsletter listed numerous other tactics employed at most locations by the NPS to separate landowners from their property, too lengthy to repeat here. However, one example involved the Craigheads:

"Whenever a ranger gets in trouble, like Merl Brooks in Voyageurs or Robert Lunger in Grand Teton, they move him up the ladder to another park as quickly as possible. Mr. Lunger failed to testify eleven (11) times in a deposition in the John Craighead condemnation trial in Grand Teton and a few weeks later he was gone (moved up to a better position in Washington)."

To make matters more difficult, Frank's cabin burned to the ground in the middle of the winter of 1978. Because it was located a quarter of a mile from a plowed road, with a lot of snow on the ground, firemen couldn't get to it to put out the blaze. Frank lost priceless photos, notes, and reports but, worst of all, he lost most of the background data for a NASA pilot study to develop satellite transmitters to be used in tracking birds. No longer having a cabin created more problems than not having a place to live, he would have to get a permit to rebuild from the NPS. And that wouldn't be obtained without a battle. A month after the fire, Esther wrote a friend, "We will definitely rebuild something when the snow melts since a house here is about as good an investment as we could make, and with the cloudy Park situation we'd better build while we can."

By November 1978, after a year of fighting the NPS, it was clear to the Craigheads they would have to resort to using the law to defend themselves from NPS actions: "We bought our land here in 1946. The park service said it wasn't interested in it, but four years later they surrounded us. The only way to fight this is to take them to court. Park policies are unfair and illegal in many cases, but we have to take them to court to prove it."

Even the government doesn't have an infinite amount of money to spend, and Teton real estate is very expensive. When the White House changed hands in January 1981, the NPS was put on an austerity program and couldn't afford to buy pricey Teton land. In the fifteen years beginning in 1966, the NPS had acquired land from 70,000 families. A December 1979 GAO report documented that the NPS already had more land than it could manage effectively. The Reagan administration had little appetite for ingesting more land it couldn't afford or maintain properly.

Frank eventually got permission to rebuild a cabin similar to his original one, but his life had changed dramatically by this time. Esther was stricken with cancer and died in 1980. Grizzlies and land and cabins had to take a back seat to what was happening in his life.

Ear-tagging and radio-tracking of grizzly bears was slowly reinstituted at Yellowstone

Park, albeit by researchers not named Craighead or their disciples, and data accumulated anew. Regrettably, humans continued to cause bears to be killed at a higher rate than grizzlies reproduce, causing researchers to revise census numbers downwards. In 1981, Knight said, "Last year, I was giving twenty or thirty years until the Yellowstone grizzly would be extinct or a remnant. This year I'm going to be more pessimistic....I'd say the way things are going, the future of the grizzly as we know it is bleak." The next summer, Knight and team accepted the fact that fewer than 200 grizzlies remained in Yellowstone Park. Their estimates came close to the Craigheads' original estimations. Frank and John were vindicated, but it was a pyrrhic victory because the bears were now facing total annihilation.

In the midst of the NPS condemnation battle, John called Jean, very upset Frank had written and was publishing results of the grizzly study on his own. All their lives, they had jointly written the results of any work they did together. Then sixty, Frank was expressing his individuality. Fortunately for him, he had already shipped the manuscript and photos for *Track of the Grizzly* to the publisher, Sierra Book Club, when his cabin burned to the ground, contents and all. Jean advised John to write something of his own. He did. John's son Johnny thought it was just another squabble like the numerous others the brothers had had since they were kids. Although deeply hurt, John never stopped talking to Frank. They each set up a non-profit organization dedicated to the study of nature and undertook projects on their own.

Frank and John continued to work and write, mostly separately but sometimes together. The grizzly population at Yellowstone rebounded, thanks in large part by the NPS's heeding the suggestions the twins had made years earlier. But the ground between the Craigheads and the NPS had been salted so badly that the twins viewed everything done at Yellowstone with skepticism. NPS employees began calling them crackpots—but not to their faces.

After living on his own several years after Esther's death, Frank married a school teacher from Vermont named Shirley Cocker in 1987. Frank was diagnosed with Parkinson's disease, but John wasn't. Because this was the first major illness one of the twins had by himself, some conjectured that a bump on his head while escaping from an angry grizzly years early or his exposure to radiation in the desert may have made him susceptible to Parkinson's disease. He and John even participated in a study of twins conducted in England. He and Shirley worked together to write his last book, *For Everything There is a Season: The Sequence of Natural Events in the Grand Teton-Yellowstone Area.*

Frank and Shirley lived life together as best they could during Frank's long illness, but the disease finally claimed him on October 21, 2001. With Shirley's loving care, he was able to live at home in his cabin overlooking the Tetons all but the last few months of his life. When the end was near, John didn't know what to do and felt helpless. His daughter Karen suggested, "Just be with him, Dad." The two who had thought as one much of their lives silently held hands. Jana eulogized her father, saying, "I am very concerned that we are not leaving the planet in very good shape for future generations. I fear my step-children, nieces and nephews and their children will not have the opportunities I had. My love of nature came from my dad and it is the greatest gift he could have given me."

John's hearing degraded to the point of near deafness as he aged, but he continued to enjoy good health almost to the end when he died in his sleep on Sunday morning, September 18, 2016, a month after his one hundredth birthday. Margaret, four years John's junior and his wife of seventy years, stayed in the house on a dead-end street in Missoula that had been their home for decades, dying barely two weeks later on October 3, 2016. Their son Johnny lives nearby and served diligently as their caregiver. Their daughter, Karen and her husband, Robert Haynam, live in the cabin John built in Moose shortly after WWII. Shirley lives in the cabin Frank rebuilt after the fire.

During their retirement years, Frank and John received numerous awards, most jointly, but a few individually. Following are a few of the honors that were bestowed on them:

1988 National Geographic Society: Centennial Award

1998 The Wildlife Society: Aldo Leopold Award (John)

2000 Audubon Society: Champions of Conservation

2000 Society for Conservation Biology: Distinguished Service Award (John)

North American Falconers Association: S. Kent Carnie NAFA-TAF Heritage Award

University of Montana: John J. Craighead Chair in Wildlife Biology

2006 The Wyoming Wildlife Foundation: Wyoming Outdoor Hall of Fame

★ ★ ★

Jean's next book, *Everglades Wildguide*, was published by the National Park Service in 1972, the same year *Julie of the Wolves* was released and the year after her father's book, *The Trees of South Florida*, was released. Jean, who had always been seeking, but seldom receiving, praise from her perfectionist father, complimented him on his latest book, "Your book is a stunner, the writing beautiful. I can't put it down." He complimented her by keeping a letter he received from Marilyn Kriney, then with publisher Thomas Y. Crowell, who wrote, "Now everything I know about what good writing is, I have learned from Jean!"

Most writers earn little or nothing; only a tiny handful get rich. Even highly successful writers like Jean Craighead George often struggle to make ends meet. In her divorce settlement, John got the stocks and bonds, Jean got the car; Jean lost the royalties from the books she co-authored with John; Jean got the family home in Chappequa but owed the mortgage. John later landed a teaching job at Penn State he kept until retirement.

A tax bill jolted Jean to accept the reality that the village of Quakers and summering New Yorkers in which she had settled had changed into a bedroom community for highly-paid executives in tony Westchester County. Keeping her children clothed, fed, and housed in that town was more than a full-time job for a free-lance writer. Seeing no way to pay the ever-increasing taxes and keep her family together at the same time, she put her house on the market. Afterwards, she walked home and dropped to her knees on the sheepskin rug next to Twig, who was warming herself at the fireplace:

"'Things are getting tough,' I said. 'I'm going to stop freelancing, sell the house, and take a job.'

"'Don't do that,' Twig said emphatically. 'We are used to feast and famine.'

"Feast and famine; that's exactly what it was, pulling in the belt one month, and going off to the lakes and rivers the next. Twig always had been a perceptive child; now she had verbalized the ecological niche to which we had become adapted: feast and famine. I surely was not going to take a nine-to-five job with that kind of support."

While researching black bears in the vicinity of Clingman's Dome in the Smoky Mountains in North Carolina for another book, oncoming hikers told Jean of a bear a quarter mile ahead on the trail. Knowing black bears aren't usually nearly as dangerous as their grizzly cousins, she made mental preparations to stop at a safe distance to sketch the bear as she continued to walk forward. Rounding a bend in the trail, she encountered an aggressive black bear. When she smelled his greasy body odor she changed course:

"There is today a branch of the Appalachian Trail that originally left the main path about twenty feet in front of the bear. It descends the mountain, then circles back up, about half a mile from where it began. I carved out that trail, at a dead run."

In spite of that scare, Jean wrote the first significant discussion of the Appalachian Trail in *The American Walk Book*. But scarier things than bears faced mothers of that era. When Jean was growing up, middle-class people using drugs was unheard of and girls in her circle seldom risked pregnancy outside of marriage. Alcohol was illegal until she was thirteen, and her parents didn't drink. Alcohol and free love quickly became lesser issues for her as drug use became rampant. Unprepared to deal with the onslaught of drugs tempting suburban teenagers at that time, Jean consulted with experts and friends and developed her own approach to parenting her children through the gauntlet of marijuana, LSD, and heroin. One of her novel approaches was to purchase the first color television in town as a means of making her home a magnet for her kids' friends. Keeping them close and in view, coupled with seeing friends harm themselves seriously were Jean's strategies for keeping her kids off drugs.

Jean in reflection along the Yellow Breeches
(Richard Ammons)

Being inquisitive Craigheads, Twig, Craig, and Luke gave Jean her share of worries, but avoided doing really stupid things and became the sort of people she'd hoped they'd become. Better yet, they all carry the Craighead naturalist gene. Jean celebrated her son's decision and was amused by his idealism when she wrote her father, "Craig is in Utah State! He is going to be an ecological engineer—make smokeless bonfires, edible tin and beer cans, fertilizing paper, pollution control house."

Craigheads are not navel-gazers; they are people of action and accomplishment. So, when Jean wrote *Journey Inward*, "a story of self-discovery," the story of her life from the end of WWII to 1982 that focused largely on her marriage, she displeased family and friends. They didn't disown her or confront her about it; they were just unhappy she wrote it.

Jean continued writing, researching, and writing some more. In celebration of her eightieth birthday in 1999, the clan assembled at Craighead for the first time since before WWII. Jean painted a bear in one of the few white spaces remaining on the kitchen wall. Adjacent to it, Craig painted a bow whale, an animal he's made his life's work studying.

Jean enjoyed good health and hoped to outlive her mother, who lived to be 103, although she began having difficulty walking and climbing when she was in her early 90s. A sore on her leg refused to heal, making a skin graft necessary. On May 15, 2012, Jean died of congestive heart failure at ninety-two years of age, but her writing career didn't end. She had completed books at the time of her death that, due to the efforts of Twig and Craig, were published afterwards. A Celebration of Jean Craighead George's Life was held in her honor on Sunday, November 11, 2012 in a packed auditorium of the Robert E. Bell Middle School in Chappaqua. The assembled crowd hushed after quite a number of friends and colleagues spoke for two hours about their experiences with Jean. Atka, a white wolf Jean had befriended at the Wolf Conservation Center in South Salem, New York fittingly took center stage as guest of honor and closed the ceremony.

The following Wednesday, with cousin Bill Craighead and friend David Masland sadly looking on, Jean's children spread her ashes across the Yellow Breeches Creek from the railroad bridge beside her ancestral home at Craighead Station where she had spent so many happy days in her youth.

APPENDIX

What it Means to be a Craighead

DURING THE COURSE OF DOING THE RESEARCH FOR THIS BOOK, it became evident that the Craigheads were no ordinary family. Family members were asked what it means to be a Craighead (whether they carried the name or not). The responses varied from lengthy, thoughtful answers to ignoring the question. The author's opinion is that Craigheads are doers not navel gazers. They immerse themselves fully in their activities and don't self-psychoanalyze every success and failure. They focus on accomplishing things.

Once, Jean Craighead George told the author, "You know more about us than we know about ourselves."

I responded, "All five of your father's generation graduated from college at a time when most people didn't go to high school."

"I thought that was normal and was just expected," she said.

This appendix consists of the answers given by those family members, followed by statements from the son of a friend who was influenced by them. Their answers and statements are not put in quotes because virtually everything was written by them. Author's interjections are in italics to differentiate them from Craigheads' actual responses.

Ruth Ann Craighead Muir

The last of your questions was the most difficult to reflect upon as I think the influence of the Craighead family was very intertwined with who I am. To tease out the specifics is a challenge, but let's give it a try. My being adopted was never a negative issue with my immediate family. They had told me I was adopted from the time I can remember. In fact they emphasized I was CHOSEN, that they had wanted me very much, and I have carried that feeling of being cherished all my life. I indeed feel grateful for somehow, and I know no details of my birth family, falling into this wonderful, interesting and talented family. My parents were loving and caring, and I had an idyllic childhood when I look back. I also gained an inquiring curiosity from my parents and the extended family around me. Although we didn't see them a lot, the Craighead scientific and environmental bent was there. I heard about it, saw some of it and read about it through Uncle Frank's writings, John, Frank and Jean's adventures and articles for the *Nat'l Geographic*, books and videos and TV specials and the interests of my own father in photography, the constellations (he knew them all) the bugs and creatures I would bring to him to identify and we would search together to answer my questions. Both parents encouraged my learning. My mother played the piano and wanted me to also. I did play but never reached her level of that skill! My father would let me come with him to his labs in the bowels of the Institute, sometimes in the evening, through tunnels and labyrinths to check on his experiments there. I remember huge vats with gauges and dials and mysterious lights and his taking notes on what he found there.

So, from all the family I was learning about the world I lived in and that observation was a way of life and interacting, recording and paying attention were part of being human. I still carry a lot of curiosity within me and love for nature. My husband and I monitor 78+ bluebird boxes at the moment and have a team of three others helping us. I am continually reading and learning and gardening—all three my favorite "hobbies."

Two years later, she added the following:

I thought on your question about capturing the essence of the Craigheads and two things stuck in my mind. I think it was Uncle Frank who once told me we are only on the earth a short time and stewards of the earth, so we should try to leave it better than we found it. That seems to fit every Craighead I have known—a sincere connection with the planet and nature. The second quality seems to me to be a huge innate CURIOSITY that permeated all that they did. I have often read in my child development course work that curiosity is one of the most steady predictors of a fulfilling and adventurous life. That seems also to fit everything I know about this gang. And what is interesting to me personally is that I have been adopted into two families—first my Craighead family and later the Muir family which gave me a link to another American naturalist, John Muir. Although we have never traced a specific link to THE John Muir, he has also become a hero of our family and by nurture, (not nature—genetics) I have come to see a further extension in this generation of his ideas. The year our son, John Muir was born, a commemorative stamp of John Muir was issued. That sheet of stamps is still in his baby book!

Bill Craighead

1. What does it mean to be a Craighead?

I'm proud to be a Craighead because of my heritage. Many of Scotch-Irish ancestors were Presbyterian ministers. So many of them became so (ministers) that I have in my posession a genealogy of Craighead Presbyterian Ministers.

They came to America in the middle to late 1600s and settled in the Philadelphia and Chambersburg, PA areas. One minister, by the name of John Craighead of the Rocky Spring Church in Chambersburg, challenged his congregation to go with him when he was going to join Washington's Army during the Revolutionary War.

Craigheads are known to have had slaves but they also helped during the underground railroad, to help free the slaves (The Emancipation Proclamation). It is not surprising to find black people with the name of Craighead. I have met some of them in both Harrisburg and Philadelphia.

2. What are the Craighead traits that make them different from Smiths, Jones or Rockefellers?

Ambitious, self reliant, strong-minded, caring, opinionated, competitive, ambitious, intelligent and well-educated, and self-reliant.

3. In what ways do you think you are typically Craighead?

Small in stature, interested in sports, fishing and hunting, nature and the environment.

4. In what ways are you not typically Craighead?

You've got me here.

Barbara Hallowell

Whew! You ask a tough question. I have always wondered myself, but never got very far when asking my mother:

"Oh, we were just outdoors a lot, country living, living on the creek and farm and all. The fellows were interested in creek creatures as bait for fishing and simply as interesting creatures. Of course, interest ran to the fish they were catching, too, how they lived and their biology.

"Mother was a great gardener, very involved in keeping it blossoming through the seasons. And she had a flock of chickens which she loved. They'd talk to her and she to them. They were friends."

Yet Mother gave no details about what kind of flowers, any other animal/bird affiliations, etc. Mother described how "we," which included girls as well as boys, tied long threads to the bodies of big bumblebees that did not sting and then let them fly off, only to be retrieved. Grandmother Craighead (Agnes) let the kids go swimming in the creek even during thunderstorms, seeming unconcerned about any danger. "She loved a thunderstorm and got me to loving them, too," said Mother—and she passed that along to me, an incorrigible storm watcher, though with great respect for the electricity involved. My kids stayed INside during them, but as soon as the electricity passed, I encouraged them to splash in puddles and mud in their bare feet. I also inherited Agnes's love of chickens, having had them at every home where I could.

Uncles Frank and Gene were interested in insects and birds. Most kids are, if given a chance. Parents squelch many budding naturalists. Probably John Craighead or Bill Craighead could answer how Frank and Gene got so interested. My parents' generation certainly passed it all along to our generation, as we all have passed it on to our kids. So—I suspect there was a whole lot of curiosity and investigation that went on in those imaginative minds that, apparently encouraged by parents—or if not ENcouraged, at least not DIScouraged—became not just a hobby but a lifetime work.

I never heard anyone mention Grandfather Charles's interests of any sort. I think he was so swamped with trying to keep afloat and raise five kids through college, etc. Again, maybe my cousins can fill in some.

My mother Ruth was not vastly knowledgeable of nature <u>facts</u>, though she reveled in botany courses at Swarthmore and dissected a cadaver and eventually taught biology along with her Latin. But she had one VERY IMPORTANT trait which certainly got me started—she had intense appreciation of the outdoor world. I suspect that Agnes had the same but do not know, nor do I know anything in that line about Charles C. C. The <u>two major characteristics</u> which seem to pervade the whole clan are great <u>curiosity</u> and keen <u>observation</u>. As a leader of nature walks through the years, I had uncountable comments like, "I can't believe all you see when you go out!" Though not all of my eleven grands are nature oriented, they at least are all good observers, as are their Hallowell parents, all Craighead descendents. The in-laws have not been helpful with encouraging this, nice as they are. It's just not in their upbringing. Both Tom, my husband, and I have been notably observant, and all three of our grown children are.

Too, Mother, with infinite patience and much interest, let me indulge in a WIDE variety of pets as a child and teenager, and I was encouraged by an elderly lady (probably younger than I am now!) with Mother and Dad's support—he constructed a wonderful shade control mechanism for it—to have a quite extensive (for a 11-15 year old) wild flower garden. Mother taught nature at a camp in Maine one summer, my sister and I as campers there, and from that I fell in love with ferns—at age 9! I ended up writing what is now a highly popular little pocket guide for native ferns of central and eastern US and eastern Canada—co-authored with my daughter. As a child, I was always wondering what would happen if—e.g. if I buried that robin I found dead. I dug it up a week or so later and was revolted to find it a mass of maggots! But I learned! What if I plant the seed I found in my grapefruit—it had a wee sprout. I did. It grew for five years to about four feet tall until, when we went away for several weeks, the house caretaker did not understand he was to water it. He felt AWFUL, for he loved growing things.

Our Craighead clan was encouraged to look and find out and try it out, and I feel that is the heart of the Craighead nature bent. Get an idea and pursue it, with parents encouraging. Even before I was in high school I had trained a falcon, raised a laughing gull chick to maturity, had a burrowing owl for two years and wrote an article on it for *Nature Magazine,* raised tropical fish in a room in our attic, made a collection of nearly 100 pressed wild flowers, raised canaries in my patient mother's dining room, etc.etc. How lovely it was to have no texting devises, Blackberrys, TV, cell phones, etc. to keep me occupied!!!!

I could go on and on, but that's more than enough! It all boils down to the fact that I do not know <u>what</u> my grandparents did to instill such a love of the outdoor world in their descendents, but whatever it was, it was GOOD, it worked, and I appreciate it! It has given me a happy life—and yes, my husband was a naturalist, too, though his work was as an organic chemist for DuPont. But our many trips all concentrated on natural history. What a wonderful time we had together! Now, I'll start to cry! Yes, I sure do miss him.

Barbara wrote this less than three months after her husband, Tom Hallowell, died after a long illness with both Parkinson's disease and Alzheimer's.

As I mull it over now, as I have many times before, I feel that Agnes and Charlie must have enjoyed the outdoors themselves and just let the five kids take it all in by osmosis rather than first hand teaching. I don't know. That's simply my hunch.

Well, maybe this might be a wee bit of help to you. I find it delightful to think on!

Jean Craighead George

From my Scotch Craighead ancestors I have inherited a sense of "clan" and enjoy the comradeship it brings with it. People write me that they are "Craigheads" and I bond with them.

Our branch of the family feels particularly good about being a "Craighead" in that we have a written genealogy that tells about Craigheads who were ministers and preaching for "the revolution and later anti-slavery."

Most of those ancestors were successful, and so are most Craigheads today, which makes one proud. They are MDs, scientists, writers, teachers, as well as successful Bohemians. We love the rebellious members of the clan and learn from them.

What really ties us together, however, is the image of those beautiful homes in the Cumberland Valley of Pennsylvania, their lands, waters and skies. As for me, it's specifically that house at Craighead Station. It means "Craighead."

Jean was asked the question in separate parts to allow her to focus on specific aspects of being a Craighead during a time she was particularly busy at ninety years of age. The second part of the question asked how Craigheads are different from the Smiths, Jones, and Rockefellers. The third and fourth parts are obvious from her answers.

We are not much different from the Jones with the exception of our liking to think of things slightly outrageous and doing them. For instance; painting on the kitchen walls, initiating the first animal tracking of grizzly bears by radio, writing non-anthropomorphic animal books, living twenty years in the Arctic, being the first of the America falconers, mapping the Potomac River islands, keeping a black snake in the walls of the house, dumping water through a register in the living room ceiling at Craigheads on an unsuspecting person, and encouraging the bees that made a hive under the bathroom window at Craigheads to chase us around the yard by getting them periodically mad at us.

All these things and more—and then—get this—being surprised that anyone thought these deeds were not the norm.

Those 3rd and 4th questions are hard to answer. I'll try.

3. I am typically Craighead in that I have energy, complete things I've started, like people, and stir up fun. (used to)

4. I'm not like a Craighead in that I had a career as a woman. Most Craighead women had to mind the hearth, even in my generation. The generation after me are breaking the crystal ceiling. Also I am more liberal. The Craigheads were conservatives—at least my folks' generation were.

David Yates

During the last years of Dad's [John Yates] life, he often had me drive them to Craighead Station to revisit one of his favorite childhood places where many fond memories would be recalled. My father's father was a Presbyterian minister and Dad's sister Ruth had a long-term childhood malady that required she sleep outdoors for fresh air. The family had an outdoor porch constructed for Ruth. Their neighbor in Harrisburg, PA, also a minster, owned a stone home on the Yellow Breeches Creek—across the creek from Craighead Station—with a suitable porch. The family doctor advised "country air" for Ruth and arrangements were made to rent the stone home for entire summers.

Dad and sisters Ruth and Dorothy became good friends with John, Frank, and Jean Craighead. Dad raised and trained a Sparrow Hawk, which would join the row of raptors at Craighead Station. Some of Dad's fondest memories were of summer evenings spent gathered around the piano singing songs. As a young lad, I was in awe of John's and Frank's adventures detailed in *National Geographic* and seen on TV while studying Grizzly Bears in Yellowstone. One episode that stands out clearly was John and Frank being chased by a Grizzly that came out from its anesthetic stupor too rapidly. One brother ran to their station wagon while the other dove into their home-made bear-trap and tripped the catch to slam shut the trap-door. The Grizzly took on the station wagon and Craighead continued filming from within while driving off to escape.

Hearing those stories first-hand during summer picnics at Craighead Station was a remarkable experience for me. You can see Dad's Princeton College art on the kitchen wall and Aunt Dot's D.Y. initials (she clearly recalls Jean Craighead encouraging her to sign the wall) near the end-wall door. During those last visits with Mom and Dad to Craighead Station, we would peer through the windows while Dad would regale us with his memories. In my mind's eye, I could see and hear the ivories being tickled and those young men and women whose lives were yet to be lived laughing and singing once again.

MEMORIES OF CRAGHEAD

(Tune - It Ain't Gonna Rain No More)

1. Oh, the Yellow Breeches Creek flows down
    Right past the Craghead's door
    It's not so deep 'cause Bill can wade
    Across from shore to shore.

    It starts up to the Westward
    Where the injuns use to roam
    And wanders slowly downward
    Right past the Masland's home.

    Chorus

    Oh, it ain't gonna rain no more, no more
    It ain't gonna rain no more
    For another inch or two will put
    It on the kitchen floor.

2. On a summer night when the moon shown bright
    The frogs made too much noise
    So Gene and Merve took the old canoe
    And I think they took the boys.

    And the very next night was just as bright
    But the Creek was very quiet
    And the neighbors said that Gene and Merve
    Were on a frogleg's diet.

    Chorus

    Oh, it ain't gonna rain no more, no more
    It ain't gonna rain no more
    That bullfrog made his last mistake
    When he croaked at half past four.

3. Oh, the bees are making honey
    Right near the bathroom seat
    It wouldn't be so bad except
    They seem to like fresh meat.

    There's Carolyn and Myra
    And also Peg and Ruth
    Four finer girls you never found
    Underneath one roof.

    They're always bright and cheerful
    They always tell the truth
    They'd like to please those doggone bees
    But they're not puncture proof.

    Chorus

    Oh, it ain't gonna rain no more, no more
    It ain't gonna rain no more
    Those bees can't read the "Keep Out" sign
    That's on the bathroom door.

4. The kitchen walls at first were blue
    Then later they were white
    Then the artists took a crack at them
    And now they're quite a sight.

    There are fish and rats and dogs and cats
    And a lady with a towel
    And Spike is there so true to life
    You can almost hear him howl.

Chorus

Oh, it ain't gonna rain no more, no more
It ain't gonna rain no more
The twins arrived with one lone hawk
And now they each have four

5. At the house party there were things to see
    And also sounds to hear
    Louise and Zim jumped into bed
    Thinking Gene was nowhere near.

    And the croquet balls rolled down the stairs
    And then out the front door
    But the strangest sound we heard that night
    Was Herbert Schaffner's snore.

    Chorus

    Oh, it ain't gonna rain no more, no more
    It ain't gonna rain no more
    That's not the thunder that you hear
    It's Herbert Schaffner's snore.

6. Oh, Bob Moorhear swung on the swing
    He was having lots of fun
    Till Villa said "I'll show you
    How it should be done".
    She swung back to the dock again
    But forgot what to do.

    So she swung back o'er the water
    A large part of her got wet
    If it hadn't been for Eddie
    She'd be swinging out there yet.

    Eddie was a hero
    He jumped in with all his clothes
    He saved her from a watery grave
    As everybody knows.

    Then Isabel yelled "It's ready"
    And we knew t'was time to eat
    Villa hurried up the stairs
    She had to dry her feet.

    As we ate our steaks and onions
    Our belts grew good and tight
    And we gathered round the fireplace
    As the evening turned to night.

    Then Charlie stepped up to the front
    His voice was strong and fine
    He said "Let's sing that good old song
    I mean 'Sweet Adeline' ".

    So we all raised up our voices
    We made the welkin ring
    The natives stopped for miles around
    Said "Hark the angels sing".

    Chorus

    Oh, it ain't gonna rain no more, no more
    It ain't gonna rain no more
    For the sun is shining down upon
    The Craghead's open door.

D. C. '53

BIBLIOGRAPHIC NOTES

PART I Who Are the Craigheads?

The dates of discussions of the Craigheads with friends and neighbors occurring before the start of work on this book were not recorded at the time and the sources have since died.

"The trip with the twins…," interview of David S. Masland, December 14, 2009

While doing some genealogical work, The Descendants of Charles Cooper Craighead (1849-1926) and Agnes Alberta Miller (1859-1924), Barbara G. Hallowell

Jean mentioned her hypothesis, interview of Jean Craighead George, September 30, 2009

"You know more about us…," conversation with Jean Craighead George, May 20, 2011

Their first National Geographic article, Life with an Indian Prince, Frank Jr. & John Craighead, Archives of American Falconry, Boise, Idaho, 2001, xv

1. The Dangerous Boys Train Their First Hawks

The bulk of the information for this chapter was derived from the twins' notes in the Afterword and Addendum to *Hawks in the Hand: Adventures in Photography and Falconry,* Frank Jr. & John Craighead, Lyons & Burford, 1997. These sections were not included in the original 1939 edition.

Today, the 100-mile trip, email conversation with Jean Craighead George, April 1-6, 2011

becoming minor celebrities, The [Washington] Evening Star, November 20, 1933, D-4

set the city-wide record, The [Washington] Evening Star, May 25, 1932, 32

2. Craigheads Come to Pennsylvania

"From my Scotch…," Jean Craighead George essay on what it means to be a Craighead, March 24, 2010

Truman, David McCullough, Simon & Shuster, 1992, 16

"…and terrible businessmen." interview of Jean Craighead George, September 30, 2009

Background on the Scots-Irish came from *Albion's Seed: Four British Folkways in America,* David Hackett Fischer, 1989, Oxford University Press

Genealogical information on Rev. Thomas Craighead and his descendants was found in *The Craighead Family: A Genealogical Memoir of Descendants of Rev. Thomas and Margaret Craighead, 1658—1876,* Rev. James Geddes Craighead, 1876

Information regarding Rev. Thomas Craighead's service to Presbyterian churches in Pennsylvania was derived from Early History of the First Presbyterian Church or Meeting House of Carlisle, Pennsylvania: Congregation from 1730 or '34 to 1757, Church from 1757 to 1835, Samuel Line Huston, 1921 and History of the Big Spring Presbyterian Church, Newville, Pennsylvania, 1737—1898, Gilbert Ernest Swope, 1898.

Information regarding Rev. John Craighead's service was found in History of Rocky Spring Church and Addresses Delivered at the Centennial Anniversary of the Present Edifice, August 23, 1894, Wylie S. S, & Pomeroy, A. Nevin, 1895.

Information about Craigheads in the Revolutionary War was found in *Presbyterians in the Revolution,* W. P. Breed, 1876.

Information regarding property ownership was found in Will of Thomas Craighead, 1803, Cumberland County Court House, Cumberland County, Pennsylvania and Patent Index and 1700s Tax Lists, Bosler Memorial Library, Carlisle, Pennsylvania.

3. Charles and Agnes Craighead

Location and route of South Mountain Railroad was documented in *Atlas of Cumberland County Pennsylvania: From Actual Surveys By and Under the Direction of F. W. Beers,* F. W. Beers & Company, New York, 1872.

Genealogical information about John Weakley Craighead found in *The Craighead Family: A Genealogical Memoir of Descendants of Rev. Thomas and Margaret Craighead, 1658—1876*, Rev. James Geddes Craighead, 1876

"very deep thinker…," Eugenics Record Number 57576, 8

"very hospitable…," Eugenics Record Number 57576, 8

Richard Reynolds Craighead's military record found in *History of the Pennsylvania Volunteers, 1861-65*, Samuel P. Bates, Harrisburg, 1868-1871

Description of the railroad right-of-way purchase is found in Releasle from John W. Craighead to South Mountain Iron Company, December 24, 1868, Cumberland County Court House, Carlisle, Pennsylvania.

Post-Civil War occupants of Mansion Farm identified from 1870 and 1880 Federal Censuses.

"common school," Eugenics Record Number 57576, 5

Junior partner, [Harrisburg] *Patriot*, August 25, 1886

Ruth recalled, The Descendants of Charles Cooper Craighead (1849-1926) and Agnes Alberta Miller (1859-1924), Barbara G. Hallowell

A source of willing workers, The Red Man and Helper, November 14, 1902

Decades later, email conversation with Jean Craighead George, December 23, 2009

"of good business qualities…," Eugenics Record Number 57576, 8

Daughter Ruth, The Descendants of Charles Cooper Craighead (1849-1926) and Agnes Alberta Miller (1859-1924), Barbara G. Hallowell

PART II Focus on Education

4. Rebecca Craighead

was born at home in 1888, The Descendants of Charles Cooper Craighead (1849-1926) and Agnes Alberta Miller (1859-1924), Barbara G. Hallowell

In November, 1902 [Harrisburg] *Patriot*, November 20, 1902, 3

"Nature is God's Mirror," Carlisle High School Commencement program, June 14, 1906

Class of 1910, Matriculation Records, Dickinson College

"When she first…" 1911 *Microcosm*, 62

secret handshake, letter from Bessie Craighead to Ethelyn Merriken Hardesty, May 19, 1902

Pi Beta Phi, The Dickinsonian, May 8, 1912, 3

"Greek, Latin, nature," Eugenics Record Number 57576, 5

"She is always…" 1911 *Microcosm*, 62

"He often calls…" 1911 *Microcosm*, 65

dominie, a Scottish word for teacher or minister

"Foggy" 1911 *Microcosm*, 62

"Just why Hanover…" 1911 *Microcosm*, 65

After three years, Faculty Minutes, Dickinson College, 1906-1909

Netcong, First Annual Letter of the Class of 1910, Dickinson College, 1916

On May 23, 1913, The Descendants of Charles Cooper Craighead (1849-1926) and Agnes Alberta Miller (1859-1924), Barbara G. Hallowell

Rebecca returned, Harrisburg City Directory, 1912, 1913

she married Findlay, The Dickinsonian, April 22, 1914, 5

One such event [Harrisburg] *Patriot*, January 31, 1913, 3

Portraying herself as being engaged [Harrisburg] *Patriot*, January 3, 1913, 7

On April 2, Rebecca resigned [Harrisburg] *Patriot*, April 3, 1914, 6

This revelation created such a scandal… Philadelphia Inquirer, April 3, 1914

Rebecca left Harrisburg [Harrisburg] *Patriot*, April 1, 1914, 3

Elizabeth Craighead Findlay, Aiken Standard, March 15, 2010

Shortly after, Passenger List, S. S. Cabrillo, 1916

Rebecca kept, First Annual Letter of the Class of 1910, Dickinson College, 1916

After returning, Allentown City Directories 1918-1921

Nancy, was born, Bethlehem City Directories 1923-1941

One conjectured, interview of Barbara Hallowell, August 30, 2010

She ended up, Recorder of Deeds, Deed Book J, Volume 10, Page 275

The only time, interview of Jean Craighead George, September 30, 2009

Jennie Fox Beiler, The Morning Call, February 28, 1990

Rebecca spent, Aiken Standard and Review, September 13, 1967

5. Frank Cooper Craighead

Little Lord Fauntleroy Jean Craighead George interview, September 30, 2009

"I was interested" Western Forest Entomology History: An interview with Dr. Frank C. Craighead, Sr., Elwood R. Maunder, March 1977, 2

"dull, but with a particular gift for mechanics" Eugenics Record Number 57576, 8

Apparently, Dicky The Tech Tattler: Commencement 1911, Vol. II, No. 9

Just after his 12th birthday The Red Man and Helper, November 14, 1902

His own first school Western Forest Entomology History: An interview with Dr. Frank C. Craighead, Sr., Elwood R. Maunder, March 1977, 2

"My first contact" Letter from Frank C. Craighead to Alfred G. Wheeler Jr., December 10, 1973

"[H]e awakened to new worlds" Journey Inward, Jean Craighead George, E. P. Dutton, New York, 1982, 32

He received his Carlisle High Program for Seventy-First Commencement Carlisle High School, June 11, 1908

History of Entomology in the Pennsylvania Department of Agriculture, 1975

"Dr. Baker was head of the school then" Western Forest Entomology History: An interview with Dr. Frank C. Craighead, Sr., Elwood R. Maunder, March 1977, 2

"I went there as a sophomore." A Forester's Log: Fifty years in the Pacific Northwest: An interview with George L. Drake, Elwood R. Maunder, 1958-1968, 41-42

"Then later in the summer" Western Forest Entomology History: An interview with Dr. Frank C. Craighead, Sr., Elwood R. Maunder, March 1977, 3

"Back in the days" Joseph E. Ibberson interview, November 4, 2009

Forest entomology was an emerging field History of Entomology in the Pennsylvania Department of Agriculture, 1975

"Gee, ain't this a peach of a bug?" The 1912 LaVie, Penn State College, 79

shy and sensitive email message from Jean Craighead George, July 30, 2010

The Department of Agriculture (USDA) Federal Entomology: Beginnings and Organizational Entities in the United States, 1854–2006, With Selected Research Highlights, Department of Agriculture, Agricultural Research Service Agriculture Information Bulletin Number 802, July 2008

"In entomology, but not in forests" Western Forest Entomology History: An interview with Dr. Frank C. Craighead, Sr., Elwood R. Maunder, March 1977, 8

"He was a very independent person" Western Forest Entomology History: An interview with Dr. Frank C. Craighead, Sr., Elwood R. Maunder, March 1977, 7

Weekends found him paddling Naples Daily News, December 19, 1991

When her father died Naples Daily News, April 12, 1993

Carolyn got a 97 Jean Craighead George interview, October 1, 2009

Being a man of science Eugenics Record Number 57576

He described Carolyn Eugenics Record Number 57575

The analysis done by prominent eugenicist letter from Charles B. Davenport to F. C. Craighead, January 29, 1915

"I guess we didn't turn out too bad." telcon with Jean Craighead George, December 23, 2009

The young couple set up housekeeping Naples Daily News, December 19, 1991

"Lord no." email message from Jean Craighead George, April 1, 2011

both by breech birth email message from Jean Craighead George, July 26, 2010

Frank Jr. and John email message from Jean Craighead George, July 21, 2010

"Mother was extraordinary" Naples Daily News, December 19, 1991

While starting a family Western Forest Entomology History: An interview with Dr. Frank C. Craighead, Sr., Elwood R. Maunder, March 1977, 2, 8

In 1920, the year after Jean was born Western Forest Entomology History: An interview with Dr. Frank C. Craighead, Sr., Elwood R. Maunder, March 1977, 9-10

"Almost as soon as we could walk" Naples Daily News, December 19, 1991

"Our whole family" Western Forest Entomology History: An interview with Dr. Frank C. Craighead, Sr., Elwood R. Maunder, March 1977, 10

Frank bought an old house Interview of Jean Craighead George, October 1, 2009

As head of the Bureau Interview of Jean Craighead George, October 1, 2009

Fords at first, Chevys later email message from Jean Craighead George, April 1, 2011

"Each summer, aunts, uncles and cousins" Journey Inward, Jean Craighead George, E. P. Dutton, New York, 1982, 33

"I always stood for gracious living" Journey Inward, Jean Craighead George, E. P. Dutton, New York, 1982, 46

Although Frank was not flirtatious Journey Inward, Jean Craighead George, E. P. Dutton, New York, 1982, 53

"When he returned" Journey Inward, Jean Craighead George, E. P. Dutton, New York, 1982, 40

"Lord no." email message from Jean Craighead George, April 1, 2011

"everyday problems of the parents" We Two Together, Robert F. Griggs, 271

"A party with these girls" We Two Together, Robert F. Griggs, 272

"sissy" interview of John Craighead, November 12, 2009

6. Eugene Miller Craighead

Eugene Miller Craighead was born WWII Registration Card U1221, April 27, 1942

1893 WWI Registration Card No. 161, May 29, 1917

According to church records Register of First Presbyterian Church, Carlisle, Pa., Pastorate of A. N. Hagerty, 1893

*His son believes…*email from Bill Craighead, August 18, 2012

The trout in the Letort conversation with Ed Shenk, July 2012

Like Rebecca and Frank [Harrisburg] Patriot, January 7, 1909, 3

In addition to serving Commencement Argus, Harrisburg High School, June 1912

"Egghead" The 1916 LaVie, Penn State College, 107

Gene worked his way email from Bill Craighead, June 17, 2012

He also received WWI Registration Card No. 161, May 29, 1917

Myra Eby's parents announced [Harrisburg] Patriot, August 25, 1917, 3

"The auspicious occasion" Tyrone Daily Herald, August 12, 1918, 3

The wedding was performed by [Harrisburg] Patriot, August 10, 1917, 3

Myra Catherine Eby Commencement Argus, Harrisburg High School, June 1912

In the fall of their Senior year [Harrisburg] Patriot, October 10, 1911, 3

Evidence that they didn't date [Harrisburg] Patriot, February 2, 1912, 2

Myra visited Ruth [Harrisburg] Patriot, July 16, 1912, 3

The fall after high school [Harrisburg] Patriot, January 7, 1913, 3

LaSell Seminary for Young Women [Harrisburg] Patriot, April 2, 1913, 3

After finishing her formal education [Harrisburg] Patriot, October 12, 1915, 2

When the United States entered WWI [Harrisburg] Patriot, November 21, 1917. 1, 5

Gene survived the war email from Bill Craighead, June 14, 2010

After the war 1920 Federal Census, January 12, 1920

In March, Myra gave birth The Descendants of Charles Cooper Craighead (1849-1926) and Agnes Alberta Miller (1859-1924), Barbara G. Hallowell

They continued living with the Ebys Harrisburg City Directory, 1920, 1922, 1923

Gurnsey The [Gettysburg] Star and Sentinel, October 4, 1924, 3

The move was made History of Entomology in the Pennsylvania Department of Agriculture, 1975, 20

Their second, and last, child The Descendants of Charles Cooper Craighead (1849-1926) and Agnes Alberta Miller (1859-1924), Barbara G. Hallowell

Gettysburg newspapers frequently published The Gettysburg Times, May 12, 1926, 2

Myra loved the beautiful Victorian The [Gettysburg] Star and Sentinel, October 4, 1924, 3

A case in point is telcon with Bill Craighead, March 25, 2010

Myra electrified the house interview of Jean Craighead George, September 9-10, 2009

Sam went to the local email from Bill Craighead, June 14, 2010

"On weekends my father" email from Bill Craighead, June 14, 2010

Gene's favorite trick interview of Jean Craighead George, September 9-10, 2009

Always the jokester email from Jean Craighead George, June 11, 2010

The only known serious incident interview of Jean Craighead George, September 9-10, 2009

In the mid to late 1930s interview of Jean Craighead George, September 9-10, 2009

In the 1930s letter from Frank Craighead to Alfred Wheeler, March 27, 1974

He returned to government work History of Entomology in the Pennsylvania Department of Agriculture, 1975, 20

7. Ruth Craighead Gawthrop

Ruth Craighead was born The Descendants of Charles Cooper Craighead (1849-1926) and Agnes Alberta Miller (1859-1924), Barbara G. Hallowell

My father went with horse Unpublished notes written by Ruth Craighead Gawthrop in 1966 after spending Christmas with her daughter, Barbara, in New Jersey

Ruth's daughter observed, email from Barbara Hallowell, September 2, 2012

Agnes's maiden sister Growing Up in Kennett, Barbara G. Hallowell, 1988-89, 14

On Sundays, Charles hitched Old Maud Growing Up in Kennett, Barbara G. Hallowell, 1988-89, 8

When barely eight years old [Harrisburg] Patriot, April 20, 1903, 2

When ten [Harrisburg] Patriot, May 12, 1905, 6

Something happened in third grade Growing Up in Kennett, Barbara G. Hallowell, 1988-89, 8

She definitely attended Harrisburg Central [Harrisburg] Patriot, February 2, 1910, 10

She received a $10 prize [Harrisburg] Patriot, May 30, 191, 3

Her extra-curricular activities Commencement Argus, June, 1913, Harrisburg Central High School, 8

In the summer between [Harrisburg] Patriot, June 7, 1912, 9

Ruth served as Secretary Commencement Argus, June, 1913, Harrisburg Central High School, 1

She escaped with only minor Commencement Argus, June, 1913, Harrisburg Central High School, last

After graduating from Harrisburg Center 1915 Halcyon, Swarthmore College, 101, 138, 159, 166, 220, 221

Ruth remained active 1917 Halcyon, Swarthmore College, 70, 154, 178, 180, 189

Her Senior year 1918 Halcyon, Swarthmore College, 46, 185

Ruth didn't spend all her time 1915 Halcyon, Swarthmore College, 93

Graduating from college [Harrisburg] Patriot, June 28, 1918, 3

The bulk of the remainder of this section, except as noted, can be found in Growing Up in Kennett, Barbara G. Hallowell, 1988-89, 1-11

Harold and Ruth were married [Harrisburg] *Patriot*, July 30, 1919, 3

8. Charles Miller Craighead

Charles Miller Craighead was born The Descendants of Charles Cooper Craighead (1849-1926) and Agnes Alberta Miller (1859-1924), Barbara G. Hallowell, 1990

Charlie attended the Model School [Harrisburg] *Patriot*, May 28, 1910, 8

He attended elementary school [Harrisburg] *Patriot*, May 14, 1912, 9

That summer, he nearly drowned [Harrisburg] *Patriot*, July 26, 1912, 5

Charlie was involved [Harrisburg] *Patriot*, March 6, 1917, 7

In August 1917 [Harrisburg] *Patriot*, August 31, 1917, 5

At least one Argus [Harrisburg High School] *Argus*, December 1919, 26

And in a later edition [Harrisburg High School] Argus, May 1920

Charlie was also active [Harrisburg] *Patriot*, November 26, 1919,

He also performed [Harrisburg] *Patriot*, February 11, 1920, 7

He played an attendant [Harrisburg] *Patriot*, October 31, 1919, 7

He was a founding member [Harrisburg] *Patriot*, October 11, 1919, 6

The March 1920 edition [Harrisburg High School] Argus, March 1920, 8

"Charlie" is our famous [Harrisburg High School] 1920 Commencement Argus, 18

Charles Craighead graduated [Harrisburg] *Patriot*, June 15, 1920, 10

Charlie attended Penn State College 1925 La Vie, 123

Inducted into Phi Lambda Upsilon 1926 La Vie, 447

According to family lore email from Ruth Muir, August 31, 2012

In November 1929 Penn State Collegian, November 19, 1929, 2

The determination of aluminum and magnesium in zinc-base die-casting alloys, Craighead, Charles Miller, 1930

By April 1930 1930 U. S. Census, Parnassus Boro, PA, 14B

"My Dad lived…" email from Ruth Muir, July 9, 2010

He then worked as a metallurgist 1940 U. S. Census, New Kensington, PA, 19B

Shortly after that email from Ruth Muir, September 5, 2012

PART III The Next Generation

9. Frank Cooper Craighead, Jr. & John Johnson Craighead

With Eugenics Being All, Eugenics Record Number 57576

he married, Richmond Times-Dispatch, October 13, 1915, 7

Carolyn gave birth, The [Washington] Evening Star, August 123, 1916, 8

In 1920, Western Forest Entomology History: An interview with Dr. Frank C. Craighead, Sr., Elwood R. Maunder, March 1977, 9-10

Virtually identical, interview of David S. Masland, December 14, 2009

The twins shone, interview of Richard Gates Slattery, March 28, 2011

"That is true." email conversation with Jean Craighead George, March 28, 2011

Gates valued, interview of Richard Gates Slattery, March 28, 2011

"Back as far as…," For Everything There Is a Season: The Sequence of Natural Events in the Grand Teton-Yellowstone Area, Frank C. Craighead, Jr., Falcon Press, 1994, vii

Gates kayaked, interview of Richard Gates Slattery, March 28, 2011

"Spike was given…," email conversation with Jean Craighead George, June 21, 2010

Gates had a bittersweet, interview of Richard Gates Slattery, March 28, 2011

Carolyn required her children, interview of John Johnson Craighead, October 12, 2009

Jean cautioned, email conversation with Jean Craighead George, March 17, 2012

Craighead summer evenings, email conversation with William Moore Craighead, June 14, 2010

One summer night, interview of John Johnson Craighead, October 12, 2009

Eugene played a bit, interview of William Moore Craighead, October 6, 2009

"We started school," interview of Emily Coyle Jacoby, June 22, 2010

Western High School produced, http:// westernhighschool-dc.org/stars.html

Lightweight football and basketball, 1934 Westerner, Western High School, Washington, 171

"In the summer of 1934…," http://www. craigheadresearch.org/frank-craighead-legacy. html

Phi Beta Rho, 1935 Westerner, Western High School, Washington, 33

Shortly after school was out, Hawks in the Hand: Adventures in Photography and Falconry, Craighead, Frank, Jr. & John, Houghton Mifflin, Boston, 1939, 187

The twins made wrestling, The Penn State Collegian, January 10, 1936, 4

John pointed out, interview of John Craighead, October 12, 2009

Their first, The National Geographic Magazine, vol. LXXII, no. 1, July 1937, 109-134

Another 10-week trip, interview of David S. Masland, December 14, 2009

They were both awarded, The Penn State Collegian, May 16, 1939, 4

Shortly after returning home, Life with an Indian Prince, Frank Jr. & John Craighead, Archives of American Falconry, Boise, Idaho, 2001, xv-xx

On August 6, Life with an Indian Prince, Frank Jr. & John Craighead, Archives of American Falconry, Boise, Idaho, 2001, 1-270

10. Falconry

"Perhaps it was," Afterword to Hawks in the Hand: Adventures in Photography and Falconry, Frank Jr. & John Craighead, Lyons & Burford, 1997, 291-294

The bulk of the information for this chapter came from the Craigheads' notes that were added as an Addendum to Hawks in the Hand: Adventures in Photography and Falconry, Frank Jr. & John Craighead, Lyons & Burford, 1997, 295-352

"She believed in," interview of Jean Craighead George, September 30, 2009

The above log entry, email conversion with Jean Craighead George, June 25, 2010

Jean still smarted, email conversion with Jean Craighead George, June 24, 2010

Soon after starting, The Penn State Collegian, November 12, 1935, 1

A weasel owned by, interview of John Craighead, October13, 2009

11. Jean Carolyn Craighead

They forced her to eat, interview of Jean Craighead George, September 30, 2009

Diablo Twins, email conversion with Jean Craighead George, March 30, 2011

"I couldn't do a math problem," interview of Jean Craighead George, September 30, 2009

Starting in 1929, email conversation with Jean Craighead George, March 25, 2010

"My bedroom looked very much," email conversation with Jean Craighead George, May 23, 2010

"With two such brothers," Journey Inward, Jean Craighead George, E. P. Dutton, New York, 1982, 34

In Washington, We Two Together, Robert F. Griggs, Boxwood Press, Pacific Grove, California,1961, 270-271

For that, interview of Jean Craighead George, September 30, 2009

Army brat, email conversation with Florence Kelton Lentz, April 28, 2015

"I see myself," Woodrow Wilson Alumni Beacon, vol. XVI, no. 3, Fall/Oct.-Dec. 2011, 1

Jean's father gave her, interview of Jean Craighead George, September 30, 2009

12. Samuel Eby and William Moore Craighead

"On weekends my father," email conversation with William Moore Craighead, June 14, 2010

"In terms of after school," email conversation with William Moore Craighead, June 13-14, 2010

Favorite foods, email conversation with William Moore Craighead, April 6, 2011

1909 S VDB," email conversation with William Moore Craighead, June 13-14, 2010

Sam frequented, New Oxford Item, June 21, 1928, 1

Grasshopper, conversation with Jean Craighead George, date uncertain

Dave incurred Myra's wrath, conversation with David S. Masland, March 7, 2012

Spelunking, email conversation with William Moore Craighead, June 20, 2010

To say Bill idolized, email conversation with William Moore Craighead, July 2, 2010

"He had tight, curly hair," The Summer of the Falcon, Jean Craighead George, Thomas Y. Crowell Company, New York, 1962, 4

"Sam, too, was somewhat," email conversation with William Moore Craighead, June 13-14, 2010

"He had created," The Summer of the Falcon, Jean Craighead George, Thomas Y. Crowell Company, New York, 1962, 4

"Sammy was born to pick on girls," interview of Barbara Gawthrop Hallowell, August 30, 2010

recalls fighting with Sam, interview of Mary Dunfee Campbell, November 18, 2009

considered Sam a troubled, interview of Jean Craighead George, September 30, 2009

"He was a master musician," email conversation with William Moore Craighead, July 2, 2010

"At Craighead there were," email conversation with William Moore Craighead, June 20, 2010

"In 1937, I won," email conversation with William Moore Craighead, July 2, 2010

Bill and Barbara, interview of Barbara Gawthrop Hallowell, August 30, 2010

found ripe cherries, interview of John Craighead, October 13, 2009

was a mutt, email conversation with William Moore Craighead, June 20, 2010

"While in public school," email conversation with William Moore Craighead, June 20, 2010

Sam made friends, The George School 1937

"When I was about thirteen," email conversation with William Moore Craighead, July 2, 2010

Sam graduated from Penn State, La Vie 1941, 67

13. Nancy Craighead and Barbara Miller Gawthrop

Ruth Craighead married, [Harrisburg] Patriot, July 30, 1919, 3

Gawthrop family background and history comes from Growing Up in Kennett, Barbara Gawthrop Hallowell, unpublished memoir, 2010

Supplemental information was obtained during an interview of Barbara Gawthrop Hallowell on August 30, 2010

Information to fill in missing pieces was gained from an ongoing email conversation beginning on January 8, 2010

14. Ruth Ann Craighead

Charles and Peg   The Descendants of Charles Cooper Craighead (1849-1926) and Agnes Alberta Miller (1859-1924), Barbara G. Hallowell

Charles and Margaret brought...email from Ruth Muir October 11, 2012

Ruth Ann's parents lived...1940 U. S. Federal Census

My father and mother left...email from Ruth Muir July 9, 2010

She also recalled...email from Ruth Muir July 9, 2010

Part IV The War Years

They hurriedly put in place, Havens Across the Sea, compiled and edited by Ann Spokes Symond, 1992, 6-13

"I had my eleventh birthday," email conversation with Heather Champion Ashton, July 1, 2015

"To drive the British away," Havens Across the Sea, Heather Champion Ashton, compiled and edited by Ann Spokes Symond, 1992, 70

15. The Home Front

Brothers Frank, Eugene, WWII Draft Registration, Eugene Miller Craighead, April 27, 1942

Harold Gawthrop, Growing Up in Kennett, Barbara Gawthrop Hallowell, unpublished memoir, 2010

"From the time," email conversation with Ruth Ann Craighead Muir, September 3, 2013

Champion horseshoe pitcher, Battelle News, July 1944

"Music and nature," The George School 1942

Immediately after graduation, email conversation with Barbara Gawthrop Hallowell, September 22, 2013

Nancy became acquainted, email conversation with Barbara Gawthrop Hallowell, April, 29, 2014

On November 6, email conversation with Barbara Gawthrop Hallowell, September 22, 2013

Although Nancy, email conversation with Barbara J. Wilson, April 24, 2014

16. Different Paths for Bill and Sam

Extra-curricular activities summarized, The George School 1943, George School, 1943, 13

Information regarding Bill Craighead's Navy experiences came from *All Ahead Full: World War II Memoirs of an LSM 215 Veteran,* William M. Craighead, Turner Publishing Company, Puducah, Kentucky, 2003

Information regarding Sam Craighead's experiences with the World War II draft came largely from As You Were: Memoirs of World War II, William M. Craighead & Kingdon W. Swayne, Acclaim Press, Morley, Missouri, 2007, 171

Information regarding his USGS work in Alaska came from Sam Craighead's untitled and unpublished memoir covering the summers of 1943 and 1944

He married Yvonne Nichols, The Gettysburg Times, December 7, 1943, 2

Other than visiting, The Star and Sentinel, December 10, 1943, 5

Shortly after returning, Declaration of Appointee, form number 16-32865-1, January 2, 1945

17. Jean and the Twins Fight the War in Unique Ways

Jean Craighead was enrolled, The Washington Post, April 26, 1942, L4

Two days later, The Evening Independent, Massillon, Ohio, April 28, 1942, 9

needed newspaper reporters, Jean Craighead George, Alice Cary, The Learning Works, Santa Barbara, California, 1996, 60-63

Jean's pieces, New Castle, PA., News, August 8, 1942, 14

amount of cloth, The Daily Courier, Connellsville, PA., August 28, 14

"The Fall Fighters," The Washington Post, September 26, 1943, L1

"Just an Atom-Smasher," The Washington Post, October 31, 1943, L1

Jean first consulted, A Passion for Physics: Essays in honor of Geoffrey Chew, ed. By C. Detar, World Scientific Publishing Co, Singapore, 1985, 8-10

"That young man," Jean Craighead George, Alice Cary, The Learning Works, Santa Barbara, California, 1996, 66-67

*It's no surprise…*email from Twig George, May 23, 2016

Four months later, The Washington Post, January 29, 1944, 5

The War Department observed, The Michiganensian, vol. 47, University of Michigan, 1943, 142

PEM 39, The Michigan Alumnus, University of Michigan, November 7, 1942, 96-97

Meanwhile, the Navy, Adrian Daily Telegram, April 17, 1943, 8

How to Survive on Land and Sea: Individual Survival, Aviation Training Division, Office of the Chief of Naval Operations, United States Navy, United States Naval Institute, Annapolis, Maryland, 1943

Over fifty years later, The Montana, vol 22 no 2, Spring 2005, An Extraordinary Life, Vince Devlin, 14-19

PART V Maturity

18. After the War

James Lewis Craighead, The Descendants of Charles Cooper Craighead (1849-1926) and Agnes Alberta Miller (1859-1924), Barbara G. Hallowell

With the war ending, The Ogden Standard-Examiner, November 28, 1944, 12 and *The Ogden Standard-Examiner*, December 10, 1944, 7

"I bet that was," interview of Karen Craighead Haynam, October 13, 2009

Margaret "Cony" Craighead held, interview of David S. Masland, December 14, 2009

"As far as the packs," email conversation with John Willis "Johnny" Craighead, August 7, 2010

Shortly after their marriage, Journey Inward, Jean Craighead George, E. P. Dutton, New York, 1982, 5

About that time, Jean Craighead George, Alice Cary, The Learning Works, Santa Barbara, California, 1996, 81-83

At Michigan, Journey Inward, Jean Craighead George, E. P. Dutton, New York, 1982, 3-5

Looking at her tiny daughter, Journey Inward, Jean Craighead George, E. P. Dutton, New York, 1982, 43

Against Jean's strong advice, Journey Inward, Jean Craighead George, E. P. Dutton, New York, 1982, 52-54 & 80-81

John was given notice, Journey Inward, Jean Craighead George, E. P. Dutton, New York, 1982, 83-84

Jean was soon writing, Journey Inward, Jean Craighead George, E. P. Dutton, New York, 1982, 84-85

The twins' dissertation, The Washington Post Magazine, Vicki Constantine Croke, November 11, 2007, 18-34

Sam connected, The Gettysburg Times, August 27, 1946, 2

He continued to work, USGS Form9-500, July 3, 1969

Bill Craighead wasn't allowed, All Ahead Full: World War II Memoirs of an LSM 215 Veteran, William M. Craighead, Turner Publishing Company, Puducah, Kentucky, 2003, 137-148

"At that time," email conversation with William Moore Craighead, June 20, 2010

"I met Bill," interview of Betty Bakley Craighead, October 6, 2009

Betty earned her AB, 1952 Quittaphilla, Lebanon Valley College, Annville, Pennsylvania, 1952

In addition to their normal duties, www.GeorgeSchool.org, 1956 work camp trip to Wolfenbüttel, Germany

Nancy Gawthrop Wilson, email conversation with Barbara Gawthrop Hallowell, April 29, 2014

Burned out, email conversation with Barbara Gawthrop Hallowell, September 23, 2013

In April of 1950, email conversation with Barbara Gawthrop Hallowell, September 22, 2013

Tom had been, 1937 Halcyon, Swarthmore College, Swarthmore, Pennsylvania, 1937

Ruth Ann Craighead was attending, email conversation with Ruth Ann Muir Craighead, October 14, 2012

He remembered the neighbor boy, interview of James Lewis Craighead, October 6, 2009

"When I was a teenager," email conversation with Ruth Ann Muir Craighead, July 9, 2010

Jim was just nine, interview of James Lewis Craighead, October 6, 2009

Gene and Myra, interview of William Moore Craighead, October 6, 2009

"Dad said he'd bulldoze it," interview of Laurie Craighead Rudolph, April 9, 2014

"We got the first batch," interview by Elwood R. Maunder in Western Forest Entomology History, March 1977

"By reaching out," "An interview with Ralph C. Hall," Elwood R. Maunder, Forest History Society, November 1974 & March 1975

"When my Aunt Carolyn," email conversation with Ruth Ann Muir Craighead, July 9, 2010

Frank didn't live long," A Forester's Legacy: The Life of Joe Ibberson, Henry D. Gerhold, Pennsylvania Forestry Association, Mechanicsburg, Pennsylvania, 2007, 71-74

Frank and Joe, interview of Joe Ibberson, November 4, 2009

Ruth Chew, Diary, May 18-31, 1946

Charles, Peg, Ruth, email conversation, July 10, 2010

19. Grizzlies, Wolves and Everglades

Frank Jr. wrote Dave, letter from Frank Craighead, Jr. to Dr. David S. Masland, April 27, 1959

His family soon melded, interview of Mark Mullen, date not recorded

"Practically nothing was known," The Montanan, vol 22 no 2, Spring 2005, An Extraordinary Life, Vince Devlin, 16-17

"Mom was a good driver," interview of Charlie Craighead, September 16, 2014

"The two families," Journey Inward, Jean Craighead George, E. P. Dutton, New York, 1982, 126

National Geographic TV specials, https://www.youtube.com/watch?v=-QCZY6eUWVA

"…point them away from you," The Washington Post Magazine, Vicki Constantine Croke, November 11, 2007, 18-34

Jean recalled meeting, Journey Inward, Jean Craighead George, E. P. Dutton, New York, 1982, 128

Johnny recalls his high school, interview of John Willis "Johnny" Craighead, October 13, 2009

"Quite early in our work," Track of the Grizzly, Frank C. Craighead, Jr., Sierra Club Books, San Francisco, 1979, 10

A year later, Track of the Grizzly, Frank C. Craighead, Jr., Sierra Club Books, San Francisco, 1979, 205

The NPS bulldozed, Track of the Grizzly, Frank C. Craighead, Jr., Sierra Club Books, San Francisco, 1979, 199

"John, if you accept that," Track of the Grizzly, Frank C. Craighead, Jr., Sierra Club Books, San Francisco, 1979, 208-9

"One day in late May," Journey Inward, Jean Craighead George, E. P. Dutton, New York, 1982, 84-5

*His DDT studies…*email from Twig George May 23, 2016

Eight days before, Journey Inward, Jean Craighead George, E. P. Dutton, New York, 1982, 117

*Students considered him…*email from Twig George May 23, 2016

Jean hired Mrs. Davidson, Journey Inward, Jean Craighead George, E. P. Dutton, New York, 1982, 135-8

"Study the Wolves," Journey Inward, Jean Craighead George, E. P. Dutton, New York, 1982, 174

In 1915 when Frank Craighead, Craighead-sidebar, Collier County Historical Society, Friday release, undated

"Possibly I am a bit old-fashioned," letter to Gov. Reubin Askew, September 6, 1972

"It has been a long time," letter from Robert Krear to the author, 2010

"Encounters with rattlesnakes," A Forester's Legacy: The Life of Joe Ibberson, Henry D. Gerhold, Pennsylvania Forestry Association, Mechanicsburg, Pennsylvania, 2007, 71-74

20. Waters Flow and Families Grow

"Sammy was a great guy," email conversation with Michael Stoner, April 9, 2014

"He taught me how to fish," "Dad said he'd bulldoze it," interview of Laurie Craighead Rudolph, April 9, 2014

Sam retired, Social Security Death Index

Bill Craighead continued teaching, email conversation with Betty Craighead, September 28, 2013

beekeeping business, interview of Vaughn Ludwig, November 13, 2015

Tragedy struck, email conversation with Betty Craighead, April 16, 2014

"When I met her," interview of Bill Craighead, November 16, 2009

Nancy Gawthrop Wilson, email conversation with Barbara Gawthrop Hallowell, April 29, 2014

"Rather than pursue a career," email conversation with Barbara J. Wilson, April 24, 2014

In the 1950s and 60s, email conversation with Barbara Gawthrop Hallowell, September 22, 2013

The possibility of a transfer, Cabin: A Mountain Adventure, Barbara G, Hallowell, Appalachian Consortium Press, Boone, North Carolina, 1986

Tom and Barbara put together, interview of
  Barbara Hallowell, August 30, 2010

Peg Craighead continued, email conversation with
  Ruth Ann Craighead Muir, September 3, 2013

Jim Craighead Graduated, email conversation
  with Ruth Ann Craighead Muir, March 26,
  2014

21. From Career to Legacy

"You were the ablest," letter to Frank Cooper
  Craighead from Horace Marden Albright,
  August 25, 1973

"Nobody listens to me," letter from Frank Cooper
  Craighead to Horace Malden Albright, August
  14, 1973

"This project, in my opinion," letter from Frank
  Cooper Craighead to Sen. Lawton Chiles,
  April 19, 1977

"had little patience for stupid," interview of David
  Southall, January 2010

"Having nine hippie grandchildren," letter from
  Frank Cooper Craighead to Jim Buckner,
  March 13, 1974

Unfortunately, orchid thieves, observation of
  author on January 2010 visit

"Where he saw greed," The Naples Star, November
  19, 1976, 2A

The twins' research, Track of the Grizzly, Frank
  C. Craighead, Jr., Sierra Club Books, San
  Francisco, 1979, 212-230

In 1977, the NPS opened, The Post-Register,
  September 28, 1977, C11

"We will definitely rebuild…", letter from Esther
  Craighead to Dorothy Bixler, March 16, 1978

*"HARRASSMENT," National Park Inholders
  Association, Testimony of Charles S. Cushman,
  September 5, 1978*

In the midst of the NPS, interview of Jean
  Craighead George, September 30, 2009

Frank and Shirley, interview of Shirley Crocker
  Craighead, September 2014

Your book is a stunner, letter from Jean Craighead
  George to her father, September 8, 1971

"Things are getting tough," Journey Inward, Jean
  Craighead George, E. P. Dutton, New York,
  1982, 155

INDEX

ABOUT THE AUTHOR

A chance statement at a talk on the Carlisle Indian School led to Dr. Benjey researching the life of Lone Star Dietz and writing the biography of the most controversial person to grace the sidelines of a football field. Doing the research exposed him to enough information about the legendary Carlisle football program to whet his interest in learning more. That led to him writing *Doctors, Lawyers, Indian Chiefs: Jim Thorpe & Pop Warner's Carlisle Indian School football immortals tackle socialites, bootleggers, students, moguls, prejudice, the government, ghouls, tooth decay and rum.* In 2009 Dr. David Masland suggested he write a book about his lifelong friends, the Craigheads. His initial investigation convinced him that this was indeed an extraordinary family. A health crisis intervened, resulting in him writing *Prostate Cancer and the Veteran.* At last, *Glorious Times: Adventures of the Craighead Naturalists* is finished.